Visio® 2000 For Du...

2-
299

Keyboard shortcuts for working with shapes

Ctrl+A	Selects all shapes
Ctrl+B	Send shape to back
Ctrl+C	Copy
Ctrl+D	Duplicate selected shape
Ctrl+F	Bring shapes to front
Ctrl+G	Group shapes
Ctrl+H	Flip selected shape horizontally
Ctrl+J	Flip selected shape vertically
Ctrl+L	Rotate shape left
Ctrl+R	Rotate shape right
Ctrl+U	Ungroup shapes
Ctrl+V	Paste
Ctrl+X	Cut
F2	toggles between text edit and shape selection mode
F4	repeats the last formatting command on a new shape

Miscellaneous keyboard shortcuts to save you time

Ctrl+I	Zoom to 100%
Ctrl+N	New blank drawing
Ctrl+O or Ctrl+F1	Display Open dialog box
Ctrl+Q	Quit Visio
Ctrl+S	Save
Ctrl+V	Paste
Ctrl+W	Zoom to show drawing full page
Ctrl+X	Cut
Ctrl+Y	Redo
Ctrl+Z	Undo
Shift+F6	Zoom out
F2	Display a shape's text box
F7	Run spell checker
Alt+F7	Cascade open drawing windows
F9	Toggles glue on and off

Opening dialog boxes with keyboard shortcuts

Ctrl-K	Display Hyperlinks dialog box		Shift+F5	Display Page Setup dialog box
Ctrl+O	Display Open dialog box		F6	Display Zoom dialog box
Ctrl+P	Display Print dialog box		Alt+F8	Display Macros dialog box
F1	Display Help dialog box		Alt+F9	Display Snap & Glue dialog box
F3	Display Fill dialog box		F11	Display Text dialog box
Shift+F3	Display Line dialog box		F12 or Alt+F2	Display Save As dialog box
F5	Display Page dialog box			

Visio® 2000 For Dummies®

Cheat Sheet

Standard toolbar tools to know and love

↖	Pointer tool	×	Connection Point tool	🖌	Format Painter tool
A	Text tool	⊥	Stamp tool	🔍	Zoom out
⟳	Text Block tool	✏	Pencil tool	🔍	Zoom in
⬡	Connector tool	/	Line tool		

Format Text toolbar tools to know and love

A⁺	Increase font size	x₂	Subscript tool	A↑	Rotate text 90 degrees
A▾	Decrease font size	≡	Align top	⇥≡	Decrease Indent tool
ABC	Strikethrough tool	≡	Middle	≡⇤	Increase Indent tool
ABC	SmallCaps tool	≡	Align bottom	↕≡	Decrease Paragraph Spacing tool
x²	Superscript tool	≔	Bullets	↕≡	Increase Paragraph Spacing tool

Action toolbar tools to know and love

▣	Align shapes	◁	Flip Vertical	⬓	Bring to front
▦	Distribute shapes	◺	Rotate Right	⬒	Send to back
✖	Lay Out Shapes	◹	Rotate Left	⊡	Group shapes
⬡	Connect Shapes	A↑	Rotate Text	⊡	Ungroup shapes
◸	Flip Horizontal				

Wiley, the Wiley Publishing logo, For Dummies, the Dummies Man logo, the For Dummies Bestselling Book Series logo and all related trade dress are trademarks or registered trademarks of Wiley Publishing, Inc. All other trademarks are property of their respective owners.

For Dummies: Bestselling Book Series for Beginners

Visio® 2000 FOR DUMMIES®

by Debbie Walkowski

Wiley Publishing, Inc.

Visio® 2000 For Dummies®

Published by
Wiley Publishing, Inc.
909 Third Avenue
New York, NY 10022
www.wiley.com

Copyright © 2000 Wiley Publishing, Inc., Indianapolis, Indiana

Published simultaneously in Canada

For general information on our other products and services or to obtain technical support, please contact our Customer Care Department within the U.S. at 800-762-2974, outside the U.S. at 317-572-3993, or fax 317-572-4002.

Wiley also publishes its books in a variety of electronic formats. Some content that appears in print may not be available in electronic books.

Library of Congress Cataloging-in-Publication Data:

Library of Congress Catalog Card No.: 99-66725

ISBN: 0-7645-0635-8

Manufactured in the United States of America

10 9 8 7

10/SQ/QY/QS/IN

About the Author

Debbie Walkowski: I'm probably a lot more like you than you think. I don't live for computers and I'm not in love with them, either. But I am eternally grateful to have them and appreciate them tremendously because they make my work so much easier.

There was a time (almost 17 years ago?) when I knew next to nothing about computers. I took a job working for a major computer manufacturer and every day thereafter was a learning experience. Much of it was frustrating and humbling, especially in the beginning; but it was rewarding, too. In fewer than four years, I was teaching software classes and writing about software. In the last six years, I've written 15 books on popular PC software. (My degree in technical writing came in handy here.)

In all my years working in the computer industry, I've never forgotten how it feels to be a beginner. My goal is — and always has been — to make the process of figuring out new software as painless and enjoyable as possible for the reader.

Dedication

In memory of my mother, Barbara Jeanette Williams, 1923–1999.
The brightest smile and the warmest heart were hers, both filled with love.

Acknowledgments

Some books are more fun to write than others. The people you get to work with determine that almost entirely (and a good product always helps!). In this case, I had the best of both worlds: a great product and great people — what could be better?

Let me start with the folks at Visio Corporation, a truly top-notch, sophisticated, quality organization. I had the pleasure of learning about this young company four years ago and was highly impressed then. My opinion hasn't changed a bit. Thanks to Stacy Dellas, Corporate Trainer, who was enthusiastic about this project from the beginning and helped us get it off the ground. She was never too busy to talk or answer questions, and she accommodated my every need. And special thanks to Charlie Zaragoza and Lorrin Smith–Bates, Visio's top trainers. They answered many questions for me and were willing to e-mail me from any place in the world! Charlie pulled together "Answers to Ten (Or So) Burning Questions about Visio," presented in The Part of Tens. Another Part of Tens chapter, "Ten of the Best Visio Tips," comes from Charlie's and Lorrin's expertise as Visio trainers.

At IDG Books Worldwide, Inc., thanks to Joyce Pepple, acquisitions editor, who pitched this book internally and made it fly. Thanks to two *terrific* partners, Andrea Boucher, project editor, and Stacey Mickelbart, copy editor. They really know their stuff, and I could never have asked for a more supportive, helpful team. Credit for the quality of this book rests entirely on their shoulders. They had great ideas, offered terrific suggestions, and really kept me calm. Thanks also to Jim McCarter, who took the time to painstakingly test every step in this book to ensure its technical accuracy. On the *Visio 2000 For Dummies* revision, thanks to Ed Adams, acquisitions editor, Jade Williams, project/development editor, Christine Berman and Tonya Maddox, copy editors, and Eric Butow, technical editor. They worked many hours and did a terrific job making sure this revision was the best it could possibly be.

Thanks also to Lisa Swayne, who made this opportunity possible. And a special thanks, as always, to my number one supporter, my husband, Frank. I could never do half of what I do without him.

Publisher's Acknowledgments

We're proud of this book; please send us your comments through our online registration form located at www.dummies.com/register/.

Some of the people who helped bring this book to market include the following:

Acquisitions, Editorial, and Media Development

Project Editor: Jade L. Williams

> *(Previous Edition: Andrea C. Boucher, Stacey Mickelbart)*

Acquisitions Editor: Ed Adams

Copy Editors: Christine Berman, Tonya Maddox

Technical Editor: Eric Butow

Editorial Manager: Leah P. Cameron

Media Development Manager: Heather Heath Dismore

Editorial Assistant: Beth Parlon

Production

Project Coordinator: E. Shawn Aylsworth

Layout and Graphics: Karl Brandt, Beth Brooks, Angie Hunckler, Kate Jenkins, Brian Massey, Barry Offringa, Tracy Oliver, Jill Piscitelli, Brent Savage, Jacque Schneider, Brian Torwelle, Mary Jo Weis, Dan Whetstine, Erin Zeltner

Special Art: Angie Hunckler, Jacque Schneider

Proofreaders: Laura Albert, Marianne Santy, Rebecca Senninger, Toni Settle, Charles Spencer

Indexer: Nancy Anderman Guenther

Special Help
Amanda Foxworth
Visio Corporation

General and Administrative

Wiley Technology Publishing Group: Richard Swadley, Vice President and Executive Group Publisher; Bob Ipsen, Vice President and Group Publisher; Joseph Wikert, Vice President and Publisher; Barry Pruett, Vice President and Publisher; Mary Bednarek, Editorial Director; Mary C. Corder, Editorial Director; Andy Cummings, Editorial Director

Wiley Manufacturing: Carol Tobin, Director of Manufacturing

Wiley Marketing: John Helmus, Assistant Vice President, Director of Marketing

Wiley Composition Services: Gerry Fahey, Vice President, Production Services; Debbie Stailey, Director of Composition Services

Contents at a Glance

Cartoons at a Glance

By Rich Tennant

page 51

page 7

page 129

page 271

page 223

Fax: 978-546-7747
E-mail: richtennant@the5thwave.com
World Wide Web: www.the5thwave.com

Table of Contents

Introduction

● ●

*I*t's 11:45 a.m., and your stomach is telling you that it's time for lunch. As you're putting on your jacket and heading for the door, your phone rings. It's your boss telling you that she needs a really impressive Visio drawing (impressive enough to present to clients) illustrating your organization's logical network, and she needs it by the end of the day today. You immediately break out in a cold sweat. You're not an artist and you've never used Visio before. So much for lunch. You take off your jacket, sit down, fire up Visio, stare blankly at the screen, and wonder where on earth to begin.

Thankfully, this scenario is hypothetical — but it isn't far-fetched. Bosses make requests like this every day. If you're not prepared, you may find yourself in a state of panic. So, if you're not an artist and need to create a Visio diagram — anything from software flowcharts to office furniture and fixture layouts — don't worry; this book is for you. *Visio 2000 For Dummies* leads you through the process of using Visio in as little time as possible. And believe me, I understand that your time is at a premium; you don't have hours to pore over a new software program and figure it out in-depth. In most cases, you have a rush job to do, and getting it done is your primary concern.

About This Book

This book is for everyone out there who has a job to do. And the job is *not* to learn Visio well enough to teach it; the job is to decipher Visio well enough so that you can create a drawing or diagram, whatever the level of complexity.

With this in mind, *Visio 2000 For Dummies* is designed to make you productive as quickly as possible. You find good, basic, useful information that helps you accomplish your goals rather than equipping you to write an essay on the history and virtues of Visio. You find real-world examples and figures that *show* you how to do something rather than just tell you. You find concise step-by-step instructions for accomplishing specific tasks rather than vague "it happens sort of like this" statements.

How to Use This Book

Don't feel that you have to sit down and read this book cover to cover. Part I is designed to get you up and running, and Part II gives you the basic tools for creating drawings. From there, choose what you want to read about. If you need help drawing shapes, there's a chapter just for that. If you want to incorporate layers in a diagram, there's a chapter for that, too. After you've mastered the basics and you consider yourself a die-hard Visio junkie, check out Part IV, which covers creating custom templates, styles, and shapes, and how to share Visio files with data from other programs and vice versa. But, hey — if you never get to the die-hard junkie stage, don't worry about it. You'll still know a whole lot more about Visio than you ever thought you would.

Whatever Visio level you are on, be sure to glance through Part V, "The Part of Tens." Here you find answers to common questions, examples of cool Visio wizards and stencils, tips, and really cool drawings and diagrams that were created using Visio.

Concentrate on these parts

If you've never used Visio, work your way through at least Part I and Part II of this book. These two parts give you the minimal knowledge required to successfully turn out Visio drawings, although not necessarily highly sophisticated drawings. When time permits and you want to know a little more about a particular topic, take a look at Part III.

Skip these parts if you want

If you're new to Visio and just want to know enough to create simple drawings or diagrams, you can safely skip Part IV, which I have affectionately deemed as being for die-hard Visio junkies. Clearly, not every reader will become devoted. Browse through Part III for the features that you find useful, and glance at Part V for anything interesting that pops out at you.

On the other side, if you've used Visio before, you can safely skip Parts I and II, which offer basic getting-up-and-running information.

How This Book Is Organized

Visio 2000 For Dummies is organized into five distinct parts and an appendix.

Part I: Starting with Visio 2000 Basics

This section lays the groundwork for your success with Visio. Every software program has its unique personality; Visio is no exception. Here you find conceptual information about Visio, get the Visio terminology down, discover how to recognize and work with what's on the screen, start Visio, save and open files and workspaces, and how to close Visio.

Part II: Creating Basic Drawings

If you're in a hurry, this section teaches you the basics of creating a *simple* drawing. I go over the basic elements of a Visio drawing, and how to implement them into your drawing. I also show you how to add and manipulate text, as well as how to work with margins and tabs, indentation, alignment, spacing, and more. You also see how to manipulate a drawing's *connectors,* the lines that connect one shape to another. (They're more than just simple lines, as you'll soon discover.) Finally, you get to see your drawings on paper in printed form.

Part III: Customizing Your Work

Here you move into the intermediate features of Visio. Find out how to place shapes precisely on a drawing, create your own shapes, enhance and manipulate shapes, do some more sophisticated stuff with connectors, work with pages and layers, and use wizards to create drawings.

Part IV: For the Die-Hard Visio Junkie: Using More Advanced Stuff

Certainly not every user needs to pursue this section! Here I show you how to create custom templates and styles, how to store data in shapes and report on that data, customize shapes using a ShapeSheet spreadsheet, and protect your shapes and drawings from inadvertent changes. You also see how to use Visio drawings with other programs and on the Internet.

Part V: The Part of Tens

One of the most entertaining sections of every *For Dummies* book, "The Part of Tens," is a set of various collections. In *Visio 2000 For Dummies,* you find answers to ten burning questions about Visio, plus check out ten of Visio's coolest wizards and stencils, ten best tips, and ten sample drawings from the makers of Visio.

Appendix: Stencil Gallery

Be sure to check out the appendix, which offers a stencil gallery — a visual tour of stencils included with Visio Standard, Technical, and Professional versions. The appendix is a great reference for finding the shapes that you want.

Conventions Used in This Book

Here's a summary of the conventions used in this book:

- ✔ When directions indicate that you type something, for example, "Enter **13** in the size box," the characters you type appear in bold.

- ✔ When I say "click," I mean to click your left mouse button. If you need to right-click, I specify "right-click."

- ✔ When I say "drag," I mean to click and hold the left mouse button as you move the mouse. Release the mouse button when you're done dragging.

- ✔ The term *shortcut menu* refers to the pop-up menus that appear when you right-click something on the screen. When I want you to select a command from the shortcut menu, directions specify *right-click.* (Shortcut menus are not available for all elements in a drawing.)

- ✔ You can select commands using toolbar buttons, menu commands, or the Alt key. Because toolbar buttons are by far the fastest method, I always list them first, followed by the menu command. (When toolbar buttons aren't available, I list only the menu command.) I specify a menu command by saying "Choose File⇨Save," which means to click the File menu to open it and to then choose the Save option.

Icons Used in This Book

The following icons are used in this text to call attention to specific types of information:

The Tip icon indicates information that's likely to save you time if you read it, or information that will make you say to yourself, "Wow, I never knew that!" Be sure to read this stuff.

When you see a Technical Stuff icon, I try to explain in lay terms something that is bogged down in technical jargon. You won't find too many of these icons, but when you do, you may want to take a gander.

Definitely pay attention to the Warning icons; they're designed to warn you of impending doom, or at the very least, a possible problem you'd just as soon avoid.

Remember icons are designed as a gentle nudge rather than a blatant slam to the head. In other words, "Remember this — it may be important to you someday!"

I use this funky little icon to point out weird stuff that Visio does every now and then.

This icon draws attention to the dos and dads that are new to Visio 2000, the latest and greatest version.

Assumptions

I assume that if you're reading this book, you have a reasonable working knowledge of Windows 95, Windows 98, or Windows NT 4.0, as one of these is required to run Visio. For this reason, I don't spend any of your valuable time in Chapter 1 describing how to find your way around Windows or how to work with dialog boxes. If you need to review these concepts, see *Windows 98 For Dummies,* by Andy Rathbone (IDG Books Worldwide, Inc.).

Part I
Starting with Visio 2000 Basics

AFTER HIS FLOWCHART DETERIORATED TO STICK FIGURES, DONALD THE TECHNOPHOBE DECIDED TO GIVE VISIO A TRY.

In this part . . .

So the boss says you gotta learn Visio and you barely even know what it is, huh? This is the place to start. You've seen other programs, but Visio is a whole different animal. It's not nearly as intimidating as you might think! Here you discover what Visio is and does, discover to "speak" Visio, and see how to find your way around the screen. You also read about how to print; something you'll no doubt find very useful if you want to be productive!

Chapter 1

Visio 101

● ●

● ●

Close your eyes for a minute and picture the amount of visual information that comes to you in any given day. Magazines, newspapers, reports, television programs, and presentations illustrate a great deal of information in the form of charts, tables, graphs, diagrams, and technical drawings. These graphic elements often convey ideas far more quickly and clearly than long, boring paragraphs. You don't typically think of charts, diagrams, and graphs as *art,* but they are graphical, and this is where Visio comes in.

Although Visio is very easy to use, you can benefit from a bit of explanation before you jump right in. This chapter lays a solid foundation for your knowledge of Visio. In this chapter, I help you become familiar with what you see on the screen and understand conceptually how Visio works.

Getting the Scoop on Visio

In simple terms, Visio is a diagramming tool for business professionals, many of whom are self-confirmed non-artists. Although Visio is often referred to as a *drawing* tool, it really isn't, because it requires no artistic ability. It's more accurate to say that Visio is a tool for creating visual aids. That's comforting, because even in highly analytical, non-art related careers, you may be called upon to create a chart, diagram, or — perish the thought — a *drawing!* If the suggestion of drawing *anything* strikes terror in your heart, Visio can help.

Visio's grab bag of icons — or *shapes,* as Visio calls them — represents all sorts of things from computer network components, to office furniture, to boxes on an organization chart. You simply drag the shapes that you want into the drawing area and arrange and connect them the way that you want. You can add text and other graphical elements wherever you like.

For those of you with a computer-aided design background, *don't think CAD with Visio!* Although the finished product — a drawing — may look similar, Visio and CAD-based systems are entirely different animals. If you're a self-confirmed CAD snob, that's okay! But don't underestimate or misunderstand Visio. Visio and CAD-based systems have different purposes and work entirely differently.

Examining Visio products

Visio doesn't make four distinct variations of its product just to confuse you. Each one addresses a slightly different audience, although each uses the same core technology. That means that each product's basic operating functions are the same. In this book, I address the basic functions that are common to each product. The following list tells you how each product differs from the others:

✔ **Visio Standard:** Designed for mainstream business professionals such as salespeople, general managers, financial analysts, and project and product managers. It includes over 1,300 Standard shapes that help you communicate typical business information in a graphical form.

✔ **Visio Professional:** Widens the audience of Standard users to include network managers and designers, database designers, and software developers. Visio Professional gives you the tools to diagram and document things like networks, software, and databases. It includes the 1,300 Standard shapes plus an additional 1,300 Professional shapes.

✔ **Visio Technical:** Addresses the needs of professionals in specialized fields like facilities management, engineering (electrical, civil, mechanical, fluid dynamics, and so on), and architecture. You can use its more than 2,500 Technical shapes in combination with the 1,300 Standard shapes to create space plans, schematics, heating, ventilation, and air conditioning designs, and CAD drawings.

✔ **Visio Enterprise:** Builds on Visio Professional. It includes over 14,000 shapes to help you automatically diagram LANs and WANs, databases, and software designs at the highest levels.

Taking a quick peek at some of Visio's features

Visio is often a misunderstood product, especially by those who've never used it. I'm amused when I hear people say "Oh, Visio! That's that org chart package, isn't it?" That's like saying, "Oh, the space shuttle! That's that thing NASA built that's sort of like an airplane, right?" Well, not exactly!

Although Visio is a whiz at creating organization charts, its sophistication reaches well beyond! The following list describes some of the things you can do with Visio:

- ✔ **Report on data:** Suppose you draw an office layout plan that includes cubicle walls, fixtures, office furniture, and computer equipment. You can store each piece of furniture and office equipment with data such as its inventory number, owner, and current location. The computer equipment shapes can also include data about the manufacturer, hardware configuration, and Internet address assigned to it. From this drawing, you can generate property, inventory, and location reports. See Chapters 13 for more information on storing and reporting on data in shapes.

- ✔ **Use the drill down feature:** Jump quickly from an overview drawing to a detailed drawing. For example, you can draw an overview map of a worldwide computer network and double-click the name of a city to see a drawing of that city's computer network. This drill-down feature is possible because Visio lets you define a shape's behavior when you double-click it. See Chapter 13 for more information.

- ✔ **Use hyperlinks:** Jump from a Visio drawing to a different drawing, to a document outside of Visio, or to a location on the Internet. I discuss this feature in more detail in Chapter 14.

- ✔ **Generate drawings from data:** Suppose you have organization chart data (employee name, employee title, manager reporting to, and so on) stored in a text or spreadsheet file. You can generate an organization chart automatically from this data using Visio. Or, suppose you manage projects and you have project tasks and durations stored in a spreadsheet file. You can automatically generate a Gantt chart from this data using Visio.

Visio also provides impressive interaction with other applications. You can:

- ✔ Include data or objects from other programs in your Visio drawings.

- ✔ Create charts and diagrams from data stored in other programs.

- ✔ Create drawings and charts in Visio that you can later export to programs like Microsoft PowerPoint and Microsoft Project.

- ✔ Use your Visio drawings on the Internet, either as HTML pages or as a part of your Web page by e-mailing drawings to your friends.

Familiarizing Yourself with Visio Lingo

Like all software programs, Visio uses certain unique terminology. You need to be familiar with some of the following terms before you begin creating diagrams and drawings.

- **Drag and drop:** The method Visio uses to create drawings. What are you dragging and where are you dropping it, you ask? You drag shapes and you drop them onto a drawing page.

- **Shapes:** Probably the most important element of Visio. Shapes represent objects of nearly any conceivable kind — office furniture in an office layout diagram, road signs in a directional map, servers in a network diagram, boxes on an organization chart, bars on a comparison chart. Visio contains literally thousands of different shapes. You can draw your own shapes, too, as I show you in Chapter 8.

- **Master shapes:** Shapes that you see on a stencil. When you drag a shape onto the drawing page, you're copying a master shape onto your drawing page, making it just one *instance* of that shape. In other words, the master stays on the stencil. Visio makes the distinction between *master shapes* and *instances* of shapes. But my advice is, don't clutter your mind with such hair-splitting detail!

- **Stencils:** Tools Visio uses to organize shapes so that you can find the one you're looking for. A stencil is nothing more than a *collection of related shapes*. If you want to create an office layout diagram, for example, you use the office layout stencil, which includes shapes such as walls, doors, windows, telephone jacks, panels, furniture, plants, and electrical outlets. (Sorry, no reclining chairs or big-screen TVs are included with this stencil.) Stencils are displayed in a special window on the left side of the screen so that the shapes are always available while you're working. (Of course, you can minimize the window if it gets in your way.)

- **Templates:** Plans for particular types of drawings. When you need to create a drawing, Visio makes life easy for you by providing templates that define certain characteristics of the drawing so that the drawing is consistent in its properties. For example, when you use a Visio template for a specific type of drawing, Visio automatically opens one or more appropriate stencils, defines the page size and scale of your drawing, and defines appropriate styles for things like text, fills, and lines. Of course, you can change any of these elements, but the point of using a template is to maintain consistency throughout the drawing. After all, your drawing may include several pages, and you want them to look as if they go together.

✔ **Connectors:** Lines (or other shapes) that connect one shape to another. Perhaps the most common example of a connector is in an organization chart. The lines that connect the president to various groups within an organization, and the lines that run through an organization are connectors. In Visio, connectors can be very sophisticated, and I tell you more about them in Chapter 6, but for now this definition is all you need to remember.

Jumping Head First into Visio

The best way to get started with Visio is to open a new blank drawing, just so you can cruise around the screen and get a feel for what's there. You discover in Chapter 2 how to create different types of drawings.

To start Visio, follow these steps:

1. **From your Windows desktop, click Start⇨Programs⇨Visio 2000.**

   Visio displays the Welcome to Visio 2000 dialog box, as shown in Figure 1-1.

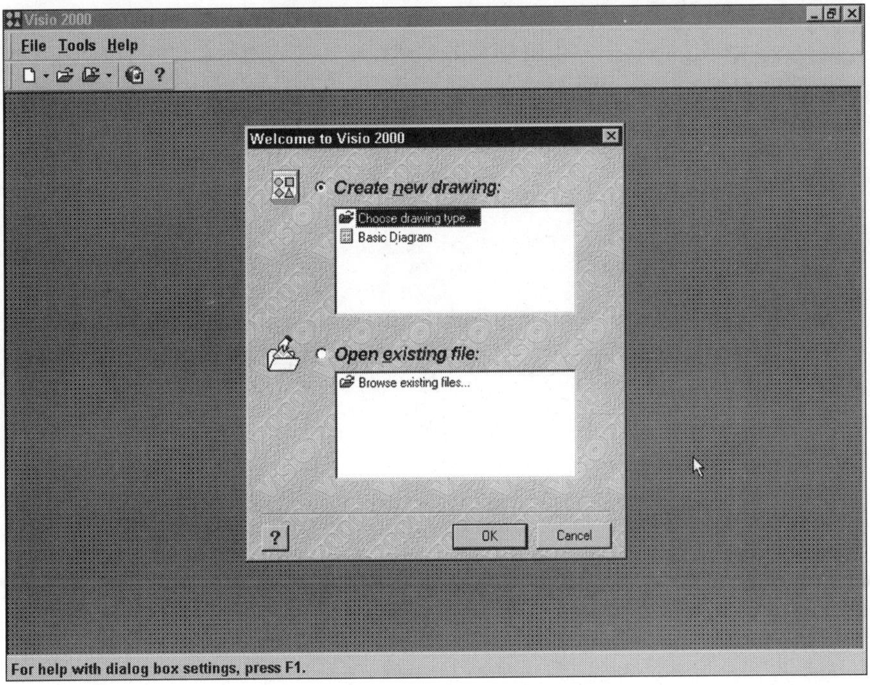

Figure 1-1:
The Welcome to Visio 2000 dialog box.

2. **In the Welcome to Visio 2000 option box, the Choose Drawing Type is already selected for you. Click the OK button.**

   Visio displays the Choose Drawing Type dialog box with a list of categories on the left, as shown in Figure 1-2.

3. **Click Other in the category list on the left to create a drawing without a template.**

   The only drawing type available is Blank Drawing that appears on the right of the screen.

4. **Click Blank Drawing and then click the OK button.**

   Your blank drawing appears, as shown in Figure 1-3.

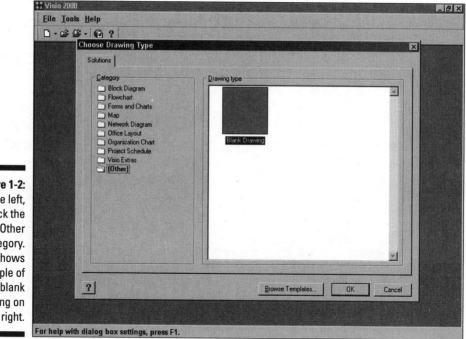

Figure 1-2:
On the left, click the Other category. Visio shows a sample of the blank drawing on the right.

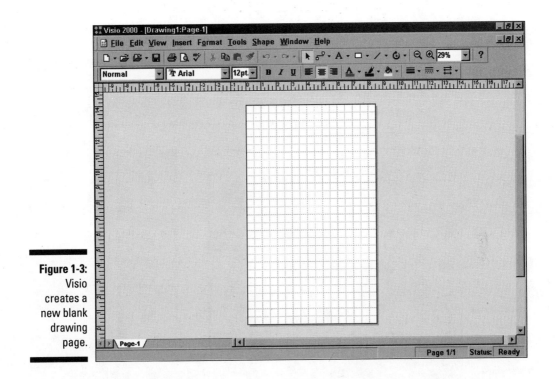

Figure 1-3:
Visio
creates a
new blank
drawing
page.

Getting familiar with the Visio screen

A typical Visio working screen looks like the one shown in Figure 1-4. In this figure, the drawing is a simple office layout. The drawing area is bounded by rulers on the top and at the left of the screen, and by scroll bars on the bottom and at the right. To the left of the bottom scroll bar is the navigation area, which displays tabs for each page in the drawing.

In this example, the Office Layout Shapes stencil appears on the left side of the screen. The Visio menu bar appears at the top of the window under the title bar. Beneath the menu bar are two open toolbars: the Standard and Format toolbars. The status bar, which provides information about your drawing, appears along the bottom of the drawing area. Note that one of the shapes in the drawing is selected, so the status bar displays the shape's width, height, and angle.

Stencil   Rulers   Selected shape   Menu bar   Toolbars

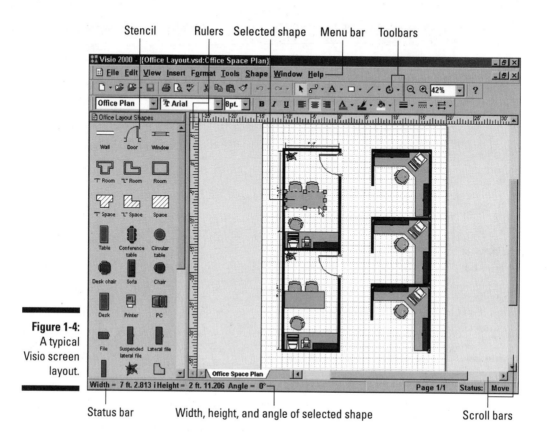

Figure 1-4:
A typical
Visio screen
layout.

Status bar   Width, height, and angle of selected shape   Scroll bars

Checking out the menus

Visio's menu bar contains some typical menus found in almost every
Windows application (like File, Edit, Format, and Help). Even so, I suggest
you review the contents of each menu for commands that you may not
expect. The following bullets describe menus and commands that are unique
to Visio:

- **Tools:** On this menu you find all kinds of tools for working with Visio
  shapes, the Visio drawing page and the drawing itself, Visio's color
  palette, rulers, grids, and so on.

- **Shape:** The Shape menu contains commands for sizing, positioning, flipping, rotating, and grouping shapes, and for choosing a drawing's color
  scheme. You also find commands on this menu for changing the stacking
  order of shapes and doing some really creative things like "fragmenting"
  and "intersecting" shapes. (See Chapter 8 for more details.)

Working with toolbars

Visio has a dozen or so toolbars, two of which are displayed automatically when you start the program. The two default toolbars are Standard and Format (refer to Figure 1-4). You can hide either of these, or display additional toolbars as well. After you begin to recognize the buttons, it's much faster to use the toolbar buttons rather than select the menu commands. I include a lot of these buttons on the Cheat Sheet at the beginning of this book to help you out.

To hide or display toolbars, right-click anywhere in the toolbar area. On the shortcut menu that appears, click a toolbar name. Those that have a check mark next to them are displayed; all others are hidden.

In keeping with Microsoft Windows compatibility, all Visio toolbars can be docked at different locations on the screen. Just grab the vertical bar at the left end of any toolbar and drag it to a new location on the screen. The toolbar automatically becomes its own window, and you can position it anywhere you like on the screen by dragging the title bar.

If you're a real toolbar fanatic, you can customize existing toolbars or create your own. Customizing means adding buttons you use most often or deleting buttons you never use. Creating your own means picking and choosing all the buttons you like.

Creating a toolbar

To create a custom toolbar:

1. **Choose View⇨Toolbars⇨Customize.**

   Visio displays the Customize dialog box, as shown in Figure 1-5.

2. **Click the New button.**

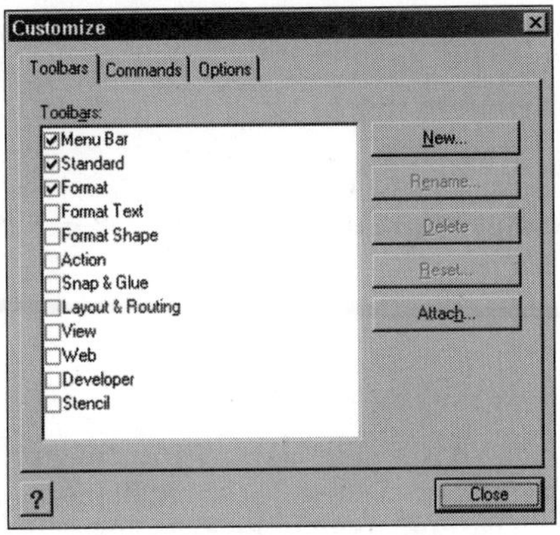

Figure 1-5:
Use the
Customize
dialog box
to modify a
toolbar's
buttons.

3. **In the New Toolbar dialog box, enter a name and click the OK button.**

   Visio adds the new name to the toolbars list and displays a new, blank toolbar in the customize box. (It's small, but it's there!)

   Drag the new blank toolbar up into the toolbar area.

Modifying a toolbar

If you just want to add a button here or there, consider modifying an existing toolbar rather than creating a new one. Follow these steps to add the buttons you want to your custom toolbar:

1. **Display the toolbar that you want to change.**

2. **Choose View➪Toolbars➪Customize.**

   Visio displays the Customize dialog box.

3. **Click the Commands tab, which displays categories on the left and commands on the right.**

4. **Find the button that you want to add by clicking a category on the left and then scrolling the commands list on the right.**

5. **Drag the button from the dialog box to the location on the toolbar where you want the button to be added.**

   Yes, that's right. Drag it right out of the dialog box onto the toolbar!

   When you release the mouse button, the new button becomes part of the existing toolbar.

Deleting a toolbar

To delete a tool from a toolbar, follow these steps:

1. **Display the toolbar that you want to change.**

2. **Right-click the toolbar to display the shortcut menu and click Customize.**

   Visio displays the Customize dialog box.

3. **Drag the button that you want to delete off of the toolbar.**

   Repeat if you want to delete additional buttons.

4. **Click the Close button to close the Customize dialog box.**

Closing Visio

When you're ready to close Visio, choose File➪Exit. If you haven't recently saved all open files, Visio prompts you to do so for each file. Choose Yes to save or Cancel to return to Visio without saving the drawing.

Getting Help When You Need It

To get help on a Visio topic, choose Help⇨Visio Help. Visio displays the Help dialog box (see Figure 1-6), which contains tabs for Contents, Index, and Favorites. As the name implies, the Contents tab lists items in a format similar to a table of contents in a book. If you want to look up a topic like you would in the index of a book, choose the Index tab.

When you find a really great Help topic that you'd like to refer to at another time, display the topic; then click the Favorites tab. The topic is saved in a list of favorites so that you can find it again easily.

Visio's Help menu also contains these commands:

✓ **Help⇨Search:** When you choose this command, Visio asks you what you would like to know. Enter a phrase or sentence and then click Search to display a list of topics.

✓ **Help⇨Shape Basics:** Choose this command if you want help specifically with working with shapes (selecting, moving, adding text, changing, connecting, and so on).

✓ **Help⇨Developer Reference:** If you're a developer, choose this help option to point you to developer's resources.

✓ **Help⇨Visio on the Web:** To connect to Visio's home page or other locations on the Internet, choose this command.

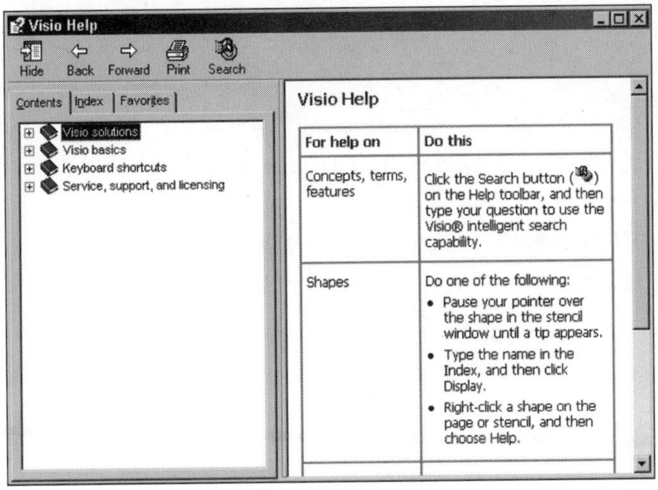

Figure 1-6:
The Visio Help dialog box is similar to that of other Windows-compatible programs.

For help on	Do this
Concepts, terms, features	Click the Search button (🔍) on the Help toolbar, and then type your question to use the Visio® intelligent search capability.
Shapes	Do one of the following: • Pause your pointer over the shape in the stencil window until a tip appears. • Type the name in the Index, and then click Display. • Right-click a shape on the page or stencil, and then choose Help.

Like many Windows programs, Visio also uses tool tips. When you point to a button on a toolbar and pause without clicking, a tip pops up to tell you the name of the button. This is especially helpful when you're learning Visio. Visio expanded the concept of tool tips to its stencils. When you point to a stencil shape without clicking on it, a tip pops up and gives the name of the shape and a description (see Figure 1-7).

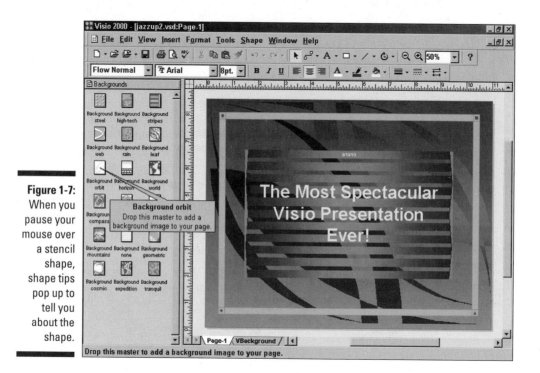

Figure 1-7:
When you pause your mouse over a stencil shape, shape tips pop up to tell you about the shape.

Chapter 2

Creating Visio Drawings

. . . .

In This Chapter

▶ Using templates to create drawings

▶ Working with more than one drawing at the same time on the screen

▶ Arranging stencils on the screen

▶ Opening additional stencils

▶ Saving drawings and workspaces

▶ Opening existing drawings and workspaces

▶ Navigating a drawing successfully

▶ Viewing drawings in different ways

. . . .

*I*n this section, I go into more detail about working with Visio drawings: creating documents using a template, arranging stencils, saving drawings and workspaces, and so on. It's not essential that you know all of these things to begin working with Visio, but it sure helps a lot!

Using Drawing Templates

A *template* is a model for creating a drawing. Think of it as a style sheet that automatically sets up certain characteristics of the drawing — like the page size, page orientation, the drawing scale, and the types of shapes you may need to use. Templates have two purposes and advantages: to make creating drawings easier and to maintain consistency throughout multi-page drawings. You don't have to create templates (unless, of course, you want to); Visio includes dozens of them for creating different types of drawings.

Visio's startup procedures were changed in Visio 2000 to make starting Visio and creating a new drawing as simple as it can possibly be. Thus, the dialog boxes that you see when you start Visio ask you to choose a drawing type rather than a template, as it was called in previous versions. In fact, they are the same thing. It's my hunch that this change was made because the term *drawing type* is less intimidating for some users than the word *template*.

To create a new drawing by using a template, follow these steps:

1. **From your Windows desktop, click Start⇨Programs⇨Visio 2000.**

   Visio displays the Welcome to Visio 2000 dialog box (see Figure 2-1). The Create New Drawing option is already selected for you.

2. **In the Welcome to Visio 2000 dialog box, Choose Drawing Type is already highlighted for you. Click the OK button.**

   Visio displays the Choose Drawing Type dialog box, as shown in Figure 2-2.

3. **Click a category on the left.**

   On the right side of the dialog box under Drawing Type, you see a sample of each type of drawing available in the current category. Use the scroll bars, if necessary, to see all drawing types available in a category.

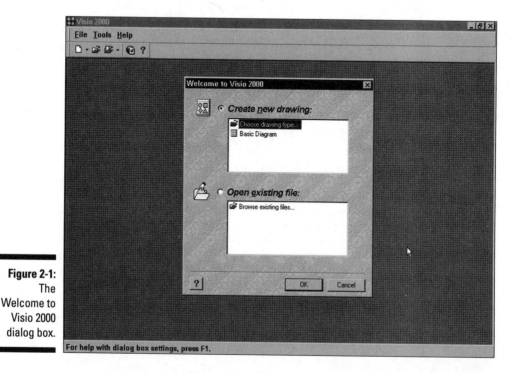

Figure 2-1:
The Welcome to Visio 2000 dialog box.

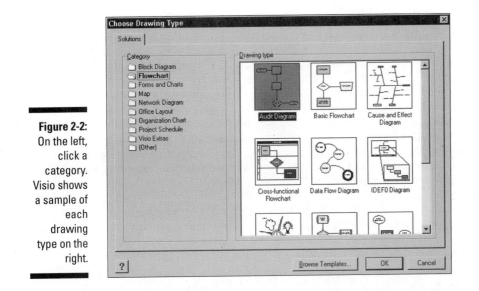

Figure 2-2:
On the left,
click a
category.
Visio shows
a sample of
each
drawing
type on the
right.

4. **Click a drawing type and then click the OK button.**

Visio creates a new drawing page. One or more stencils are automatically
opened on the left side of the screen (see Figure 2-3). See the "Opening
additional stencils" section later in this chapter.

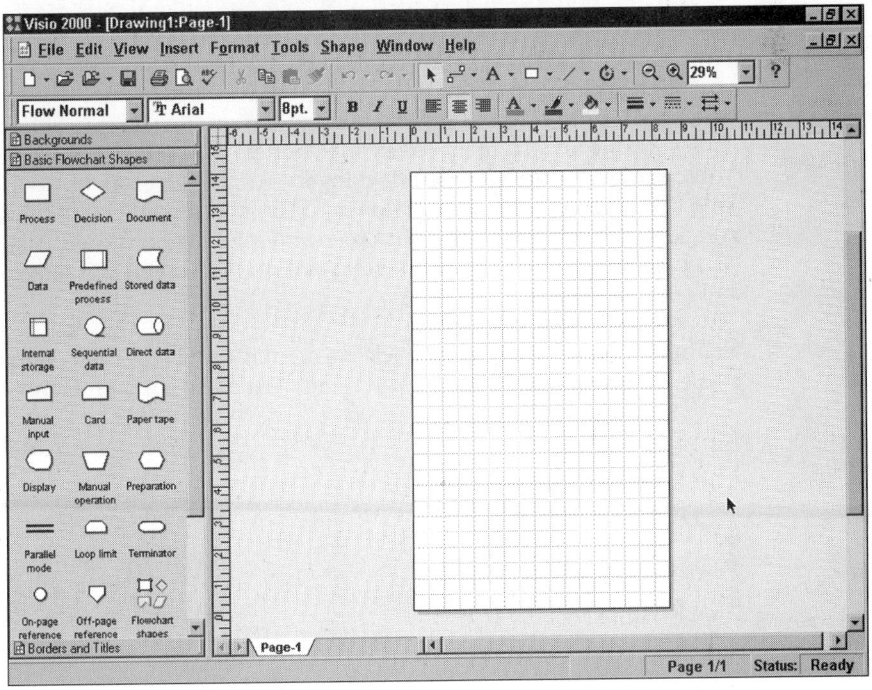

Figure 2-3:
Visio
creates
a new
drawing
page for
the type of
drawing that
you want to
create.

Visio practically begs you to use a template to create a drawing! You didn't know it until now, but whenever you start Visio and choose a drawing type, you automatically create a new drawing using a template. For example, if you want to create a business form, you choose the Forms and Charts category, then the Form Design drawing type when you start Visio. This ensures that your new drawing is created using the Form Design template, which sets up a page size of 8½ x 11 and a drawing scale of 1:1 (drawing size:actual size). The template automatically opens the appropriate stencil or stencils — in this example, the Form Shapes stencil. The template also specifies other settings that you may not notice right away (like a typical point size for text in a form), but you don't need to worry about these settings. You can change anything about a template that you don't like.

It's easy to create templates of your own, too. Many corporations find custom templates useful because they can incorporate their company logos and other company-specific information. See Chapter 12 for more information about creating custom templates.

Moving and arranging stencils

Some drawing types automatically open more than one stencil, so you can have as many open stencils as you like while you're working. (You can also open additional stencils. See the "Opening additional stencils" section later in this chapter.) In Figure 2-4, at the top of the open Office Layout Shapes stencil, two additional stencils called Basic Shapes and Callouts are also open.

The default "docking location" for stencils is on the left side of the screen. As you open additional stencils, the one most recently opened appears, and the title bars for other open stencils are stacked on the left side of the screen. This stacking arrangement saves space on your screen for the drawing area. You can change the left-sided docking location to the top, bottom, or right side of the screen. A fourth option is to "float" a stencil so that it appears in a separate window with its own Close and Minimize buttons. This option lets you place the stencil anywhere you want on the screen and move it at any time or minimize it.

To reposition a stencil, right-click the stencil's title bar, then choose the Position option from the shortcut menu. From the submenu, choose:

- ✔ Docked to Left
- ✔ Docked to Right
- ✔ Docked to Top
- ✔ Docked to Bottom
- ✔ Floating

Open stencils

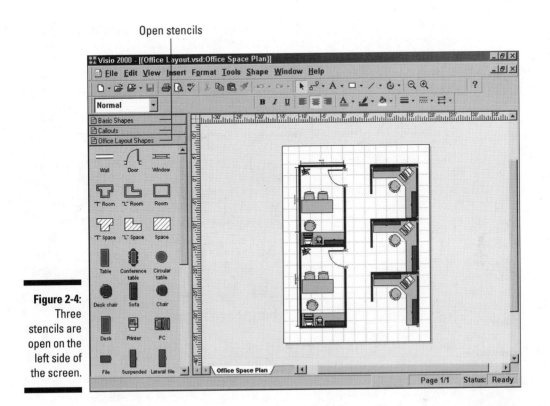

Figure 2-4:
Three
stencils are
open on the
left side of
the screen.

In Figure 2-5, one stencil is moved to the right side of the screen while the others remain on the left. You can arrange stencils any way you like. Be aware that the more stencils you display at once, the smaller your view of the drawing area becomes.

 Rather than right-click on the title bar of a stencil to move it, you can simply drag the stencil's title bar, and the stencil automatically becomes a floating window. As you drag the stencil window toward any of the edges of the screen, it snaps into place at the top, bottom, right, or left side of the screen.

To close a stencil, right-click the title bar and then choose the Close option from the shortcut menu.

Opening additional stencils

If you ever want to use a shape that's not available on the open stencil, you can open as many stencils as you want until you find the shapes that you need for your drawing. For example, suppose you decide that you want to add a mini-calendar to a business form so that your employees can't exclaim, "I didn't know there was a meeting today!" A calendar shape is available on the Calendar Shapes stencil.

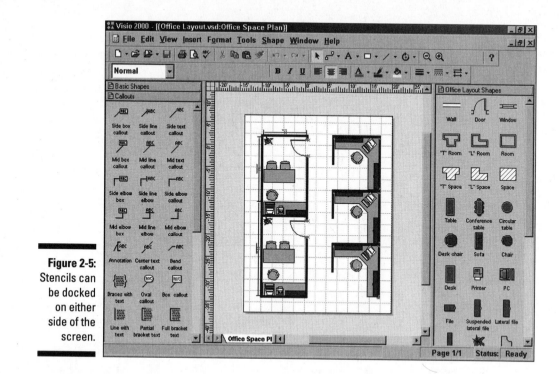

Figure 2-5:
Stencils can
be docked
on either
side of the
screen.

If you're not sure which stencil you need to open, check out the Shape Explorer in Chapter 4. It helps you find the shapes you need by searching for a description that you supply.

To open a stencil, follow these steps:

1. **With your drawing displayed on the screen, choose File⇨Stencils.**

   Visio displays a submenu listing categories of stencils, as shown in Figure 2-6. Notice that each category appears with an arrow on the right, indicating there is a submenu for each particular category.

2. **From the bottom portion of the submenu, click a stencil category.**

3. **From the submenu, click a stencil name.**

   Visio opens the stencil and displays it on the left side of the screen. For more information about arranging stencils, see the "Moving and arranging stencils" section earlier in this chapter.

Stencil category   Stencil name

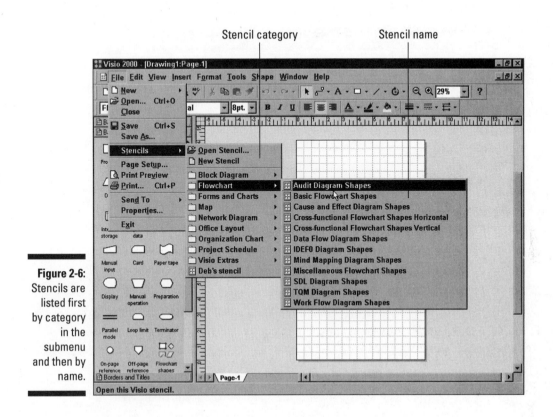

Figure 2-6:
Stencils are
listed first
by category
in the
submenu
and then by
name.

Saving a drawing

After you spend a lot of time creating a drawing, you may want to save your
file. In fact, don't wait until you finish a drawing; save it frequently from the
minute you start creating it!

When you save a file for the first time, Visio displays a Properties dialog box.
In this dialog box you can store information about the file that makes it easy
for you to find and identify the file later, such as title, subject, author, manager, company, category, keywords, and description. In addition, you can
choose whether to save a preview picture, which helps you identify the file
in the Open dialog box before you open the file. The preview feature is especially nice because you can often identify a file more quickly visually than by
its name. To save a file for the first time, use these steps:

1. **Choose File⇨Save.**

   Visio displays the Save As dialog box, as shown in Figure 2-7.

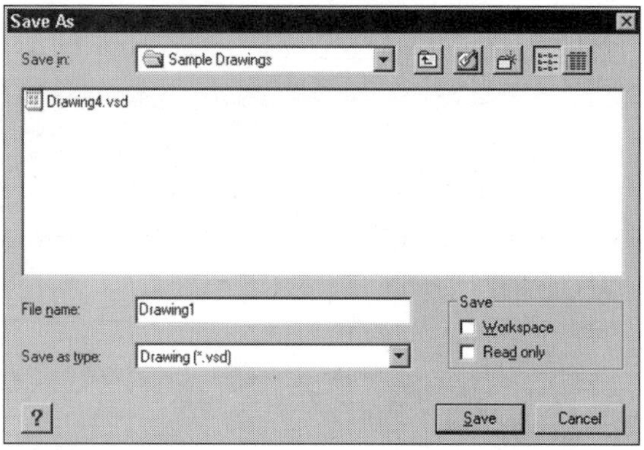

Figure 2-7:
Type a
filename in
the Save As
dialog box.

2. **In the Save In box, click the folder where you want to store the file.**

   Click the down arrow to choose a new folder if necessary.

3. **Type a name in the File Name box.**

4. **If the .VSD file extension is not selected in the Save As Type box, select it now.**

   VSD is the file extension Visio uses for all drawings.

5. **Click the Save button.**

   Visio displays the Properties dialog box, as shown in Figure 2-8.

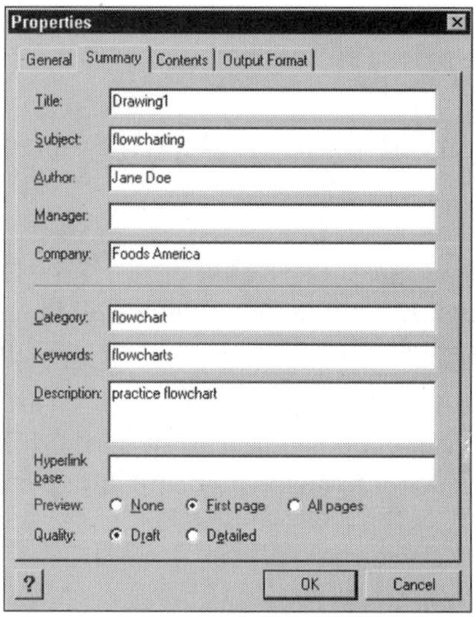

Figure 2-8:
Enter
information
in the
Properties
dialog box
to help you
identify your
file.

6. **Fill in as many of the fields as you want in the Summary tab to help you identify the file (all fields are optional).**

7. **To save a preview of the file, click the Draft or Detailed button.**

   The Draft option saves shapes only; the Detailed option saves all objects in the drawing and therefore increases the file size.

8. **To conserve file space when saving a Preview, click the First Page Only option.**

9. **Click the OK button. Visio returns to your drawing.**

Saving your workspace

Because you can spend a lot of time opening additional stencils and arranging them on the screen, Visio lets you save your screen arrangement along with your drawing. This feature saves you the time you'd spend opening the same file and stencils and arranging them on your screen the next time you want to work. Visio calls this *saving your workspace* and performs this function automatically whenever you save a file (unless you change this option). The check box for this option appears in the lower right corner of the Save As dialog box (refer to Figure 2-8). To turn off this feature, remove the check from the Workspace box. When you save the file, Visio uses the filename for your drawing with a .VSW file extension (instead of the typical .VSD file extensions for drawings).

If you have more than one drawing file open and want to save your workspace, you can do this, but you must choose a new filename. Note that saving a workspace doesn't automatically save changes to each open drawing. Be sure to save changes to each drawing individually.

To save a workspace when you have more than one drawing open, use these steps:

1. **Choose File⇨Save Workspace.**

   Visio opens the Save Workspace dialog box. The default file type in the Save File As box is Workspace (.VSW).

2. **In the File Name box, enter a unique filename.**

3. **Click the OK button.**

Following a step-by-step method for creating drawings

You've seen it before. It's that Okay-What-Do-I-Do-Now? blank stare that creeps across someone's face when they start up a new program. (Of course, no one's ever witnessed that expression on *your* face!) As they say, it always pays to "have a plan," and with Visio, there's no exception. At least with a plan, you can *pretend* you know what you're doing!

Use this checklist whenever you create a new drawing using a template:

- ✔ Know what kind of drawing you want to create so you can choose an appropriate drawing type.

- ✔ Start a new drawing by choosing that drawing type, which opens the template automatically (see the preceding section on "Using Drawing Templates").

- ✔ Open any additional stencils that you may want to use (see the preceding section on "Opening additional stencils").

- ✔ If you want your drawing to have multiple pages, add them now (see Chapter 9).

- ✔ Drag and drop shapes from the stencil onto the drawing (see Chapter 4).

- ✔ Connect the shapes (see Chapter 6).

- ✔ Add text to the drawing (see Chapter 5).

- ✔ Apply a color scheme to the drawing (see Chapter 7).

- ✔ Save the drawing or workspace (see the preceding section on "Saving your workspace").

- ✔ Print your document (see Chapter 3).

Of course, the process can be far more involved than this; creating background pages, adding layers, incorporating hyperlinks, inserting objects from other programs, and so on. But this is the basic process you follow each time you create a drawing. Refer to this list until you're comfortable working with Visio.

Opening an existing drawing

Visio makes it easy for you to open an existing drawing. The Welcome to Visio 2000 dialog box that appears when you start Visio lists recently opened drawings, or you can browse for others to open.

To open an existing Visio drawing when you start Visio, follow these steps:

1. **From your Windows desktop, click Start⇨Programs⇨Visio 2000.**

   Visio displays the Welcome to Visio 2000 dialog box (refer to Figure 2-1).

2. **Choose the Open Existing File option.**

   Visio automatically highlights the Browse Existing Files option.

3. **Recently opened files appear in the selection box. If one of these is the file you want, click the file's name and then click the OK button.**

   If the file that you want to open isn't listed, be sure Browse Existing Files is still highlighted and then click the OK button.

   Visio displays the Open dialog box.

4. **Select the file that you want to open and click the Open button.**

   Visio displays your drawing.

Opening more than one drawing at a time

While you're working in Visio, you can work with more than one drawing at a time. Just open a saved drawing or workspace at any time. The file you open becomes the active drawing (or workspace); any other drawings that are already open are still open. All open drawings are listed at the bottom of the Window menu.

To open a drawing or workspace while working in Visio, follow these steps:

1. **Choose File⇨Open.**

   Visio displays the Open dialog box.

2. **In the Look In box, choose the folder where your file is located.**

3. **In the Files of Type box, choose either All Visio Files (*.VSW*), or a specific file type such as Drawing (*.VSD).**

4. **In the document list, click the file that you want to open.**

5. **Click the OK button.**

After you're running Visio, the quickest way to open a file you've recently used is to check the File menu. The files you've most recently opened are listed at the bottom. Just click a filename to open the file.

If you want to view more than one drawing on the screen at the same time, choose Window⇨Tile, or Window⇨Cascade. After all your drawings are open, you can drag a window border to resize it or drag the title bar to position a window where you want it to appear on the screen. For more information on arranging windows on your screen, see *Windows 98 For Dummies,* 2nd Edition, by Andy Rathbone (IDG Books Worldwide, Inc.).

Navigating through a drawing

Often drawings contain multiple pages, and you need to be able to move from one page to another quickly. The drawing shown in Figure 2-9 contains four pages. The name of each page appears on a tab at the bottom of the drawing window on the navigation bar. To move from one page to another, just click the page tab. Visio highlights the page that's currently displayed.

If the navigation bar isn't wide enough to display all page names, put your mouse over right end of the navigation bar until the pointer changes to a double-headed arrow. Now you can drag the navigation bar to the right until it displays all the page tabs in your drawing.

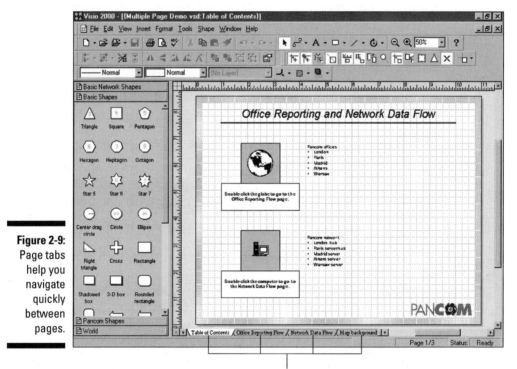

Figure 2-9:
Page tabs
help you
navigate
quickly
between
pages.

Page tabs

Zeroing in on a Drawing

As you work on a drawing, it's nice to be able to zoom in on a particular area. Visio gives you several options for zooming in and out. The typical way is to use one of the zoom buttons on the Standard toolbar. Next to the Zoom button (the one that displays a percentage) is a drop-down arrow. When you click this arrow, a drop-down list of percentages (25%, 50%, 75%, 100%, 150%, 200%, and 400%) is displayed, along with three other options. Just click the percentage you want or click one of these:

- ✔ Last — to return to the last percentage used
- ✔ Width — to display the width of the page
- ✔ Page — to display the entire page

(You can also find these options on the View menu by choosing View⇨Zoom, but it's quicker to use the Zoom button.)

To the left of the Zoom button on the Standard toolbar are two other zoom buttons: Zoom Out and Zoom In. They look like magnifying glasses with - and + symbols in them. Click the Zoom Out (-) button to view more of the drawing; click Zoom In (+) to get a closer view.

The keyboard/mouse shortcut for zooming in is Ctrl+Shift. When you press and hold these keys, you see the mouse pointer change to a magnifying glass with a +. Click the left mouse button to zoom in; click the right mouse button to zoom out. To zoom back out again to display the entire drawing, press Ctrl+W.

When you're zoomed in close, you can pan through a drawing by using the scroll bars, but it's quicker to use another mouse shortcut. Hold down the right mouse button as you move the mouse in the direction you want to go. Visio automatically readjusts your view of the drawing.

Using the Pan and Zoom window

When you're working on an enormous drawing, it's easy to lose your bearings when you zoom in on a specific area. And using the scroll bars or the right mouse button to pan through a drawing can get cumbersome. A great way to keep your perspective on a drawing and navigate at the same time is by using the Pan and Zoom window, shown in Figure 2-10. This tiny window gives you a full-page view of your drawing and marks the area you're currently "zoomed in" on with a red rectangle. You can use the red rectangle simply to keep an eye on the area you're working in, or you can move the rectangle to a different location in the drawing.

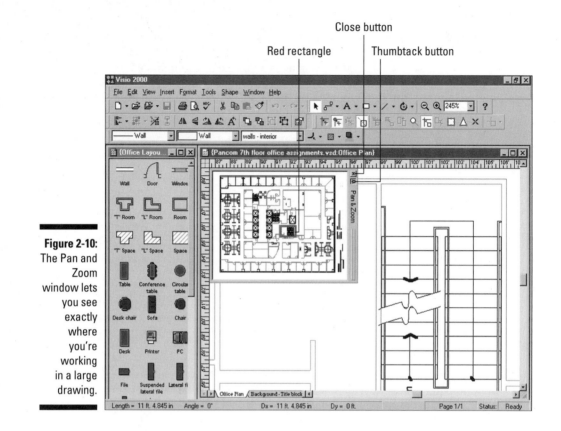

Figure 2-10:
The Pan and
Zoom
window lets
you see
exactly
where
you're
working
in a large
drawing.

To use the Pan and Zoom window, follow these steps:

1. **Choose View➪Windows➪Pan & Zoom from the submenu that appears.**

   Visio displays the Pan and Zoom window. The red rectangle outlines the
   area of the drawing you're currently viewing.

2. **You have three options:**

   • To zoom in on a different area of the drawing, place your mouse
     over the red rectangle until the mouse pointer changes to a four-
     headed arrow. Drag the red rectangle to a new location in the
     drawing.

   • To move to a completely different location in the drawing, point
     anywhere outside of the red rectangle and drag the mouse pointer.
     A new rectangle is drawn automatically and Visio shifts your view
     of the document.

- To resize the red rectangle (which changes the size of the area you view in the drawing), move the mouse pointer over the red rectangle until the mouse pointer changes to a two-headed arrow. Click and drag the arrow in any direction to resize the rectangle. Visio automatically shifts your view of the drawing to the boundaries defined by the red rectangle.

Like other windows, you can make the Pan and Zoom window a floating window by dragging it anywhere on the screen. Or, you can dock it along any edge of the drawing area just by dragging it (it snaps into place along the edge it's closest to). Notice that when the window is docked, the Thumbtack button is depressed (see Figure 2-10) to show that the window is "thumbtacked" in place. Clicking on the thumbtack and then moving the mouse away from the window is like removing the thumbtack. The window rolls up like a window shade to keep from blocking your view of the drawing. The title bar for the window shade is still docked along the edge of the drawing area. When you want to use the window again, just move your mouse over the title bar and the window reappears.

Using the Drawing Explorer

The Drawing Explorer is like "central database administration" for your drawing. It keeps track of a truckload of data (some you might think trivial!) about a drawing, such as:

- Number and name of foreground and background pages
- Order of pages
- Shapes used on a specific drawing page
- Layers used on a specific drawing page
- Styles used throughout the drawing
- Master shapes used throughout the drawing
- Fill pattern, line pattern, and line ends used in the drawing

Why would you possibly care about this kind of information? For some drawings, you may not care and won't even bother to open the Drawing Explorer. But just knowing that the information is readily accessible is a great help. Suppose, for example, you used a shape in a drawing that you want to use again, but you don't know remember the name of it. Go to the Drawing Explorer, and you'll find the name of the shape. Suppose you used a particular pattern and fill that you want to use again. Go to the Drawing Explorer to find it. Besides just *finding* this information, though, you can also use Drawing Explorer to modify data, copy it, paste it, and so on.

The Drawing Explorer, a separate window, displays information about a drawing in a hierarchical format. It is modeled after Windows Explorer, which uses the tree structure, folder and document icons, and the + and − symbols that indicate whether a folder has contents. In Figure 2-11, the first line in the Drawing Explorer window displays the path name for the drawing. Below the name are various folders, some of which are open, to illustrate the hierarchical format of the information.

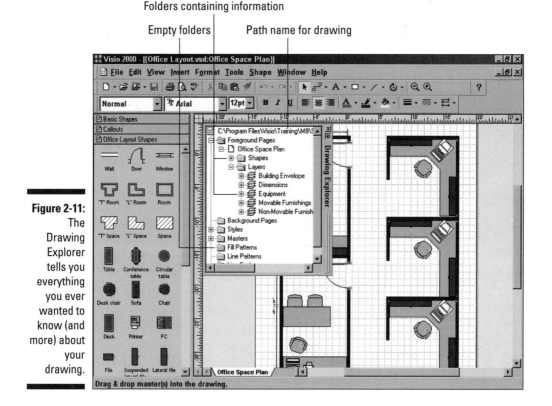

Figure 2-11:
The
Drawing
Explorer
tells you
everything
you ever
wanted to
know (and
more) about
your
drawing.

To open the Drawing Explorer, choose View➪Windows, then choose Drawing Explorer from the submenu. Use Drawing Explorer the same way you use Windows Explorer; click the + symbol to the left of a folder to see its contents. You can right-click any folder or folder entry to display a shortcut menu. The options available on the menu are unique to the item you click. For instance, if you right-click the folder Foreground Pages, the shortcut menu lets you insert or reorder pages.

The best way to learn about Drawing Explorer is to play with it: open and close folders, and right-click everything. You'll soon become familiar with the type of information that's available and your options for using it.

If you open an existing drawing while the Drawing Explorer window is open, it remains open and reflects the data of the current drawing. To close the Drawing Explorer, click the Close button in the upper-right corner of the window.

You can move, dock, or auto-hide the Drawing Explorer window using the same methods used for the Pan and Zoom window. Refer to the "Using the Pan and Zoom window" section earlier in this chapter.

Chapter 3

Printing Pages Hot Off the Press

. . . .

In This Chapter

▶ Getting familiar with Visio's printer lingo

▶ Discovering how Visio "thinks" about printing

▶ Getting a look at your drawing before you print

▶ Preparing oversize drawings for printing

▶ Making adjustments: margins, position, and scale

▶ Adding titles, dates, filenames, page numbers, and so on

. . . .

*F*or the most part, printing in Visio is a breeze — not much different than printing from any other Windows application. However, because Visio drawings can sometimes be non-standard sizes or multiple pages, you need to know about some special printing considerations. In this chapter, I show you everything you need to know to print your drawings successfully.

Understanding Printing Terms

Almost every application has some new terminology to learn, and Visio is no exception. When it comes to printing, most of the terminology is logical, so it's easy to remember. You need to understand Visio definitions of the following terms:

✔ **Drawing page:** Refers to the drawing area that you see on the screen represented in white.

✔ **Page orientation:** The direction a drawing prints on the paper. When you hold a sheet of paper the *tall* way, the orientation is called *portrait*. When you turn the page a quarter turn so that you're holding it the *wide* way, the orientation is called *landscape*.

✔ **Page Setup:** Defines how your drawing page is set up in Visio; that is, its size and orientation. You can change page setup by choosing File⇨ Page Setup.

✔ **Printed page:** The paper on which you print your drawing.

✔ **Printed drawing:** The final result; that is, your drawing as printed on paper by your printer.

✔ **Printer Setup:** Defines the page size and orientation that your printer uses when you print. When you're printing with a 1:1 ratio (drawing size: actual size), Page Setup and Printer Setup settings must match in order to print successfully. You change printer setup by choosing File⇨Page Setup⇨Print Setup.

✔ **Tile:** When a drawing is too large to print on a single sheet of paper, Visio *tiles,* or breaks up, the drawing into separate pages. Each tile prints on a separate sheet of paper. Visio marks where the drawing will tile with a wide gray line, which is visible in Print Preview (see the "Previewing Your Drawing" section later in this chapter).

Setting Up Your Printer with Visio

When you create a drawing in Visio, the drawing page is represented by the white area in the drawing window. You can see the size of the drawing page by looking at the vertical and horizontal rulers along the edges of the drawing area. You can determine the orientation of the drawing page by whether the page is wider than it is tall (landscape) or taller than it is wide (portrait). Choosing File⇨Page Setup tells you the same information. In Figure 3-1, the drawing is landscape on 8½ x 11-inch paper.

The most important concept to keep in mind when printing is that you're printing with a 1:1 ratio for drawing size and actual size. To print successfully, the settings for your printer must match the settings for the drawing page. But you're in luck, because when you use a template to create a drawing, Visio takes care of matching these two settings. You can print your drawing correctly just by selecting File⇨Print.

But, suppose you change something about the drawing — for example, the print orientation. If the template is set for portrait orientation and you change the drawing to landscape, the drawing will not print correctly. Likewise, if your drawing is 8½ x 14 inches and your printer is set up to print on 8½ x 11-inch paper, the complete drawing doesn't print. All printer settings must match drawing page settings. To figure out how to make these changes, see the "Solving Printer Problems" section later in this chapter.

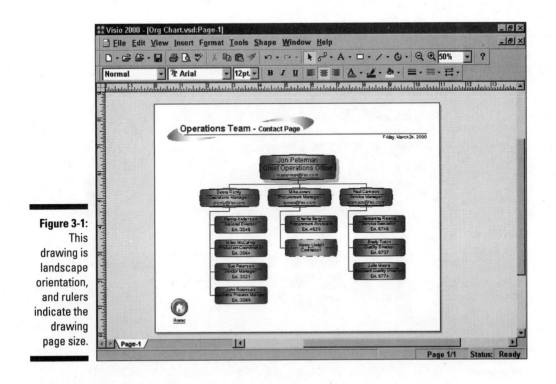

Figure 3-1:
This
drawing is
landscape
orientation,
and rulers
indicate the
drawing
page size.

Previewing Your Drawing

Previewing your drawing lets you see how it will look on the printed page before printing. Your drawing probably isn't nearly as exciting as a Roger Ebert movie review, but it's definitely more important! Figure 3-2 shows how a drawing looks in Preview window.

Previewing a drawing gives you a chance to see that everything in the drawing is placed exactly where you want it, and to check for the correct placement of shapes, balance, symmetry, readability, and so on. Also, check to see that all shapes fall inside the wide gray lines around the edge of the paper, which indicate the drawing's margins. These page margins are only visible in Preview. Shapes that fall across the margin lines don't print completely.

Previewing a drawing also shows you if your drawing page size and orientation match the same settings for your printer. In Figure 3-3, you can see that the printer is expecting to print on 8½ x 11-inch paper in portrait orientation because that's where the preview displays the margin lines.

Notice in Figure 3-2 and Figure 3-3 that the preview screen has its own toolbar. The first four buttons — New Drawing, Open, Save, and Print Page — also appear on the Standard toolbar; the remaining buttons are described in Table 3-1.

Preview menu and toolbar

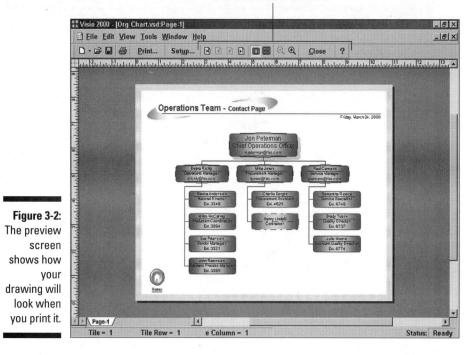

Figure 3-2:
The preview
screen
shows how
your
drawing will
look when
you print it.

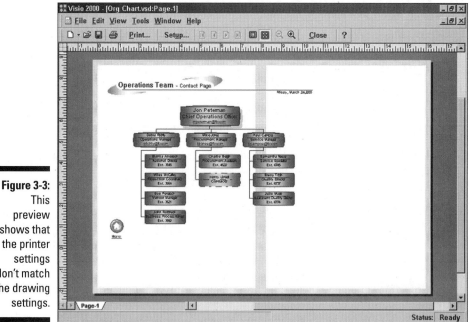

Figure 3-3:
This
preview
shows that
the printer
settings
don't match
the drawing
settings.

Table 3-1	Preview Toolbar Buttons
Button	*Function*
Print...	**Print:** Prints the current page as shown.
Setup...	**Page Setup:** Displays the Page Setup dialog box (refer to Figure 3-4).
	First Tile: When you select the Single Tile option, clicking this button displays the first tile.
	Previous Tile: When you select the Single Tile option, clicking this button displays the tile before the one currently displayed.
	Next Tile: When you select the Single Tile option, clicking this button displays the tile after the one that's currently displayed.
	Last Tile: When you select the Single Tile option, clicking this button displays the last tile.
	Single Tile: Lets you view a single tile at a time in a drawing that's tiled.
	Whole Page: Lets you view all tiles in a drawing at the same time.
	Zoom Out: Reduces your view in the Preview window so that you can see more of the drawing.
	Zoom In: Magnifies your view in the preview window. (You see less of the drawing.)
Close	**Close:** Closes the Preview window and takes you back to Normal drawing view.
?	**Help:** Changes the mouse pointer to a question mark; displays help on the item that you click.

Solving Printer Problems

So, when you run into printing problems, how do you solve them? Remember the most important principle of printing with Visio: You have to make your Page Setup and your Print Setup match.

Begin by looking at your drawing in Print Preview. If the drawing looks good to you on the screen (it fits without overflowing, and so on), you probably want to print it with the current settings. Follow these steps:

1. **Choose File➪Page Setup.**

2. **In the Page Setup dialog box (shown in Figure 3-4), select the Print Setup tab.**

   Check to see that the Paper Size (standard 8½ x 11 or other) and the Paper Orientation (portrait or landscape) are correct for the paper you're printing on.

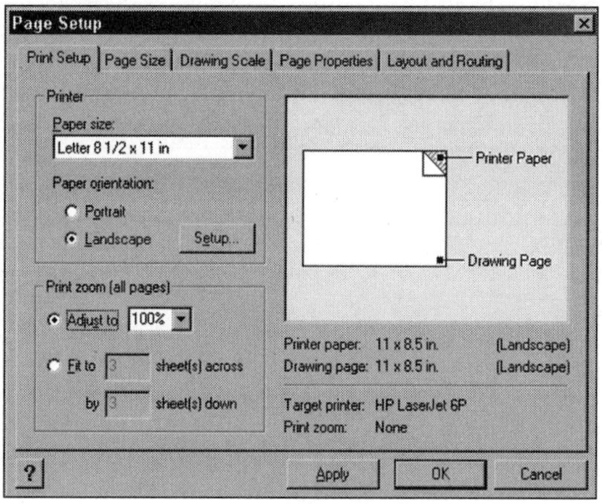

Figure 3-4:
The Print Setup dialog box shows printer settings.

Page Setup	
Print Setup	Page Size	Drawing Scale	Page Properties	Layout and Routing	

Printer

Paper size:
Letter 8 1/2 x 11 in

Paper orientation:
○ Portrait
● Landscape   Setup...

Printer Paper

Drawing Page

Print zoom (all pages)
● Adjust to 100%
○ Fit to 3 sheet(s) across
by 3 sheet(s) down

Printer paper: 11 x 8.5 in.   (Landscape)
Drawing page: 11 x 8.5 in.   (Landscape)
Target printer: HP LaserJet 6P
Print zoom: None

Apply   OK   Cancel

3. **Select the Page Size tab.**

   Visio displays the dialog box, as shown in Figure 3-5.

4. **In the Page Size box, click the Same As Printer Paper Size option.**

5. **Click the OK button.**

If you want to save the settings you choose in the previous steps as default settings, click Apply in Step 5, then click the OK button.

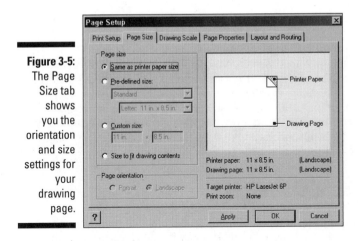

Figure 3-5:
The Page
Size tab
shows
you the
orientation
and size
settings for
your
drawing
page.

Changing margin settings

If your drawing doesn't quite fit on the page, you can sometimes tweak the margin settings enough to fit the drawing on the page. Before you consider this option, think about the aesthetic appeal of the drawing. You don't want your drawing to look like you squeezed a Chevy Suburban into a parking space marked for a compact car. If you have room to breathe in your drawing, narrowing the margins may work.

Be aware, however, that many printers can't print within ½ an inch of the edge of the paper (top, bottom, or sides). I recommend that you keep your margins at least ½-inch wide or more. Check your printer's manual to determine your printer's capabilities.

To change margin settings, use these steps:

1. **Choose File⇨Page Setup.**

   Visio displays the Print Setup tab in the Page Setup dialog box (refer to Figure 3-4).

2. **In the Print Setup dialog box, click the Setup button (next to the portrait and landscape options).**

3. **In the Margins box, enter the new margin measurements in the Left, Right, Top, and Bottom boxes (enter fractions as decimals, such as .5 for ½ inch).**

4. **Click the OK button to close the Print Setup dialog box.**

5. **Click the OK button again to exit Page Setup.**

If you want to save the settings you choose in the previous steps as default settings, click Apply in Step 5 and then click the OK button.

Now that you're back at your drawing, choose View➪Page Breaks. This command displays the margins as gray lines around the outer edges of the drawing page. Check to make sure that all your drawing shapes fit within the new margins. If the shapes still don't fit on a single drawing page, consider scaling the drawing when you print. See the "Reducing and enlarging printed drawings" section later in this chapter.

Centering a drawing

If you create a drawing that doesn't take up an entire page, you may want to center it on the page before you print it. You can do this by selecting all of the shapes on the drawing and moving them manually, but this method isn't very accurate (and is way too time-consuming). Visio makes it easy and exact by providing a command that does it for you. When you choose Tools➪ Center Drawing, Visio automatically centers all shapes in the drawing between the top, bottom, right, and left edges of the paper. When you print the drawing, it appears in the center of the page.

Reducing and enlarging printed drawings

When you create an *oversized drawing* (larger than the paper in your printer), you can see in Print Preview that the drawing doesn't print on a single sheet of paper. One option is to change the *print scale* (the reduction or enlargement of the printed drawing) until it fits on a single sheet of paper. Conversely, when a drawing is too small — so small that it's difficult to read — you can enlarge the print scale and make it easier to read when you print it.

Keep in mind that the print scale is completely different from the *drawing scale,* which is the size of the actual drawing. I show you how to change the drawing scale in Chapter 7.

Altering the print scale of a drawing

To alter the print scale of a drawing, use these steps:

1. **Choose File➪Open to display your drawing.**

2. **Choose File➪Page Setup.**

   Visio displays the Print Setup tab in the Page Setup dialog box (see Figure 3-4).

3. **In the Print Zoom section of the dialog box, click the Adjust To option.**

   Enter a number smaller than 100 percent to reduce the printed size of the drawing. Enter a number greater than 100 percent to enlarge the printed size of a drawing.

4. **Click the OK button to close the Page Setup dialog box.**

You may expect your drawing to change on the screen, but it doesn't. This is because you've altered the *print* scale only, not the *drawing* scale. (It's just like reducing or enlarging a page on a photo copier — your original doesn't change; only the copied result changes.) To check that the change will take place when you print, click the Print Preview Tool button or choose File⇨ Print Preview. The Print Preview shows you exactly how the drawing will fit on the paper. If you need to print the drawing at regular scale, be sure to follow the previous steps to change the percentage back to 100 before you print again.

Tiling a drawing

Suppose you don't want to reduce your drawing so that it fits on a single sheet of paper. Another option for printing oversized drawing is to specify exactly how many sheets of paper that you want your drawing to fit on. This is called *tiling* a drawing.

Use these steps to specify the number of sheets a drawing prints on:

1. **Choose File⇨Open to display your drawing.**

2. **Choose File⇨Page Setup.**

   Visio displays the Print Setup tab in the Page Setup dialog box (see Figure 3-4).

3. **In the Print Zoom section of the dialog box, click the Fit To option and then enter the number of sheets across and the number of sheets down.**

4. **Click the OK button to close the Page Setup dialog box.**

   If you have Page Breaks displayed (View⇨Page Breaks), you can see how Visio tiles your drawing across the number of pages you specify. Or, you can see the page breaks by clicking the Print Preview toolbar button.

Fitting the drawing on the number of pages you specify doesn't affect the actual scale of the drawing — just the printed copy.

Printing Your Documents

If the settings for your drawing page and your printer match, you're ready to print. Follow these steps:

1. **Choose File➪Open to display your drawing.**

2. **Choose File➪Print.**

   Visio displays the Print dialog box, as shown in Figure 3-6. (Note that your Print dialog box may look slightly different depending on the printer you're using.)

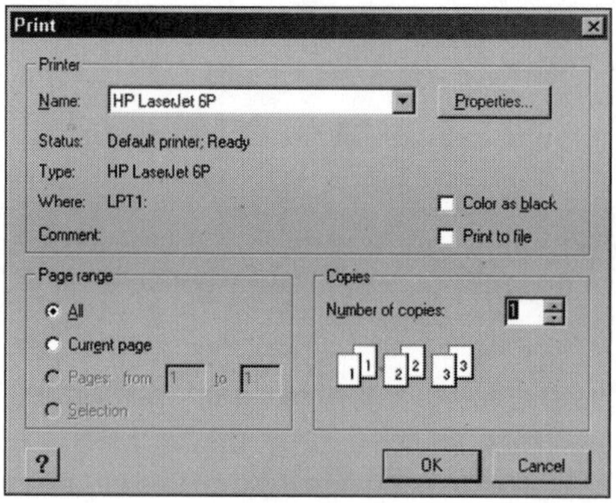

Figure 3-6:
Use the
Print dialog
box to
specify how
you want to
print your
drawing.

3. **In the Printer Name box, select the correct printer.**

   (This is only necessary if you have access to more than one printer.)

4. **In the Page Range dialog box, indicate which pages you want to print.**

   • **All:** Prints all pages in the drawing.

   • **Current:** Prints the page that is currently displayed on the screen.

   • **Pages:** Prints a range of pages; enter the first page number in the From box and the last page number in the To box.

5. **In the Copies box, enter the number of copies that you want.**

6. **Click the OK button to print.**

See? That wasn't so hard.

Some Windows applications also give you the option of printing a group of selected pages, such as 2, 4, and 7. Visio doesn't provide this option. To print a group of selected pages, you need to print each page individually by entering in the Pages option from 2 to 2, printing that page, entering from 4 to 4, printing again, and so on.

Adding Headers and Footers to a Drawing

A *header* refers to text that appears at the top of each page of a drawing; a *footer* is text that appears at the bottom of each page. Headers and footers are optional. If you decide to add them to a drawing, you can include text such as a title, filename, date, or automatic page numbers. You decide where you want them to appear in the header or footer area — left, center, or right.

To add a header or footer to a drawing, follow these steps:

1. **Choose File⇨Open to display your drawing.**

2. **Choose View⇨Header and Footer.**

   Visio displays the Header and Footer dialog box, as shown in Figure 3-7.

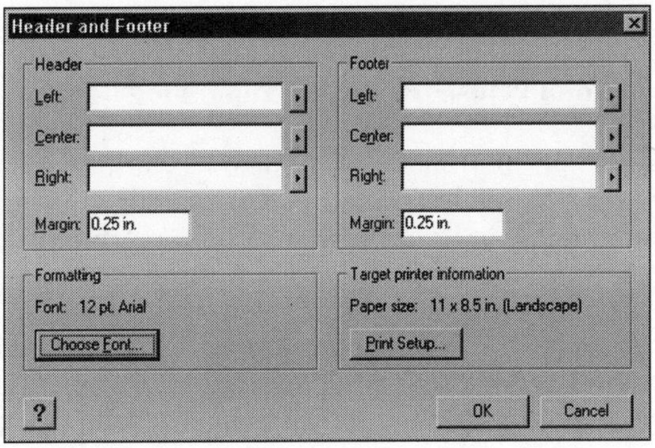

Figure 3-7: Type the text for headers and footers in this dialog box.

3. **In the appropriate Header or Footer text box (Left, Center, Right, and so on), type the information that you want to appear.**

4. **In the Margins area, enter a size for the header margin and footer margin.**

   You can type up to 128 characters in each header or footer box. I can't imagine why you would want that much information, but if you do, be sure to estimate the space you need when entering a margin size.

5. **To format the header and footer text, click the Choose Font button, which displays the Font dialog box, as shown in Figure 3-8.**

   Formatting applies to all header and footer text; you can't format each one individually.

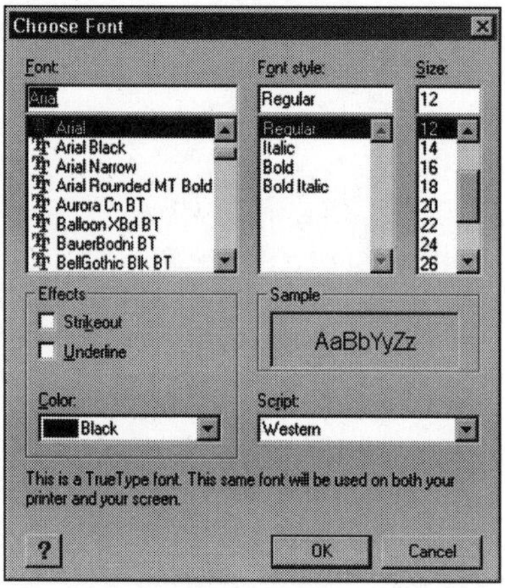

Figure 3-8:
Use the Font
dialog box
to format
header and
footer text.

6. **In the Font dialog box, choose a font, size, style, special effects, and color for the header and footer text.**

7. **Click the OK button to close the Font dialog box.**

8. **Click the OK button to close the Page Setup dialog box.**

Click the Print Preview Tool button or choose File⇨ Print Preview to see how your header and footer text will look when you print your drawing. (Header and footer text is only visible in Print Preview or on the printed drawing.)

In a tiled drawing, Visio prints headers and footers on each tile. When you have to tile a drawing to print it, you may want to put header and footer information on a background page (a separate page that works as an "underlay") instead. See Chapter 9 for details about creating background pages.

To add common text — time, date, filename, and page number — to a header or footer, click the arrow to the right of the Header and Footer text boxes (refer to Figure 3-7). The complete list of items you can automatically insert includes

- ✔ Current date (long)
- ✔ Current date (short)
- ✔ Current time
- ✔ File extension
- ✔ Filename
- ✔ Filename and extension
- ✔ Page name
- ✔ Page number
- ✔ Total pages printed

When you click one of these items in the dialog box, Visio enters a formatting code in the text box. Note that you can use more than one of these items for each text box. For example, if you want a centered header to include the page number, page name, and filename, click all three options for the Header Center text box. Be sure to add punctuation or spaces between each entry.

Part II

Creating Basic Drawings

The 5th Wave — By Rich Tennant

"Don't let Mort work on the office diagram next time."

In this part . . .

1f you don't have a whole lot of time to spend reading about Visio, this is definitely the part to focus on. There is a lot of the basic stuff here: how to get some basic shapes into a drawing, how to connect shapes, and how to throw some text in there, too, so you can describe your drawings. What more do you need to know?

Chapter 4

Discovering What Visio Shapes Are All About

Shapes are the most important elements of Visio; they're the building blocks that you use to create diagrams, drawings, charts, and graphs. Regardless of the type of drawing that you need to create — a flowchart, a network diagram, an architectural drawing, a project timeline — you can create each drawing by using shapes. In this chapter, I show you all the different types of shapes in Visio and how to work with them.

Discovering What's In a Shape

If you think you may not have enough shapes to choose from when you're building your drawings, think again. Visio Standard includes more than 1,300 shapes; Visio Professional and Technical contain nearly twice and three times as many shapes, respectively. Shapes are stored on *stencils,* which are collections of related shapes that are displayed in their own window on your Visio screen. You create most drawings by using stored Visio shapes, but you also can create and store your own shapes. Chapter 8 covers creating and storing shapes.

A shape can be as simple as a single line or as complex as a network component for a computer system. Unlike clip art, shapes have certain "smart" characteristics. If you add text to a shape and then move the shape, the text moves along with it.

If you resize a shape at its corner, the shape maintains its height and width proportions. Shapes with glued connectors (like the lines that connect boxes on an organization chart or flow chart) stay connected when you move them. Some shapes are easy to customize, such as the number of slices in a pie chart. A complex shape can contain special programming that makes the shape behave in a particular way. For example, a bar chart shape from the Charting Shapes stencil adjusts the length of its bars automatically after you type in a percentage for one of the bars (see Figure 4-1).

You can control a particular aspect of a shape, such as the angle and direction of the vanishing point of a three-dimensional shape like a cube. (The *vanishing point* is the point at which the lines of a three-dimensional object converge.) You can store data with a shape; for example, tracking capital equipment and generating inventory reports. (For more information about storing data in shapes, see Chapter 14.) Now you know why Visio shapes are called *SmartShapes*. Many of them have built-in brainy behavior.

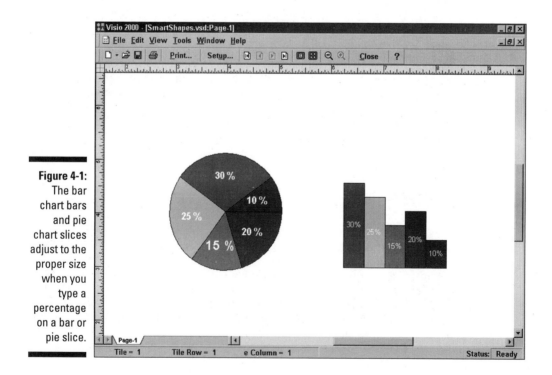

Figure 4-1:
The bar chart bars and pie chart slices adjust to the proper size when you type a percentage on a bar or pie slice.

Examining open and closed shapes

Shapes can be classified as either *open* or *closed,* as shown in Figure 4-2. An open shape is one in which the endpoints aren't connected, such as a line, arc, or an abstract shape. A closed shape is a fully connected object such as a polygon.

What difference does it make whether a shape is open or closed? You can fill a closed shape with a color or a pattern. You can't fill an open shape, but you can add endpoints such as arrows and other symbols.

Comparing one- and two-dimensional shapes

All Visio shapes are either one-dimensional or two-dimensional. Two-dimensional shapes have length and height. When you select a two-dimensional shape with the Pointer tool, you can see its *handles* (see Figure 4-3).

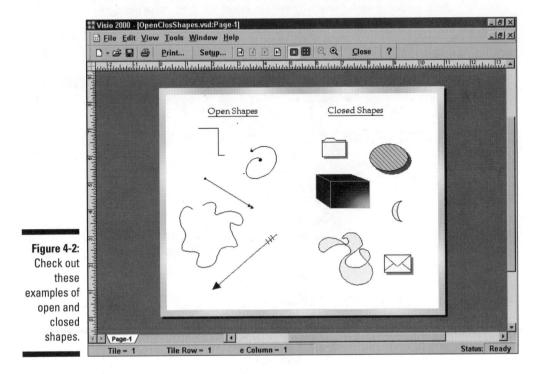

Figure 4-2:
Check out these examples of open and closed shapes.

Handles are green squares that appear at the corners and sides of a shape. (Later you see that handles can look different when you select a shape using a different tool.) The handles enable you to change the shape's length and height. Even a non-rectangular shape (such as a pie chart) displays a rectangular *frame* with side and corner handles when the shape is selected. A frame is a green dotted line that fully encloses a shape.

A line is an example of a one-dimensional shape. It has only two *endpoints* — small green boxes — that are visible when you select the line (see Figure 4-4). The beginning point — that is, the point from which you begin drawing — contains an x; the endpoint contains a (+) symbol.

You can resize the length of a one-dimensional shape, but not its height; a one-dimensional shape has no height. (A line has *thickness,* which you can alter by using a formatting command. Thickness is not the same as height.)

An arc is considered a one-dimensional shape, although it may seem to be two-dimensional. Notice in Figure 4-4 that an arc has only two endpoints; it doesn't have a frame with handles at each corner and side. The handle at the top of the arc is called a *control handle,* which enables you to adjust the bend of the arc. See the "Controlling Your Shapes" section later in this chapter, to find out more about working with control handles on other types of shapes.

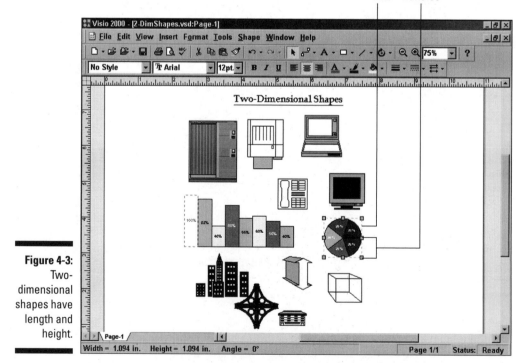

Figure 4-3:
Two-dimensional shapes have length and height.

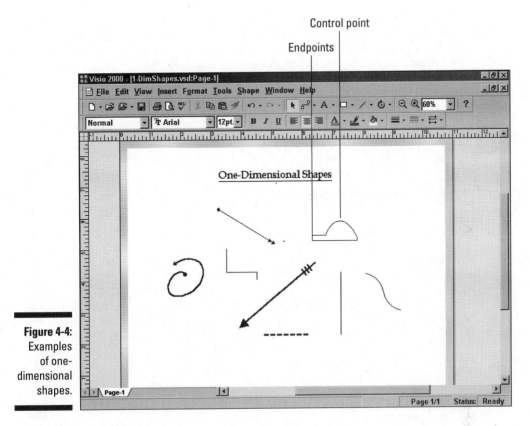

Control point

Endpoints

Figure 4-4:
Examples
of one-
dimensional
shapes.

You see a shape's handles only when the shape is selected. The type of handle you see depends upon the tool that you use to select the shape. You see more examples of both throughout this chapter.

Dragging Shapes into Your Drawing

So, how do you get shapes into a drawing? You drag 'em in. It's almost too simple. On the stencil, position the mouse pointer over the shape that you want in your drawing, click and *hold down* the left mouse button; then drag the shape into the drawing area. Release the mouse button when the shape is where you want it. (As simple as it is, don't be embarrassed if you click a shape, then click the drawing area and wonder why your shape isn't there. This may happen a couple of times before you remember to hold the mouse button and *drag!*)

You can drag a shape into a drawing as many times as you want — the master shape stays on the stencil. As you drag a shape into your drawing area, you see an outline of the shape on the screen. When you release the mouse button, the actual shape appears in your drawing. The shape may not be exactly the size that you want. (If you just can't wait to adjust it, see the "Sizing up your shapes" section later in this chapter.)

Remember that you can open as many stencils as you need when you create a drawing. Just choose File⇨Stencils.

Selecting Shapes

Believe it or not, selecting a shape in a drawing is even easier than dragging it onto a drawing — just click the shape. When you select a shape, its green handles become visible. You need to select a shape before you can move it, copy it, delete it, or change it in any other way.

Sometimes you may want to perform the same task (such as moving or copying) on several shapes at a time. To select more than one shape, hold down the Shift key as you click each shape that you want to select. The green handles are visible on the first shape that you select. If you select more shapes, the handles are blue.

You can also select shapes by dragging a *selection box* around them (see Figure 4-5). A selection box fully encloses the shapes you want to select. Select the Pointer Tool button (the one that looks like an arrow) on the toolbar, and then drag the mouse around the shapes that you want to select. As you drag the mouse, you draw a selection box around the shapes. You must fully enclose all the shapes that you want to select; if you cut across a shape, it isn't selected. You know the shapes are selected because you'll see their selection handles. (The first shape's handles appear in green; the remaining shapes' handles appear in blue.)

If you select a bunch of shapes and then decide to exclude one of them, you can deselect it without deselecting all of the shapes. Hold down the Shift key and click that particular shape again. You can tell that you successfully deselected the shape because the selection handles disappear. To deselect all shapes, click in any blank area of the drawing, or press Esc.

Press Ctrl+A to select all shapes in a drawing quickly, or choose Edit⇨ Select All.

Handles   Selection box

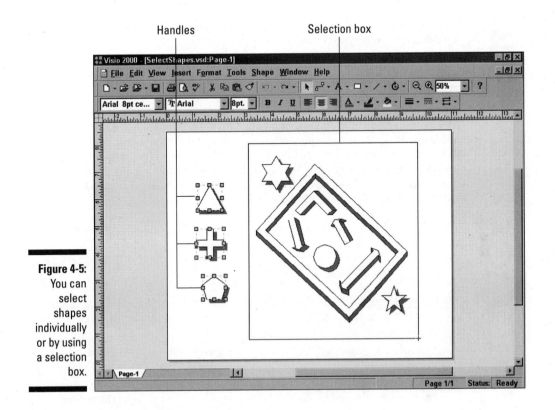

Figure 4-5:
You can
select
shapes
individually
or by using
a selection
box.

Manipulating Your Shapes

You can manipulate shapes after you drag them into your drawing. In this
section, I describe some of the most common ways that you can alter shapes.
Table 4-1 shows several toolbar buttons that you can use to alter shapes.

Table 4-1	Tools on the Standard Toolbar
Button	*Function*
✂	Cut
📋	Copy
📋	Paste
🔨	Stamp

To drag a shape, you have to click the shape with the left mouse button and hold the button as you move the shape.

Moving shapes

After you have shapes in your drawing, you may want to move them around. Moving a shape is simple; just drag the shape wherever you want it. As you drag a shape, watch the vertical and horizontal rulers. The shape's position is highlighted on the ruler. If you want to place a shape 3 inches from the top border of your drawing and 2 inches from the left border, you can see where using the rulers aligns the shape's frame.

You can restrict the movement of a shape by holding down the Shift key as you drag the shape. If you drag the shape horizontally, it moves only to the right and left, and keeps its vertical position. If you drag the shape vertically, it moves up and down and keeps its horizontal position.

See Chapter 7 for additional information on how to snap shapes into alignment by using rulers, a grid, and alignment commands that can make the placement of your shapes more exact.

Nudging shapes

Visio 2000 lets you *nudge* shapes, a great feature that saves you time when you reposition shapes. Nudging is essentially bumping a selected shape by using the arrow keys on the keyboard. When you nudge a shape, the shape moves in tiny increments, usually to the nearest ruler subdivision. Variables such as the ruler scale, grid, and the zoom percentage you use can determine how much the shape moves. It's best to use this feature when you want to move a shape only slightly.

Try this quick and easy way to reposition shapes:

1. **Click the shape that you want to nudge.**

2. **Position the shape where you want it by pressing the up, down, right, or left arrow key repeatedly.**

If you want to nudge several shapes at the same time, just hold down the Shift key as you select the shapes you want and then use your arrow keys to nudge the selected shapes as a unit.

Copying and pasting shapes

To copy a shape, select the shape that you want to copy. You can then use one of these four methods to copy the shape:

- ✔ Press Ctrl+C
- ✔ Click the Copy button on the Standard toolbar
- ✔ Select Edit⇨Copy
- ✔ Hold down the Ctrl key and drag (you see a (+) symbol attached to the mouse pointer) and then release

I prefer keyboard shortcuts because they're so fast. All of these methods place a copy of the shape (or shapes) on the Windows Clipboard.

To paste the shape in a new location:

- ✔ Press Ctrl+V
- ✔ Click the Paste button on the Standard toolbar
- ✔ Choose Edit⇨Paste

A quick way to copy and paste all at once is to select a shape, then press Ctrl+D or choose Edit⇨Duplicate. The shape is pasted to the right and slightly below the copied shape. Now you can move it wherever you want.

Stamping shapes

If you need to use a shape over and over again, the stamp feature in Visio is a nifty tool that saves you dragging time. This tool works just like a rubber stamp; wherever you stamp it, the shape is pasted into your drawing. Follow these steps to use the stamping tool:

1. **Click the Stamp Tool button (refer to Table 4-1) on the Standard toolbar.**

2. **In the stencil, click the shape that you want to stamp.**

3. **Drag the mouse into the drawing area.**

   Notice that your mouse pointer now looks like a stamp.

4. **Click the mouse where you want to stamp the shape.**

   Keep clicking until you've added all the stamped shapes that you want in your drawing.

5. **Click the Pointer Tool button to switch back to the regular mouse pointer.**

Sizing up your shapes

It's likely that you may want to resize some of the shapes you use in your drawings. Use the following steps to adjust the size of your shapes.

1. **Select the shape with the Pointer Tool and do one of the following:**

   • Drag a side handle to change a shape's width.

   • Drag a top or bottom handle to change a shape's height.

   • Drag a corner handle to change the height and width at the same time.

   • To maintain a shape's height-to-width proportions, press and hold the Ctrl key as you drag a corner handle.

2. **Release the mouse button when the shape is the size that you want.**

If your shape contains text, the text reformats automatically as you resize the shape. (See Chapter 5 to find out how to enter text in shapes.)

The previous steps may seem to imply that all shapes are parallelograms. They're not; but remember that every shape has a rectangular frame, which *is* a parallelogram, so that the shape can be resized in width, height, or both proportionally.

If you want a shape to be a specific size, for example, 2 x 1.5 inches, remember to watch the status bar at the bottom of the screen as you resize the shape. The status bar displays the shape's height and width as you move the mouse. Did you know that you can click the status bar to resize a selected shape? You bet you can. When you click the status bar, a Size and Position window appears. Just fill in the height and width you want and then press Enter. (To close the window, click the Close button in the upper-right corner of the window.)

Deleting shapes

You can delete a shape in one of four ways. First select the shape and then do one of the following:

- ✔ Press the Delete key
- ✔ Click the Cut button on the Standard toolbar
- ✔ Choose Edit➪Cut
- ✔ Press Ctrl+X

Pressing the Delete key is the easiest way to delete a shape. If you think you may want to bring back the shape, use Cut. That way, the shape is stored on the Clipboard so that you can paste it in the drawing again (as long as you paste it before you cut anything else).

You can use the same method to delete more than one shape at a time. Select all shapes you want to delete (either click them or draw a selection box around them) and then delete by using one of these methods:

- ✔ Press the Delete key
- ✔ Click the Cut button on the Standard toolbar
- ✔ Choose Edit➪Cut
- ✔ Press Ctrl+X

If you delete something by mistake, you can choose Edit➪Undo (or press Ctrl+Z) to bring it back. By default, Visio has ten levels of Undo, so you can undo up to the last ten commands that you performed.

Controlling Your Shapes

You can select a shape by using the tools shown in Table 4-2. (The tool you choose depends on the task you want to perform. For example, if you want to alter the form of a shape, use the Pencil tool. To draw an abstract shape, use the Freeform tool.) A list of tools is included on the Cheat Sheet in the front of this book.

When you select a shape, it displays *selection handles* that enable you to control the shape in some way. The handles a shape displays depend on the tool that you use to select the shape. Shapes can have other types of handles — so many that you can lose track of them all!

Table 4-2	More Tools on the Standard Toolbar
Button	**Tool**
▲	Pointer tool
A	Text tool
□	Rectangle tool
○	Ellipse tool
/	Line tool
⌐	Arc tool
∿	Freeform tool
✎	Pencil tool
A	Rotation tool

Adjusting shapes with control handles

Some shapes have control handles as well as selection handles. Unless you look closely, you may confuse the two types of handles. Both handles are green squares, but control handles are darkly shaded. Control handles appear somewhere on or near the shape, and enable you to control some aspect of the shape, whereas selection handles only let you resize a shape. For example, manipulating the control handle on a cube lets you adjust the cube's vanishing point, that is, the depth and length of the cube and the angle from which you view it. (See Figure 4-6.)

In a bar chart (a shape from the Charting Shapes stencil), the control handles enable you to change the number of bars and their relative heights.

If you've ever worked in a Windows environment, you know that when you pass the mouse pointer over a tool on the toolbar, a box pops up and explains the function of the tool. Visio provides a pop-up box for control handles as well. (That's a good thing, because guessing what some control handles do can be difficult.) Another way to find out a tool's function is to right-click a shape in your drawing and then choose Shape Help from the shortcut menu.

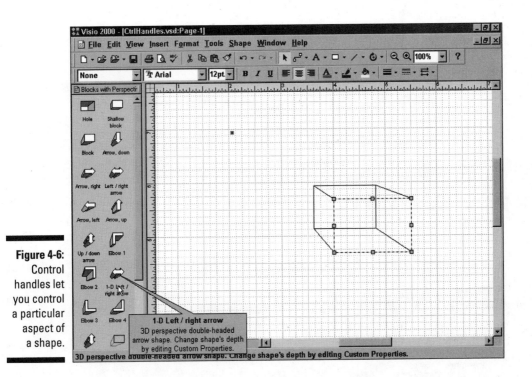

Figure 4-6:
Control
handles let
you control
a particular
aspect of
a shape.

Controlling shapes with control points

Control points are green circles that appear between vertices on certain shapes, lines, and arcs when you select them with the pencil tool. Control points are different from control handles because they let you control the "shape of a shape." So, if you want to make a straight-sided rectangle look like a bulging rectangle, you drag the rectangle's control points. If you want to change a straight-sided pentagon to a curved one, you drag the shape's control points. Figure 4-7 shows how a pentagon shape looks before and after its control points are moved. You can think of a control point as a rubber band point.

Shaping corners with vertices

Just as control points enable you to change the sides of a shape, *vertices* let you change the corners of a shape. (Technically, vertices are the points at which two lines intersect, but thinking of them as corners may be easier.) You can display vertices, green diamond-shaped points, by selecting a shape with the Line, Arc, or Pencil tools (refer to Table 4-2).

Pencil tool

Control point

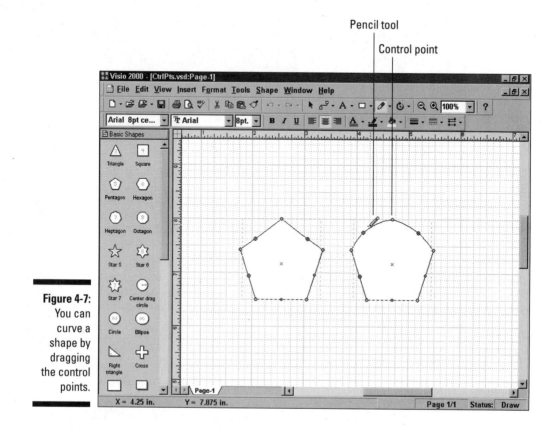

Figure 4-7:
You can
curve a
shape by
dragging
the control
points.

When you select a vertex, it turns magenta. After you select a vertex, you can drag it in any direction, changing the length and angle of the lines that form the vertex. If you want to alter the slope of a roof in a drawing, for example, drag the top vertex. (See Figure 4-8.) To find out how to add or delete vertices, see Chapter 8.

You can seldom display vertices on a shape that you drag into a drawing, particularly complex shapes. However, you can always display vertices on shapes that you draw. (After all, if a Visio shape isn't quite what you want, you may want to draw your own.) Some Visio shapes are complex enough that moving a vertex may destroy the shape. See Chapter 8 for information about drawing your own shapes.

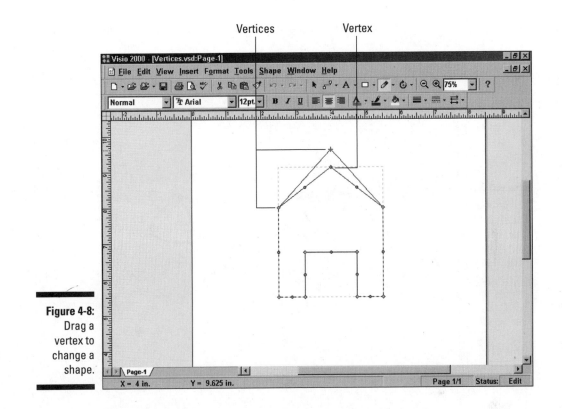

Vertices   Vertex

Figure 4-8:
Drag a
vertex to
change a
shape.

Rotating objects into place

You can rotate many Visio shapes so that you can place them at the angle
you prefer. To display a shape's *rotation handles*, click the Rotation Tool
button (refer to Table 4-2) on the Standard toolbar; then select the shape.
Rotation handles appear as round green handles at the corners of a shape's
frame. After a rotation handle appears in each corner, you can rotate the
shape starting at any corner you choose.

Notice that when you choose the Rotation tool, the mouse pointer changes to
a right angle with a curved arrow. When you move the pointer over a rotation
handle on the shape, the mouse pointer changes to two curved arrows in the
shape of a circle (see Figure 4-9). The *center of rotation*, which marks the
point around which the object moves, is a green circle with a + symbol.

Rotation handle   Center of rotation   Rotation mouse pointer

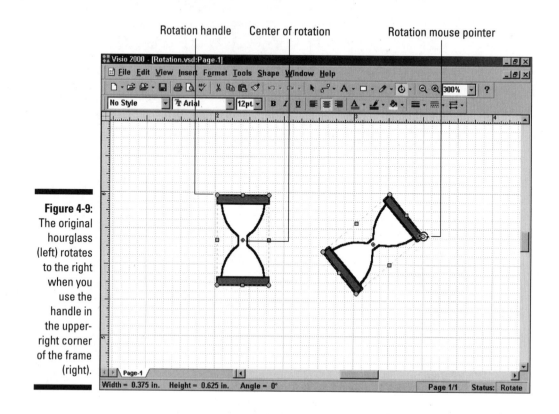

Figure 4-9:
The original
hourglass
(left) rotates
to the right
when you
use the
handle in
the upper-
right corner
of the frame
(right).

To rotate a shape, drag a rotation handle using a circular motion. The mouse pointer changes to a rotation pointer, and you see an outline of the frame as you rotate it around the center of rotation. (Check out Chapter 8 for more details on rotating shapes.)

Modifying shapes with the Eccentricity handles

In simple, non-techie terms, an elliptical shape is an oval. In Visio, an elliptical shape can also be *part* of an oval, as in an oval-shaped arc. (Circles and circular-shaped arcs are *not* elliptical shapes.) Eccentricity handles are designed to let you adjust two aspects of an elliptical shape: its angle and its *off-centeredness,* or *eccentricity.* For example, if you draw an arc, you can use the eccentricity handles to change the angle at which the arc sits relative to its endpoints, or change the eccentricity of the arc relative to its endpoints.

Eccentricity handles are visible only when you select a shape with the Pencil tool. Eccentricity handles look like a pair of green circles with a (+) inside each circle. A third green circle (also containing a (+) symbol) sits between the two eccentricity handles. This is actually a control point used for changing the *height* of a curve. A green dotted line connects all three circles. The dotted line represents the angle at which the curve sits relative to the curve's endpoints (see Figure 4-10).

To change the height of an arc, click the control point at the top of the arc and drag it in any direction. If you want your arc to angle differently, drag either eccentricity handle up or down. To change an arc's eccentricity, drag either eccentricity handle closer to or farther from the control point. (The closer the eccentricity handles are to the control point, the more circular the arc becomes.) The best way to figure out how to work with eccentricity handles is to play with them!

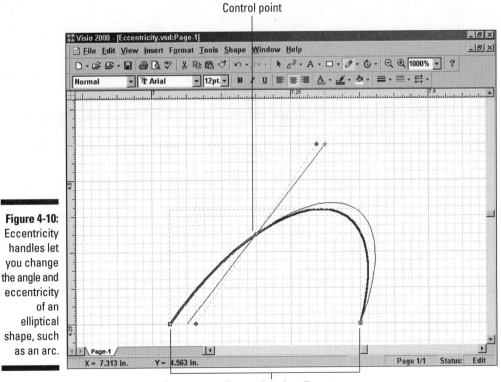

Control point

Figure 4-10:
Eccentricity handles let you change the angle and eccentricity of an elliptical shape, such as an arc.

Eccentricity handles

Using connection points

Connection points are the places on a shape where the endpoints of other one-dimensional shapes (such as lines) can connect to the shape. For example, the boxes in an organization chart have connection points where the lines connect to the boxes.

You can display connection points by choosing View⇨Connection Points. These small, blue Xs can appear almost anywhere on a shape — usually at corners, midpoints of lines, or centers of shapes (see Figure 4-11). You can clutter your screen by displaying connection points all the time! I recommend that you display them only when you need them. To turn off connection points, choose View⇨Connection Points.

Unlocking padlocked shapes

You are free to alter most shapes in Visio. However, some of Visio's more complex shapes are locked so that you can't rotate, flip, move, delete, select,

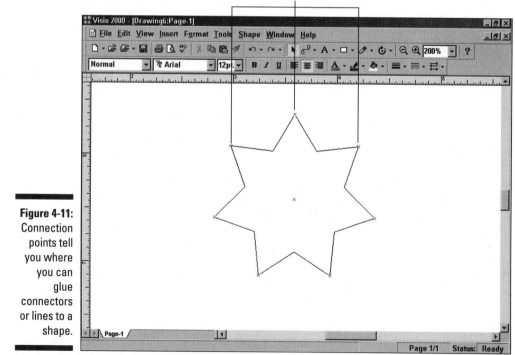

Figure 4-11:
Connection points tell you where you can glue connectors or lines to a shape.

or resize the shape. When a Visio shape is locked, you see padlocks instead of selection handles at the corners of its frame. (They're called *padlocks*, but they may look more like a nut and bolt!) Notice the padlocks that appear on the keyboard section of the laptop computer (see Figure 4-12). This measure is designed to protect you from yourself! You don't want to accidentally go mucking up one of Visio's masterpiece shapes.

When a shape is locked against changes other than the ones I just mentioned, you don't see padlocks, but you still can't make a change. You can prevent change to any shape by using a padlock. It may be a good idea to use a padlock if you know that some inexperienced Visio users are snooping around your drawings!

You can lock a shape by using the Format⇨Protection command. See Chapter 14 to find out how to protect shapes.

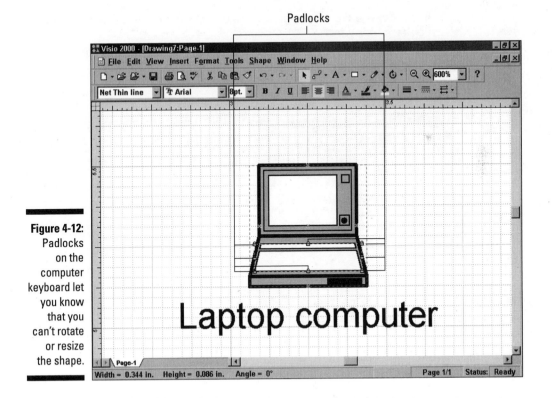

Figure 4-12:
Padlocks
on the
computer
keyboard let
you know
that you
can't rotate
or resize
the shape.

Finding the Shapes That You Want

Because Visio offers so many shapes (at least 1,300 depending on the Visio product that you have), you need a way to search for a shape. After all, when you open and close dozens of stencils, you can easily forget where you saw a shape that you like.

Shape Explorer enables you to search for a shape by its name, a stencil name, a template name, a keyword, a phrase that describes the shape you want, or the type of drawing that you want to create.

To use Shape Explorer, follow these steps:

1. **Choose Tools⇨Macros⇨Shape Explorer.**

   Visio displays the dialog box, as shown in Figure 4-13.

2. **In the Search For box, type a word or phrase that describes the shape you're looking for.**

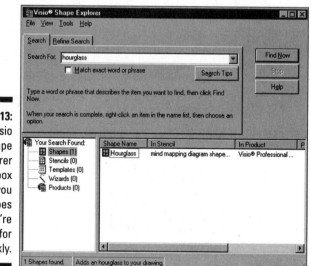

Figure 4-13: The Visio Shape Explorer dialog box helps you find shapes that you're looking for quickly.

3. **Click the Find Now button.**

   Visio searches shapes, stencils, templates, wizards, and Visio Products (Standard, Professional, Technical, Enterprise, and add-on shapes) and displays the result in the lower-right section of the dialog box. (If you see a full-color icon for the shape that you want, you can add it to your drawing. If the icon is grayed, the shape belongs to a stencil that isn't installed on your system, and you can't add it to your drawing.)

4. **To add the shape to your drawing, right-click the shape's icon and then choose Add to Drawing.**

   If you prefer to open the entire stencil that the shape is on so that you can use other shapes as well, right-click the shape's icon, then choose Open Containing Stencil.

   Still not sure which shape you want? Double-click the shape icon; the Properties dialog box appears. In the dialog box, click Show Preview to see how the shape looks.

5. **Close the Visio Shape Explorer dialog by clicking the Close button in the upper-right corner, or choose File⇨Exit.**

If you have trouble finding the shape that you want, click the Search Tips button in the Shape Explorer dialog box . It offers detailed, useful information about how to type the word or phrase so that Shape Explorer can find the shape you're looking for.

If you want to narrow your search, click the Refine Search tab in the Shape Explorer dialog box and then uncheck categories that you *don't* want Visio to search. For example, if you want to search only shapes and stencils, remove the check marks from the Templates, Wizards, and Products check boxes to speed up your search. To further refine your search, click the Details button to specify whether you want to search for names, descriptions, or keywords. Then click the OK button.

Jazzing Up Your Drawings

Some drawings and charts are appropriate without any frills or fluff. But sometimes, black shapes and text on a white background can be *really* boring. This is especially true if you plan to use your drawings as part of a presentation, or add them to a publication. If you have the flexibility to add interesting graphic elements and color, by all means, do so! Visio 2000 has some slick new features for jazzing up your drawings.

Using stencil shapes

Your first option is to add some interesting shapes to a drawing. Choose File⇨Stencils⇨Visio Extras. The submenu lists several categories of stencils that contain interesting shapes for dressing up drawings, such as:

✔ **Backgrounds Full-page themes:** that you can add as a backdrop to your drawing.

   ✔ **Clip Art:** Graphic elements that you may not want or be able to draw
     yourself.

   ✔ **Embellishments:** Cool and weird stuff like Egyptian corners, Greek
     borders, art deco frames, and wave sections.

   ✔ **Borders and Titles:** predefined page border styles and title boxes from
     elegant to technical.

Figure 4-14 illustrates some creative ways to use these stencil shapes.

Applying a color scheme

With Visio 2000, you can also apply a color scheme to your drawing. A color
scheme is a predefined set of colors assigned to various shapes, including
background shapes, used in a drawing. Figure 4-15 shows the same drawing
from Figure 4-14 with a color scheme applied. (Of course, you can't see the
color in the figure, but you get the idea!)

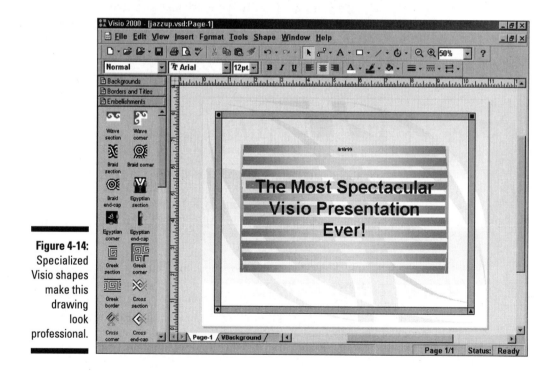

Figure 4-14:
Specialized
Visio shapes
make this
drawing
look
professional.

Figure 4-15:
Every
element of
a drawing
is colored
when you
apply a
color
scheme.

To apply a color scheme to a drawing, follow these steps:

1. **Open the drawing.**

2. **Choose Tools⇨Color Scheme.**

   Visio displays the Color Scheme dialog box, as shown in Figure 4-16.

3. **From the Choose a Color Scheme list, highlight a color scheme and then click Apply.**

   Grab the title bar and move the Color Scheme dialog box out of the way so you can see how the color scheme looks in your drawing.

4. **Repeat Step 3 to try other color schemes.**

5. **When you're satisfied with the color scheme, click the OK button.**

If you prefer, you can create your own color scheme by following these steps:

1. **Open the drawing.**

2. **Choose Tools⇨Color Scheme.**

   Visio displays the Color Scheme dialog box (see Figure 4-16).

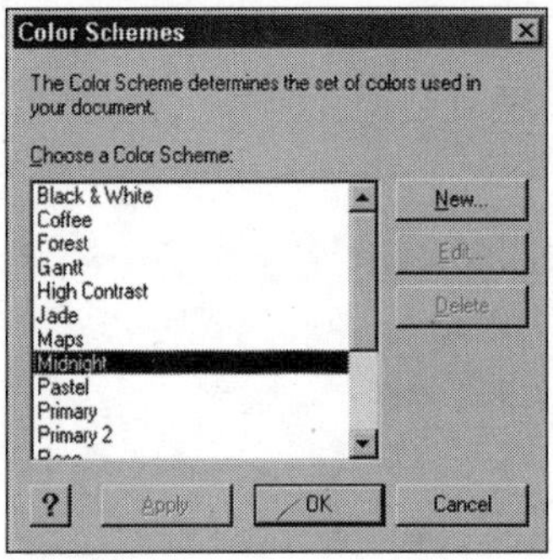

Figure 4-16:
The Color
Scheme
dialog box
offers over
a dozen
different
color
schemes for
drawings.

3. **Click the New button.**

   Visio displays the Color Scheme Details dialog box, as shown in Figure 4-17.

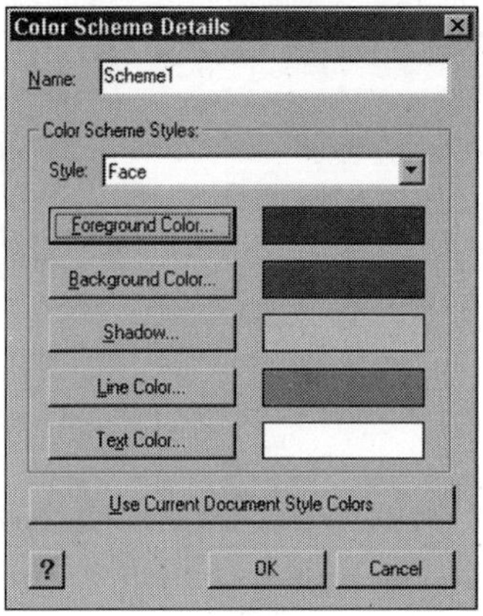

Figure 4-17:
In the Color
Scheme
Details
dialog box
you're free
to choose
the style
and colors
you want.

4. **In the name box, enter a name for your color scheme.**

5. **From the Style box, choose a style.**

   The changes you see in the drawing depend on the stencil shapes used in the drawing.

6. **Click the Foreground Color button.**

   Visio displays the Color dialog box, as shown in Figure 4-18.

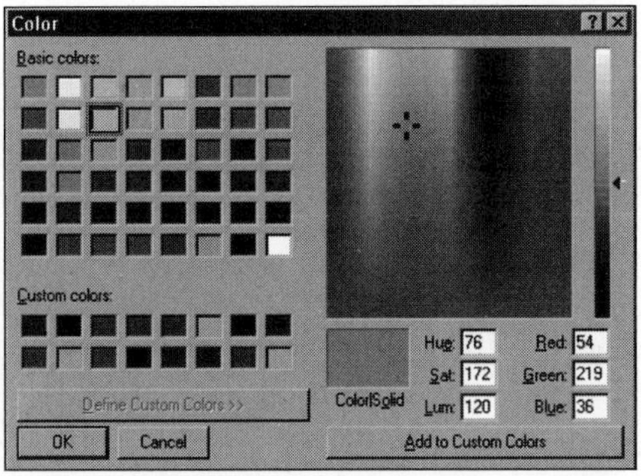

Figure 4-18:
In the Color
dialog box
you can
choose an
existing
color or
create your
own.

7. **In the Color dialog box, click a basic color or an existing custom color on the left side of the box.**

   If you prefer, you can create a custom color by dragging the site in the color map on the right and then clicking the Add to Custom Colors button.

   The custom color is added to the Custom Color selection on the left.

8. **When you've chosen a color, click the OK button.**

   Visio returns to the Color Scheme Details dialog box (refer to Figure 4-17).

9. **Repeat Steps 6, 7, and 8 for the Background Color, Shadow Color, Line Color, and Text Color buttons.**

10. **Click the OK button.**

    Visio returns to the Color Schemes dialog box. The name you gave your color scheme now appears in the list.

11. **Click your new color scheme name and then click Apply.**

    Visio applies the color scheme to your drawing.

12. **Click the OK button to close the Color Schemes dialog box.**

Notice that the Color Scheme Details dialog box has a button called Use Current Document Style Colors. If your drawing already uses a color scheme, you can click this button to base a new color scheme on the current colors used.

Chapter 5

Giving Your Drawings
a Voice with Text

Regardless of the type of drawing you create, you probably want to add text to it somewhere. I just know you want a title, label, caption, page number, description, or explanation in your drawing! You're in luck, because with Visio you can add text easily anywhere you want.

Discovering Text Blocks

All text in a Visio drawing is contained in a *text block*. A text block is a special frame for holding text. Most Visio shapes have a text block attached to them. For example, every shape in a flowchart has an attached text box; it's where you enter data to describe what's in the shape.

A shape's attached text block goes wherever the shape goes. But you won't see a text block unless you enter text in it — even then you only see the text itself. A black frame doesn't define the border of a text block; it has no color. This is convenient because you don't want a mysterious-looking empty frame lurking about when a shape doesn't have any text!

In some cases, you may want to add text to a drawing that's *not* attached to a shape. This is called *freestanding text*. A title for a drawing is a good example of freestanding text. It's obviously text, but it isn't attached to any of the shapes in the drawing.

Adding Text to a Drawing

In this section, you add text to a shape in a drawing and add freestanding text. As you work with text, you use the tools shown in Table 5-1.

To add text *to a shape* in your drawing, follow these steps:

1. **Double-click a shape to select it.**

2. **Begin typing text in the shape's text block.**

   When you begin typing, Visio immediately zooms in on the shape's text block, which appears as a frame bordered by a green dotted line. Your eyes aren't playing tricks on you! Visio zooms in for those of us who can't read 4-point type (and I contend that's most of us).

   Continue typing. Visio keeps up with you even if you enter a 400-line caption (well that may be exaggerating a bit . . .). If you enter more than one line of text, Visio thoughtfully wraps the text to the next line automatically. You can press Enter any time to begin a new line of text. If you enter more text than the text block can hold, Visio enlarges the text block as you continue to type.

3. **Click anywhere outside the text block when you finish typing.**

Voilà! You see the original shape again, along with your text. The drawing in Figure 5-1 shows how extensively you can use text in a drawing. Sometimes a "drawing" contains more text than graphics!

If you enter a lot of text, the text block may become larger than the shape itself! To make the text fit inside the shape, you have a couple of options. Enlarge the shape, and the text block (including the text in it) reformats automatically as you resize the shape. (Refer to Chapter 4 for more about resizing shapes.) If you can't enlarge the shape, you can change the size of the text block or change the text's font size. See the "Manipulating Text" section later in this chapter.

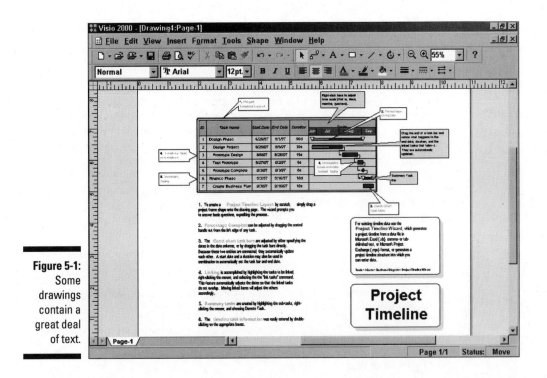

Figure 5-1:
Some
drawings
contain a
great deal
of text.

Table 5-1	Tools on the Standard Toolbar
Button	**Name or Function**
	Copy
	Paste
	Pointer tool
	Text tool
	Text Block tool (drops down below the Text tool)
	Format Painter tool

You can't tell where a shape text block is going to show up until you type something in it. If you're curious about its location before you enter text, you can display it quickly by double-clicking or selecting the shape, and then pressing F2.

The formatting of text in a text block is different depending on the shape you work with. Some shapes may display left-aligned text while others may right-align the text or orient the text vertically. Templates control the way text aligns. For more information on changing text characteristics, see the "Changing the Way Your Text Looks" section later in this chapter.

Some of you adventurous types may want to include in a drawing text that's not part of a shape. That's cool — Visio is prepared for you! You can include *freestanding text* in a drawing easily by following these steps:

1. **Click the Text Tool button on the Standard toolbar.**

   Your mouse pointer changes to look like a sheet of paper with text.

2. **Drag the pointer to draw a text box as large (or as small) as you want, or double-click, and Visio draws a text block for you.**

   Your text block is outlined by a green dotted line and an insertion point appears in the center.

3. **Type your text.**

4. **Click anywhere outside the text block or press Esc.**

Note that in Step 2, the insertion point appears in the center of the text block because the text is set to be center-aligned. For more information on changing this setting, see the "Changing the lineup" section later in this chapter.

You can also type in a text block when you use the pencil, line, freeform, rectangle, or ellipse tools to create your own shapes. You create and add text to the text block in the same way I just described. For more information about creating your own shapes, see Chapter 8.

Okay, let's clear up one thing. Technically speaking, freestanding text isn't really freestanding; it's a shape in and of itself. Visio calls it a *text-only shape*. Does that matter? Not really. You just need to know that a text block always encloses text; it never just floats around aimlessly!

Manipulating Text

In any drawing, you invariably manipulate text in *some* way, whether you edit, copy, paste, move, resize, change the alignment, alter the margins, shift the tabs, and so on. This section helps you make these changes after you enter text.

If you're familiar with word processors, you find that Visio handles text in nearly the same way as a word processor. If you're already a pro at performing these options, you can skim the sections of this chapter that discuss copying, pasting, moving, and deleting.

Editing text

Of course, the moment that you click outside a shape to set your text in stone, you may decide that you want to change some aspect of your text. Maybe you want to add, delete, or just start all over again. Changing text in Visio is easy. Follow these steps:

1. **Click the Text Tool button (the one that looks like an A) and then click a shape to display its text block (see Figure 5-2).**

2. **Click the mouse button where you want to change the text (you see the insertion point after you click).**

3. **Begin typing, selecting, deleting, or backspacing to make your changes.**

   - **To delete characters to the right of the insertion point:** Press the Delete key.

   - **To delete characters to the left of the insertion point:** Press the Backspace key.

   - **To select the text and type over it:** Highlight text by using the mouse or hold down the Shift key while you highlight text by using the arrow keys. After you highlight the text you want to delete, begin typing new text. Whatever you type replaces the text you selected.

4. **After you make changes to your text, click anywhere outside the text block.**

   Your shape or text-only shape is visible again.

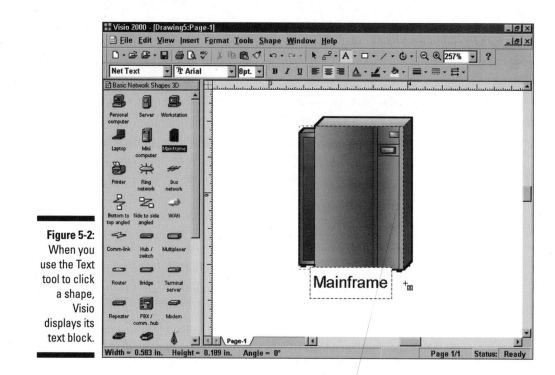

Figure 5-2:
When you
use the Text
tool to click
a shape,
Visio
displays its
text block.

You can also open a text block by clicking the Pointer Tool button (which looks like an arrow) on the Standard toolbar and then double-clicking the shape or text-only shape. But watch out! If you use this method, Visio automatically selects all the text in the shape. If you don't want to replace all the text, be sure to click somewhere in the text block to position the insertion point before you begin typing. If you begin typing without positioning the insertion point, Visio replaces your text with whatever you type. If you replace text accidentally, use Edit⇨Undo or press Ctrl+Z to bring back your old text.

Copying and pasting without glue

Sometimes you may want to copy text from one place to another — anything to avoid retyping! Actually, copying text is a good idea for another reason: consistency. If you want a chunk of text to be exactly the same somewhere else in your drawing, the best way to ensure this is to copy the text.

Don't worry about whether the text you're copying is part of a shape or is a text-only shape; you follow the same steps. First, select the text block. If you don't select a text block, but instead paste the text by clicking somewhere in the drawing, Visio pastes the text into its own text block somewhere near the middle of the drawing page. You can then move the text block where you want it.

You can copy and paste text using the following steps:

1. **Click the Text Tool button on the Standard toolbar and click a shape (refer to Table 5-1).**

   Visio displays the shape's text block.

2. **Select the text that you want to copy.**

3. **Click the Copy button on the Standard toolbar, or choose Edit⇨Copy, or press Ctrl+C.**

4. **Choose where you want to paste the text:**

   • **To paste into a shape's text block:** Double-click the shape.

   • **To paste a text-only shape:** Click any blank area of the drawing.

5. **Click the Paste button on the Standard toolbar, choose Edit⇨Paste, or press Ctrl+V.**

The text that you copy remains on the Windows Clipboard until you copy something else. If you need to paste again and again, feel free!

After you select a text block, you can choose the Copy and Paste commands from the pop-up shortcut menu quickly by right-clicking your mouse.

Moving a text block

Keep in mind that you don't know where Visio places a shape's text block until you enter some text in it. You may find that you don't like the position of a text block and want to move it. In Figure 5-3, the text block for the star on the left covers up part of the shape. You can move the text block below the star (see the star on the right) to make the text readable and make the shape more visible.

Even if you move a text block halfway across a drawing page, it still attaches to its shape. If you move a shape, any accompanying text moves with it. If you copy the shape, the text copies with it. If you paste the shape, the text pastes with it. And if you rotate . . . well, you get the idea.

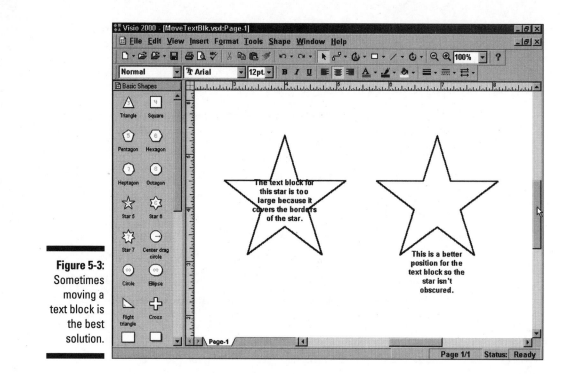

Figure 5-3:
Sometimes
moving a
text block is
the best
solution.

To move a text block independently of its shape, follow these steps:

1. **Click the Text Block Tool button on the Standard toolbar (refer to Table 5-1).**

   Your mouse pointer changes to look like a sheet of paper with lines of text.

2. **Click the shape that has text that you want to move.**

   The green text block frame and handles are visible.

3. **Move the mouse over the text block frame until it changes to a pointer that looks like a double rectangle.**

4. **Drag the text block to reposition it.**

5. **Click the Pointer tool again to bring back your normal mouse pointer.**

Moving a text-only shape is as easy as moving any other type of shape. Follow these steps:

1. **Click the Pointer Tool button on the Standard toolbar if it isn't already selected (refer to Table 5-1).**

2. **Click the text-only shape that you want to move.**

   The green selection handles and frame appear.

3. **Make sure the mouse is pointing somewhere inside the text block.**

   The mouse pointer changes from black to white.

4. **Drag the text block to a new location.**

Resizing a text block

Sometimes you may need to resize a text block to fit a shape a little better. In Figure 5-4, the text block for the star on the left is too large because it covers up part of the star's borders. The star on the right shows the text block resized.

Use these steps to resize a text block:

1. **Click the Text Block Tool button on the Standard toolbar (refer to Table 5-1).**

   When you move the mouse pointer over the text in the text block, the pointer changes to a double rectangle.

2. **Click the shape.**

   The green text block frame and handles appear.

3. **Move the mouse pointer over a side handle to resize the shape's width or over a top or bottom handle to resize the shape's height.**

   The mouse pointer changes to a double-headed arrow.

4. **Drag the handle to resize the text block.**

5. **Click the Pointer Tool button again to bring back your normal mouse pointer.**

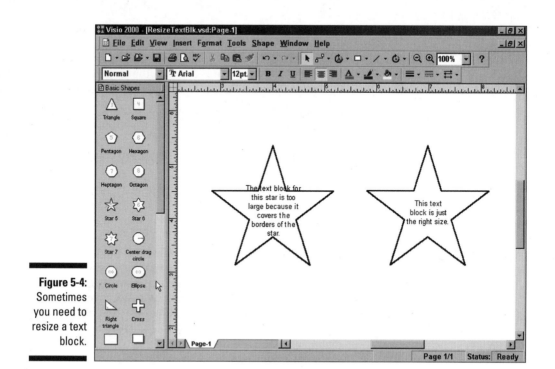

Changing the lineup

Whenever you create text in a drawing, you need to pay attention to how the text aligns. *Horizontal alignment* refers to the way characters line up left to right in a text block. In most text documents, text is left-aligned. However, center, right, and justified alignments all work well in drawings. Figure 5-5 shows an example of each style.

To change horizontal text alignment, follow these steps:

1. **Click the Text Tool button on the Standard toolbar (refer to Table 5-1).**

2. **Click the shape that contains the text that you want to change.**

   Visio displays the text block.

3. **Select the paragraph that you want to align.**

4. **Click the Align Left, Center, or Align Right toolbar button.**

   Visio reformats the selected text.

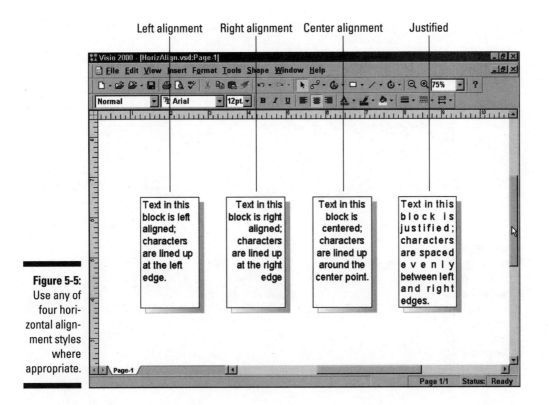

Figure 5-5:
Use any of
four hori-
zontal align-
ment styles
where
appropriate.

I recommend that you use these tools, because they're faster than choosing menu commands. If you prefer using menu commands, you can find alignment settings by choosing Format➪Text, clicking the Paragraph tab in the Text dialog box and then selecting the check box of the alignment option that you want.

Note that because horizontal alignment applies to a paragraph, you can align separate paragraphs differently in the same text block.

Vertical alignment refers to the alignment from top to bottom in a text block. When you work with a text document, you don't usually think about vertical alignment because your text appears on a page with margins. However, when your text is contained in a text block (which is really nothing more than a box), you can choose to align the text with the top or bottom of the box, or you can center the text in the box (see Figure 5-6).

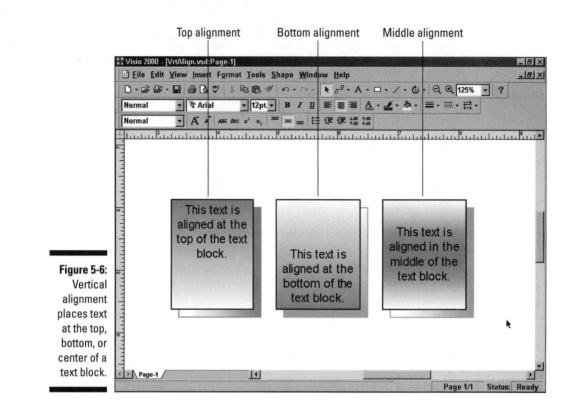

Figure 5-6:
Vertical alignment places text at the top, bottom, or center of a text block.

You can use the following tools on the Format Text toolbar to vertically align your text, as shown in Table 5-2.

Table 5-2   Vertical Alignment Tools on the Format Text Toolbar

Button	Name
	Align Top
	Align Center (Middle)
	Align Bottom

To set vertical alignment of a text block, follow these steps:

1. **Click the Text Tool button on the Format Text toolbar (refer to Table 5-1).**
2. **Click the shape that contains the text that you want to change.**

   Visio displays the text block.
3. **Click the Align Top, Middle, or Align Bottom button.**

   Visio adjusts your text.

Again, to set alignment, I recommend that you use one of the alignment tools provided on the Format Text toolbar. Using tools saves you the time it takes to select menu commands. If you prefer using menu commands, alignment settings are available by choosing Format⇨Text, clicking the Text Block tab in the Text dialog box, and selecting an option from the Vertical Alignment drop-down list.

Note that unlike horizontal alignment, vertical alignment applies to *all* of the text in a text block.

Adjusting margins

Text block margins define the white space that surrounds text in a text block. Visio sets text block margins very narrowly — about ⅛ of an inch. In most cases, these narrow margins are fine, because the outline of the text block usually isn't visible. But if you decide to outline a text block with a frame, these margins can be so narrow that the text doesn't look right. Figure 5-7 shows two text blocks. The text block on the left uses standard margins; the margins for the text block on the right are increased to ½ inch. Not only does the text block on the right look better, the words are more readable. And you don't get that claustrophobic feeling looking at it!

Visio uses *points* as the default units of measurement for text and margins. One inch is roughly equivalent to 72 points, so ⅛ of an inch is about 4 points. (I say roughly because points were originally based on the size of common typewriter fonts. Today, system fonts vary in relative size.)

Standard margins   ¹/₂-inch margins

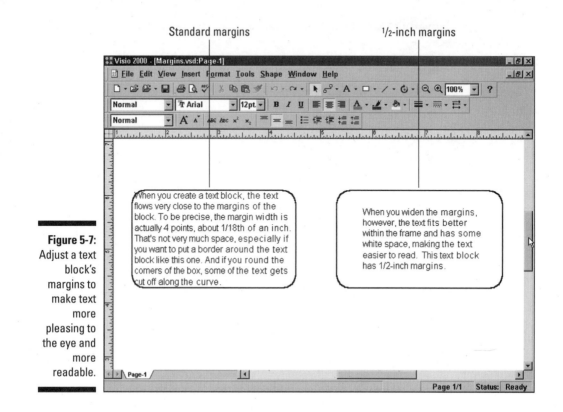

Figure 5-7:
Adjust a text
block's
margins to
make text
more
pleasing to
the eye and
more
readable.

If you prefer to have Visio measure text and margins in inches (or any of 19 other units of measure), you can change the default setting. Just choose Tools⇨Options, click the Default Units tab and then change the Text setting. The drop-down box lists all of the choices for units.

To change a text block's margins, follow these steps:

1. **Click the Text Block Tool button on the Standard toolbar (refer to Table 5-1).**

   When you move the mouse pointer over the text in the text block, the pointer changes to a double rectangle.

2. **Click the shape that has the text block you want to change.**

   The green text block frame and handles appear.

3. **Choose Format⇨Text.**

   Visio displays the Text dialog box.

4. **Click the Text Block tab, as shown in Figure 5-8.**

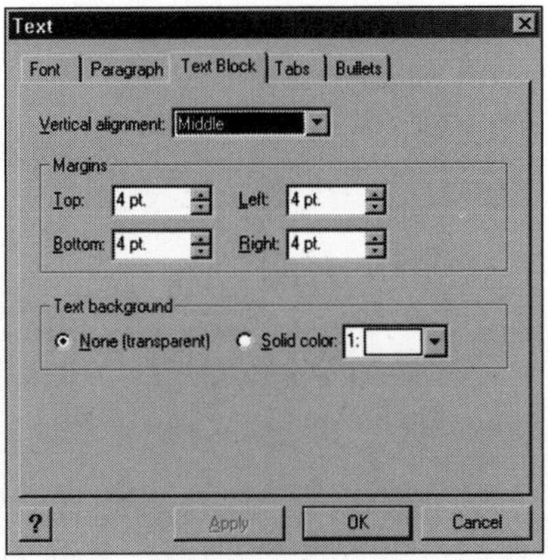

Figure 5-8:
The Text
Block tab in
the Text
dialog box
lets you set
margins.

5. **In the Top, Bottom, Left, and Right boxes, type a number.**

   Visio measures margins in points (72 points = 1 inch). If you prefer to
   use inches, enter them as decimal numbers and type **in** after the number
   (such as .5 in).

6. **Click the Apply button if you want to make more changes in the Text
   dialog box.**

7. **To return to your drawing, click the OK button.**

When you right-click your shape and choose Format⇨Text, the Text dialog
box pops up quickly.

Picking up the tab

Some types of text call for a tabular format, even in a drawing. You may want to
include a simple table in a drawing, with items aligned in rows and columns. To
create this type of layout, you need to set *tab stops* (or just *tabs*) — the points
where you want your cursor to jump when you press the Tab key.

You can set tabs to be left-aligned, right-aligned, centered, or decimal-
aligned. You can see examples of each in Figure 5-9. When you use a decimal-
aligned tab, be sure to type the decimal point in your entry. If you don't enter
a decimal point, the entry is left-aligned.

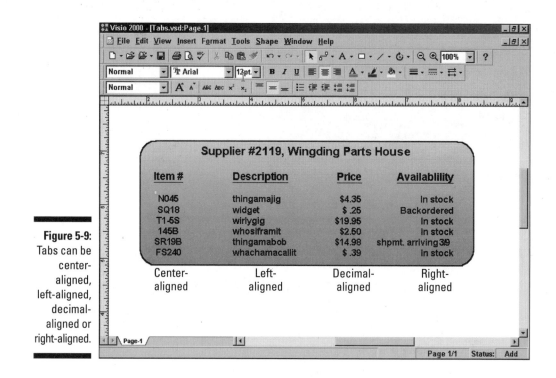

Figure 5-9:
Tabs can be center-aligned, left-aligned, decimal-aligned or right-aligned.

Follow these steps to set tabs for a text block:

1. **Click the Text Block Tool button on the Standard toolbar (refer to Table 5-1).**

   When you move the mouse pointer over the text in the text block, the pointer changes to a double rectangle.

2. **Click the shape with the text that you want to alter; the green text block frame and handles appear.**

3. **Choose Format⇨Text.**

   Visio displays the Text dialog box.

4. **Click the Tabs tab, as shown in Figure 5-10.**

5. **To add tabs, enter a number in the Tab Stop Position box (or click the up or down arrows) and then click the Add button.**

6. **In the Alignment box, choose an alignment style (Left, Center, Right, or Decimal) and then click the OK button.**

   Visio returns to the Tabs dialog box.

7. **Click the OK button.**

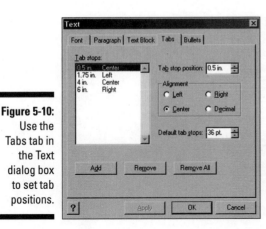

Figure 5-10:
Use the
Tabs tab in
the Text
dialog box
to set tab
positions.

When you return to your text block, you can use the tabs by pressing the Tab key.

To remove tabs, use the same dialog box, highlight the tab to remove and then click the Remove button.

Creating bulleted lists

Bulleted lists are very common in drawings and diagrams — probably because they help summarize and separate material. Fortunately, creating bulleted lists in Visio is easy because Visio does it for you automatically.

You can set up a bulleted format for text that you already typed, or in a blank text block. If you set up a bulleted list in a blank text block, Visio inserts and formats the bullets as you type the text.

Use these steps to created a bulleted list:

1. **In the text block, select the text that you want to format with bullets. If the text block is empty, just select the text block itself.**

2. **Choose Format⇨Text.**

   The Text dialog box appears.

3. **Click the Bullets tab to display the bullet options, as shown in Figure 5-11.**

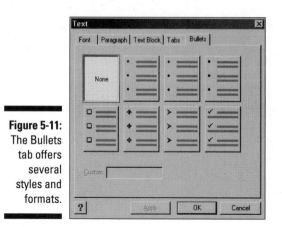

Figure 5-11:
The Bullets
tab offers
several
styles and
formats.

4. **Click a bullet style and then click the OK button.**

   Visio returns to your drawing. If you selected text in Step 1, it formats instantly. If the text block was empty, the bullets appear automatically when you begin typing.

Creating numbered lists

The process for creating numbered lists is a bit more complicated than the process for creating bulleted lists, and is not automatic. Because the process isn't automatic, it's easier to type the numbers and the text all at once. I recommend that you format the text block for a numbered list *before* you enter the text. (It isn't required, however.) The following steps show you how to manually indent a numbered list; keep in mind that you may want to alter the steps slightly for your particular text.

Follow these steps to add a numbered list to a text block:

1. **In the text block, select the text that you want to format as a numbered list. If the text block is empty, just select the text block itself.**

2. **Choose Format⇨Text.**

   The Text dialog box appears.

3. **Click the Paragraph tab to display the options on the Paragraph tab, as shown in Figure 5-12.**

4. **In the Horizontal Alignment box, choose Left.**

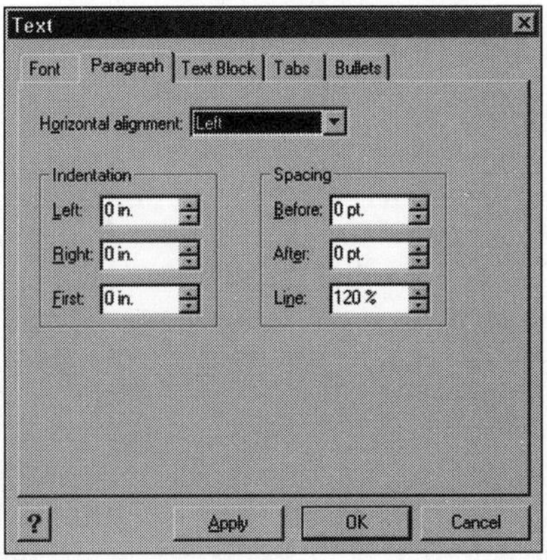

Figure 5-12:
Use the
Paragraph
tab in the
Text dialog
box to set
up the
format for a
numbered
list.

5. **In the Indentation section, type .5 in the Left box to mark the left indentation of the paragraph.**

6. **In the Indentation section, type –.5 in the First box to mark the indentation for the first line of the paragraph.**

7. **Click the OK button.**

Visio returns to your drawing.

In case you're wondering what you just did in these steps, you created a *hanging indent* (the first line hangs out to the left of the rest of the paragraph). You set the *wrap* point (the point where text wraps on the second, third, and following lines) to .5 inches.

If you haven't typed your text yet, type the number for the first item (such as 1. or I.), press Tab, and then type the text. Press Enter when you finish the first item. Repeat the process for all the items in the list.

If you already typed your text, move your insertion point to the beginning of the line for each item, type the correct number, and then press Tab. Visio reformats the existing text.

In the steps above you use .5 (½ inch) for indentation because it's a "standard" measurement. You aren't required to use that measurement; you can just as easily use .2 inches or 1.2 inches. In either case, make sure you use the same number for the Left and First (Left being positive and First being negative).

Setting the indentation and spacing of text

To set indentation for a paragraph, you use the Paragraph tab in the Text dialog box. Indenting is like widening the margins on the left and/or right sides of a paragraph (without *really* widening the margins). For example, you may want to indent a particular paragraph half an inch on the right and left sides to give it emphasis. You can also make the first line of a paragraph stand out by indenting only that line.

The Paragraph tab in the Text dialog box also lets you adjust line spacing. For example, you can automatically add extra space before or after paragraphs. Like margins, line spacing is measured in points unless you change the unit of measurement by using the Tools⇨Options command. (See the "Adjusting margins" section earlier in this chapter for more about margins.) For extra space before or after a paragraph, type a number in the Before or After box (see Figure 5-12).

To set indentation and line spacing for a paragraph, use these steps:

1. **Click the Text Tool button on the Standard toolbar (refer to Table 5-1).**

    The mouse pointer changes to look like a sheet of paper with text.

2. **In the text block or text-only shape, select all or part of the paragraph that you want to indent.**

3. **Choose Format⇨Text.**

    Visio displays the Text dialog box.

4. **Click the Paragraph tab.**

5. **To set indentation for the paragraph you selected, type a number (measured in inches or decimal inches) in the Left, Right, and First boxes.**

6. **To set line spacing for the selected paragraph, type a number (measured in points) in the Before, After, and Line boxes.**

    The Before and After boxes set the number of spaces preceding and following the paragraph; the Line box sets the spacing within the lines of the paragraph.

7. **Click the OK button to return to your drawing.**

Changing the Way Your Text Looks

When you draw a text block and enter text, Visio automatically displays the text as 12-point Arial black characters on a transparent background. Simple. Sedate. Readable. Nothing dramatic. Are existing Visio shapes set up to display anything more dramatic? Not really. You may find some variation — maybe 8-point Arial instead of 12-point — but nothing to get excited about.

If you want more pizzazz in your text, it's up to you to create it. You have the option of changing the font, size, color, and style of text. You can also designate a case, position, and language (no, Visio won't translate English into Portuguese for you!).

The quickest way to make changes to text attributes is by using toolbar buttons. Select the text that you want to change and click one of the toolbar buttons on the Format or Format Text toolbars (see Table 5-3). Some tools change the selected text immediately; others display a drop-down box where you can choose an option for changing the attributes.

Table 5-3	Text Formatting Tools on the Format and Format Text Toolbars
Button	**Name**
A˄	Increase Font Size
A˅	Decrease Font Size
12pt. ▼	Font Size
B	Bold
I	Italic
U	Underline
A ▼	Font Color

If you want, you can use the Text dialog box to change the text attributes listed in Table 5-3. To use the Text dialog box, follow these steps:

1. **Select the text that you want to change.**

2. **Choose Format⇨Text or right-click your mouse and choose Text from the shortcut menu.**

   The Text dialog box appears, as shown in Figure 5-13.

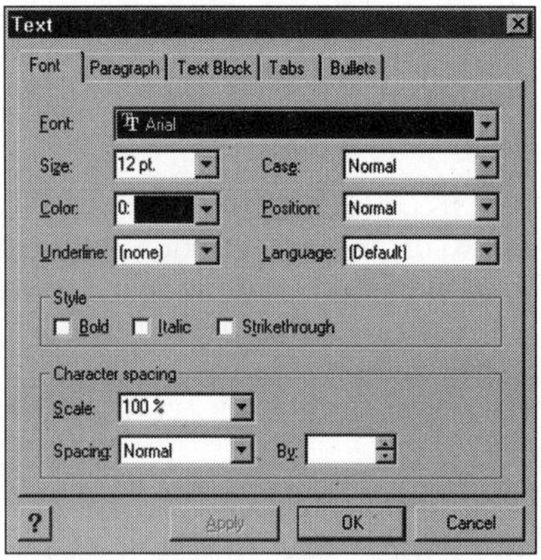

Figure 5-13:
The Font tab in the Text dialog box gives you options for changing your text.

3. **Click the drop-down box of the attribute that you want to change.**

   To change the font: Click the Font drop-down list and choose a font style.

   Unfortunately, the Font tab of the Text dialog box doesn't show you a preview of the fonts, so you can't see how a font looks before you choose it. The next best thing is to move the dialog box out of the way so that you can see your selected text. This way, when you click the Apply button you can see how the text looks without closing the dialog box and starting all over again.

   • **To change the text size:** Click the Size drop-down list and choose a point size for the selected text.

   • **To change the text color:** Click the Color drop-down list and choose a color for the selected text.

   • **To change the case:** Click the Case drop-down list and choose Normal (the default setting), All Caps, or Initial Caps.

   • **To change text position:** Click the Position drop-down list and choose Subscript or Superscript.

   • **To change the language of the Spell Checker:** Click the Language drop-down list and choose a language other than English.

- **To change the style:** Click the check boxes for Bold, Italic, Underline, or Small Caps.

4. **Click the Apply button.**

5. **Repeat Steps 3 and 4 if you want to try other options.**

6. **Click the OK button.**

    Visio returns to your drawing and reformats the selected text.

Adding a colorful background

If you aren't satisfied with colorful characters alone, you can change the background color of a text block as well. Just think of all the wonderful color combinations that you can come up with! Remember, though, your text needs to be *readable.* The more contrast between the text and background colors, the better.

An important thing to realize about text blocks is that they're transparent, which means that if your text block falls over the outline of a shape, the shape shows through, obscuring the text, as shown in Figure 5-14. To solve this problem, you can change the text block background to solid white (or whatever color that matches the shape underneath).

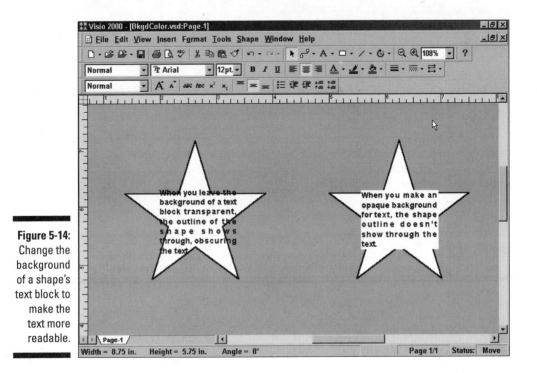

Figure 5-14:
Change the background of a shape's text block to make the text more readable.

To change the background color of a text block, follow these steps:

1. **Click the Text Tool button on the Standard toolbar (refer to Table 5-1).**

2. **Select the text block that you want to change.**

3. **Choose Format➪Text, or right-click the text block and choose Text from the shortcut menu.**

   Visio displays the Text dialog box.

4. **Click the Text Block tab, as shown in Figure 5-15.**

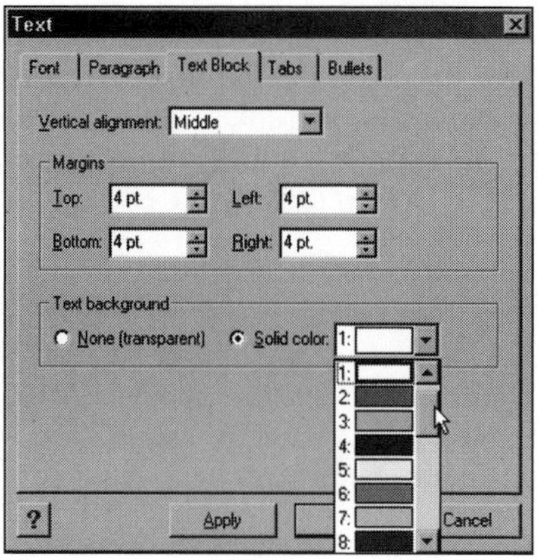

Figure 5-15:
Choose a
background
color from
the Text
Block tab in
the Text
dialog box.

5. **In the Text Background area, choose a color from the Solid Color drop-down list.**

   To make an opaque background on an unfilled shape, choose white.

6. **Click the OK button.**

Note: The previous steps change the background color of a *text block*. This is not the same thing as filling a shape with a color. The text block and the shape can fill independently of one another. See Chapter 8 for more information about filling shapes.

Copying formatting to other text

When you use your precious time and energy to set up a text block with a magenta background, chartreuse text, Elephant font, 38-point font size, underline, bold, italic, and small caps, you don't want to have to do it all over again manually to make a matching text block. This task is much simpler if you just *copy* the format — and you can. Follow these steps:

1. **Click the Text Tool button on the Standard toolbar (refer to Table 5-1).**

2. **Click the text block with the formatting that you want to copy.**

3. **Click the Format Painter Tool button on the Standard toolbar.**

   Your mouse pointer now includes a paintbrush.

4. **Click the text block that you want to copy the format to.**

   Visio applies the format instantly.

The previous steps copy all aspects of the actual text formatting. Vertical and horizontal alignment, margin settings, indentation, and tabs are considered formatting that belongs to the *text block*. If you want to copy these as well as the text formatting, use the same steps but click the Pointer Tool button on the Standard toolbar in Step 1 instead of the Text Tool button. Using this method, Visio copies all text block and text attributes to the target text block. Copying formatting not only saves you time — it ensures consistency when consistency is important to you.

Rotating text

One of Visio's most versatile features is its ability to rotate text. For most Visio shapes, the text is oriented horizontally, but sometimes you may need to rotate the text at an angle. Figure 5-16 shows a triangle on the left with a horizontal text block. In the triangle on the right, the text block is rotated and moved so that the text runs parallel to the triangle's side.

To change the rotation of a shape's text block, follow these steps:

1. **Click the Text Block Tool button on the Standard toolbar (refer to Table 5-1).**

   When you move the mouse pointer over the text in the text block, the pointer changes to a double rectangle.

2. **Click the text block.**

   The green selection handles appear, along with round rotation handles at each corner of the frame.

3. **Move the mouse pointer over one of the rotation handles.**

   The mouse pointer changes to two curved arrows in the shape of a circle.

4. **Drag the text in the direction that you want to rotate the text.**

If you want to rotate the text to a specific angle, such as 45 degrees, or 125 degrees, watch the status bar as you rotate the text. Moving in a counter-clockwise direction produces a positive angle up to 180 degrees; moving clockwise displays negative angles up to –180 degrees.

If you want the text to align with a particular part of the shape (such as a border or outline), it may be necessary to move the text block after you rotate it.

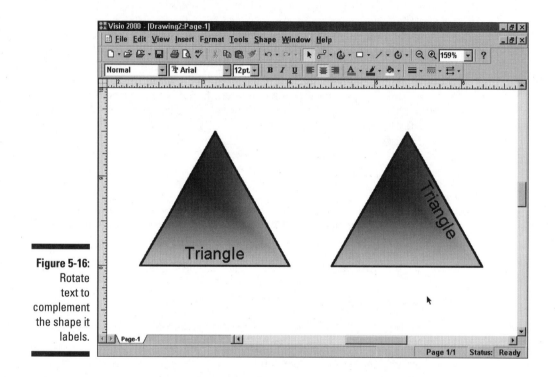

Figure 5-16:
Rotate text to complement the shape it labels.

Chapter 6

Connecting Shapes

● ●

● ●

In this chapter, I unravel the mysteries of two of Visio's most powerful features: glue and connectors. The relationship between glue, connectors, and shapes is a close one. After you understand how each one works, you can become a powerful Visio user.

Discovering Connectors

Connector is a term that is unique to Visio. The simple, non-techie explanation is that connectors are lines between boxes. In the techie world, a connector is a special, one-dimensional shape that you use to connect two-dimensional shapes to one another. This technical definition allows for the fact that connectors are not always lines; they can also be 1-D shapes such as arrows, arcs, hubs, and other specialized shapes (like an Ethernet cable) that connect 2-D shapes.

Where and why do you use connectors? You use connectors to show the following:

✔ Relationship between two shapes

✔ Hierarchy

✔ Path in a process

✔ Two connected shapes (this one seems rather obvious!)

Some drawings don't make any sense without connectors. Imagine an organization chart without connectors — you may have the president reporting to the copy room clerk! (That doesn't sound like a bad idea, does it?) You find connectors in all sorts of drawings from network diagrams, to process flowcharts, to Web page diagrams. In Figure 6-1, the 2-D executive shape in the organization chart is connected to the 2-D manager shapes; manager shapes are connected to 2-D position shapes. All of the connectors are 1-D shapes.

You can create a connector in three ways by:

✔ Dragging a special connector shape from a stencil onto a drawing

✔ Using the Connector tool from the Standard toolbar

✔ Dragging a connector from a control point one a shape to another shape

It's important to know that Visio connectors are more than just lines or shapes. Some connectors are *smart,* meaning they can reconnect to a different point on a shape (if necessary) when you move the shape. Other connectors are *dynamic,* meaning they can change their form or path around shapes depending on the shapes they're connected to. This may seem vague and meaningless to you now, but it will all become crystal clear in this chapter!

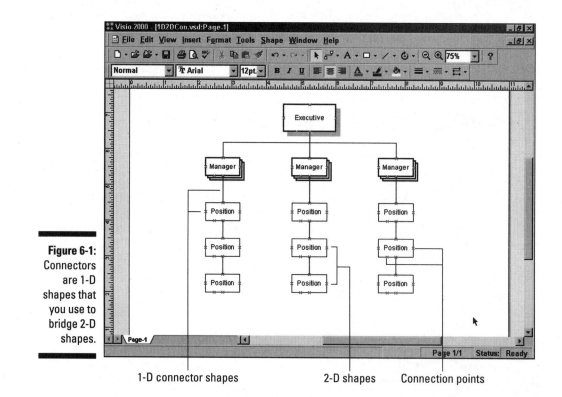

Figure 6-1:
Connectors
are 1-D
shapes that
you use to
bridge 2-D
shapes.

1-D connector shapes   2-D shapes   Connection points

In this chapter, you work with various tools on the Standard and Action toolbars. These tools are listed in Table 6-1.

Table 6-1	Toolbar Tools for Working with Connectors	
Button	*Tool name*	*Toolbar*
	Pointer tool	Standard
	Connector tool	Standard
	Connection Point tool	Standard
	Connect Shapes tool	Action

The Connection Point tool is located underneath the Connector tool on the Standard toolbar. You can access the Connection Point tool by clicking the down arrow to the right of the Connector tool.

Working with Connection Points

The blue Xs that appear on the sides of each shape are called (refer to Figure 6-1) *connection points*. Connection points are the places on a shape where you can hook up a connector.

Every shape has at least one connection point. Refer to Figure 6-1 and you see that at least one side of each shape has *two* connection points. Unfortunately, there isn't a formula for how many connection points a shape has or where you find them. One shape may have two connection points, and another may have 12. Connection points can appear inside or outside a shape, or on a line or border of a shape.

If you don't see connection points on your screen, choose View⇨Connection Points. You can toggle them on and off by using this menu command. Or, display the View toolbar on your screen (choose View⇨Toolbars⇨View). It contains a Connection Point tool that lets you toggle connection points on and off. (The Connection Point tool looks like a square with an X in the middle of each side.)

Adding connection points to a shape

Connection points appear only on your screen; they don't print when you print your drawing. If a shape doesn't have a connection point where you need it, add one! Use these steps:

1. **Select a shape.**

2. **Click the drop-down arrow next to the Connection tool on the standard toolbar; then click on the Connection Point Tool button (it looks like a blue X).**

   The mouse pointer changes to an arrow with an X.

3. **Press and hold the Ctrl key, and click the location on the shape where you want to add a connection point.**

You can add as many connection points as you like (but don't get carried away!). You can place them on a shape, inside, or outside a shape.

If you have trouble placing connection points where you want them, you may have better luck if you turn off the Snap function. Choose Tools⇨Snap & Glue. On the General tab of the Snap & Glue dialog box, uncheck the Snap check box and then click the OK button. Or, if the Snap & Glue toolbar is displayed, click the Snap button to turn off the snap function. (To find out more about how the snap function works, see Chapter 7.)

Deleting a connection point

Some shapes may have connection points that you don't want to use. You may have added connection points to a shape that you don't want to use. You can leave them there and just ignore them, or you can delete them; it's your choice.

To delete a connection point from a shape:

1. **Click the drop-down arrow next to the Connection tool on the Standard toolbar.**

2. **Click the Connection Point Tool button, which looks like a blue X.**

3. **Click the connection point that you want to remove.**

   The connection point turns magenta.

4. **Press the Delete key.**

   Voilà! The connection point is gone.

Applying Glue without the Mess

Put your sticky white glue away — you don't need it when you use Visio! *Glue* is a feature built into Visio connectors. Glue lets you stick connectors to shapes and keep them there. This may not seem to be an important function now, but it's important when you start moving connected shapes all over the place.

Creating a glueless drawing is a monotonous task. Without glue, you have to move a connector each time you move a shape. If the distance between shapes changes, you have to adjust the length of the connector. Then you have to reattach the connector to the shape after you move it. If the path between two shapes changes, you have to reroute the connector. Now, multiply those changes about 15 times, because you probably move shapes *at least* that many times in a drawing before it's done. See? Glue sounds pretty good now, doesn't it? Without glue, creating drawings is a lot more work than you ever imagined.

Choosing dynamic or static glue

Glue is such a great idea that Visio has two kinds: dynamic and static. As you see in this section, each one has a different purpose. I describe static glue first.

Static glue

Static glue forms a *point-to-point* connection between shapes. This means that if you use static glue to connect two boxes from points on the top of each box, no matter where you move the boxes, those connectors don't budge! The connectors stay stuck to the top of each box, even if the drawing makes no sense or looks goofy. Static glue is *permanent*.

In Figure 6-2, the boxes at the bottom of the figure originally were arranged like the ones at the top — with connectors attached to the tops of the boxes. Each connector uses static glue. In the bottom of the figure, as you rearrange the boxes, the connectors are *still* attached to the top of each box. And yes, it looks goofy. That's how static glue behaves. Think of static glue as stubborn and unyielding. Yet, static glue has its purpose — you may create drawings and want connectors to stay exactly where you put them.

When it's really important to you *how* shapes are connected and that connectors stay exactly where you put them, use static glue. Static glue is also good for drawings you create quickly and for drawings that you aren't likely to change a great deal.

Connectors still attached to the tops of boxes

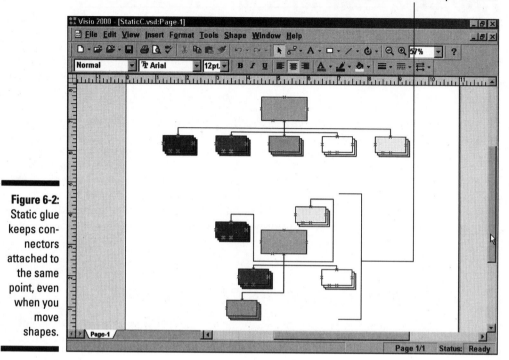

Figure 6-2:
Static glue
keeps con-
nectors
attached to
the same
point, even
when you
move
shapes.

Dynamic glue

Unlike static glue, dynamic glue is looking for adventure; it loves to travel and find new places to rest! Yet, it's a *sensible* traveler. When you move a shape that has a connector attached with dynamic glue, the connector attaches itself to a different connection point if necessary — one that makes sense in the drawing. (Of course, you can always change the connection point if you don't like it.)

Because dynamic glue can attach to any connection point on a shape, it forms what are called *shape-to-shape* connections. Figure 6-3 shows the same boxes pictured in Figure 6-2, but the connectors in Figure 6-3 use dynamic glue. If you move shapes that are connected with dynamic glue, the connectors move to more logical connection points (usually the nearest point) on each box instead of sticking to a specific connection point. Notice in Figure 6-3 that some boxes are now connected at the side instead of the top.

You want to use dynamic glue when you anticipate moving shapes around a lot, and when it's not important to you that shapes connect at specific points.

Connectors are repositioned

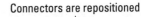

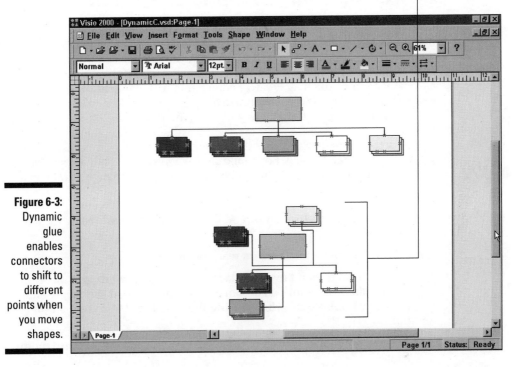

Figure 6-3:
Dynamic
glue
enables
connectors
to shift to
different
points when
you move
shapes.

Sometimes identical terminology in Visio can be confusing. For example, the term *dynamic* describes glue as well as connectors. Dynamic simply means *changeable*. Dynamic glue attaches a connector to a different point on a shape while a dynamic connector changes its shape and path, if necessary.

Identifying glue types

You need to know how to tell whether a connector uses dynamic glue or static glue. After you select a connector, look at its endpoints. You see one of two things:

- ✓ **When a connector uses static glue,** the connector's endpoints are dark red and are the size of other endpoints and selection handles. The beginning point has a + in it; the ending point has an X in it.

- ✓ **When a connector uses dynamic glue,** the endpoints are bright red and are slightly larger than other endpoints and selection handles. The endpoint contains no + or X symbols.

Switching from one glue to the other

Before I leave this sticky topic, I want to tell you how to switch a connection from one type of glue to the other. Knowing how to change glue types can be important depending on the type of drawing you create, how much you want to control connections, and how much you may want to change the drawing as you work on it. You may create a connection with dynamic glue and then decide that you want the connector to *always* stay attached to a shape's lower-left corner no matter where you move the shape.

The trick to switching glue types lies in where you point your mouse. When you point to a shape, you get dynamic glue; when you point to a specific connection point, you get static glue. Follow these steps to change a static connection to a dynamic one:

1. **Click the Pointer Tool button on the Standard toolbar (refer to Table 6-1).**

2. **Select the connector that you want to change.**

3. **Drag either endpoint away from the shape and then drag it back toward the shape until a red border appears around the whole shape. (You must point somewhere inside the shape, not to a connection point.)**

4. **Release the mouse button at the most logical connection point on the shape.**

   When you release the mouse button, the endpoint attaches. The endpoint is light red and slightly larger than other endpoints. This tells you that the glue is dynamic.

When you use dynamic glue, you don't get to choose the connection point; Visio chooses the *nearest* logical point to connect to. If you move the shape the connector is attached to, the connector may choose a different point to attach to.

You can't glue certain connectors by using dynamic glue. Dynamic glue is available only to dynamic connectors. Dynamic connectors must have visible *elbow joints,* a point on the connector at which it can bend. If you don't see elbow joints, you can use only static glue. See the "Drawing connectors" section later in this chapter for more information about dynamic connectors and elbow joints.

To change a dynamic connection to a static one, follow these steps:

1. **Click the Pointer Tool button on the Standard toolbar (refer to Table 6-1).**

2. **Select the connector that you want to change.**

3. **Drag either endpoint away from the shape; then drag the endpoint toward the connection point where you want to attach the connector.**

   A bold red appears around the connection point only.

4. **Release the mouse button.**

   The endpoint is attached to the connection point you pointed to. The connection point is dark red, which tells you that the connector is now using static glue.

Setting glue options

You may think that connection points are the only areas on a shape where you can attach connectors. In fact, you can attach connectors to connection points, guides, shape handles, and shape vertices. You also can glue to a shape's *geometry* (anywhere along the lines or curves that define the shape) even without a connection point. You can choose from five options in the Glue To box located in the Snap & Glue dialog box (see Figure 6-4).

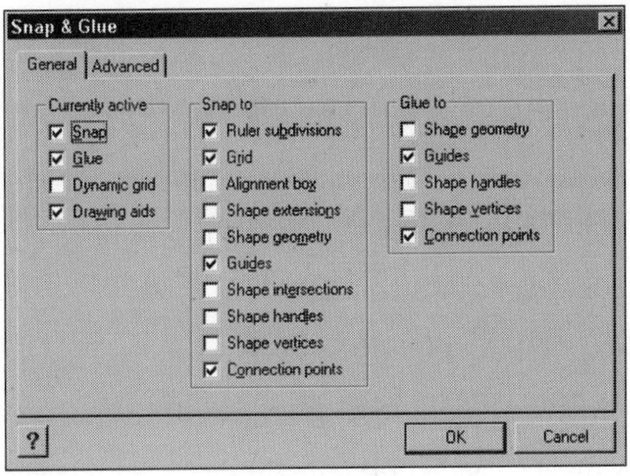

Figure 6-4:
Choose the items that you want to glue to from the Snap & Glue dialog box.

Follow these steps to set your glue options:

1. **Choose Tools⇨Snap & Glue.**

   Visio displays the Snap & Glue dialog box, as shown in Figure 6-4.

   In the dialog box, *Guides* and Connection Points are selected for you automatically. (Guides are lines that you can add to a drawing to help you position shapes accurately. See Chapter 7 for more on guides.)

   If you want to glue connectors to handles, vertices, and shape geometry, you need to click these check boxes as well. Or, you can deselect any of the five options.

2. **In the Glue To box, click the check boxes of the points that you want to glue connectors to.**

3. **Click the OK button.**

When you choose Shape Geometry, you can glue a connector to any point that defines the shape. A circle is a perfect example. A circle typically has five connection points: top, bottom, right, left, and center. When Shape Geometry is *not* selected as a glue option, you can glue a connector to only one of these five points. When Shape Geometry *is* selected, you can attach a connector to any point along the circumference of the circle. And the best part is that you can drag the connector clockwise or counterclockwise, and it stays attached to any "point" you choose along the circumference of the circle.

Gluing Connectors to Shapes

Visio offers many options for connecting shapes in a drawing. The following two actions involve using dynamic glue to connect shapes. (For more information, see the "Dynamic glue" section earlier in this chapter.)

- Connecting shapes as you drag them into your drawing
- Drawing connectors with the Connector tool and the Ctrl key

These three actions involve using static glue to connect shapes (see "Static glue," earlier in this chapter, for more information):

- Dragging connector shapes into your drawing
- Drawing connectors with the Connector tool
- Pulling connectors from control handles on shapes

The following sections discuss each of the methods for adding shapes to a drawing.

Connecting shapes as you drag them

I prefer connecting shapes as I drag them into my drawing because I can combine two steps. This method is particularly useful for process drawings such as flowcharts.

To connect shapes as you drag them, use the Connector tool on the Standard toolbar (refer to Table 6-1). This method uses dynamic glue, so if you move shapes around later, the connectors reconnect to the closest logical points. Follow these steps to connect and drag shapes:

1. **Choose File⇨Stencils to open the stencils that you want to use.**

2. **Click the Connector Tool button (refer to Table 6-1).**

   The mouse pointer changes to the Connector tool, which looks like an elbow-shaped arrow.

3. **Drag a shape that you want to use onto the drawing page.**

4. **Drag another shape into the drawing.**

   Visio uses dynamic glue to connect the two shapes automatically.

5. **Repeat Step 4 until all of the shapes that you want are in the drawing.**

6. **Click the Pointer Tool button to display the regular mouse pointer.**

As you work through these steps, you may notice that the most recent shape you dragged into the drawing remains selected. After you drag another shape into the drawing, that shape remains selected.

If the last shape you dragged isn't selected, the connector tool won't automatically connect that shape to the next one you drag. The last shape must be selected so that Visio knows which additional shape you want to connect the existing shape to.

To turn off this automatic connection feature, click the Pointer tool (it looks like an arrow) on the Standard toolbar again.

Figure 6-5 shows two boxes that were connected as they were dragged into the drawing. The Connector tool is highlighted on the toolbar, the mouse pointer is an elbow-shaped arrow, and the connector glues dynamically.

If the automatic connection feature isn't working for you, you may be trying to connect 1-D shapes. This feature automatically connects only 2-D shapes. (If you need to connect 1-D shapes — which is a rarity — you can draw connectors. See the next section to find out more about drawing connectors.)

Connector tool mouse pointer

Dynamic glue endpoints · · · · Connector tool · · · · Connector

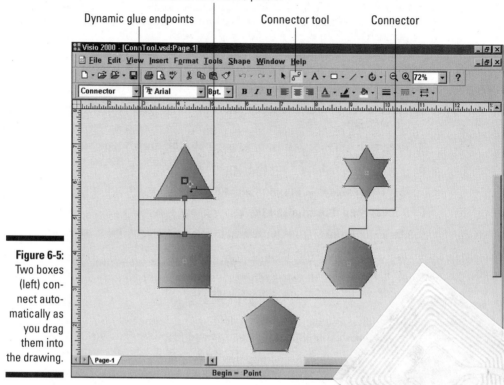

Figure 6-5:
Two boxes
(left) con-
nect auto-
matically as
you drag
them into
the drawing.

Drawing connectors

If your drawing already contains 2-D shapes, you can use the Connector tool
to go back later and make connections using either static or dynamic glue.
This tool creates dynamic connectors — the incredible, bendable, shapeable,
flexible, elbow-jointed connectors I described in the "Switching from one glue
to the other" section earlier in this chapter. If necessary (for example, to
make its way around another shape), the connector bends to form an elbow-
joint connector like the one shown in Figure 6-6.

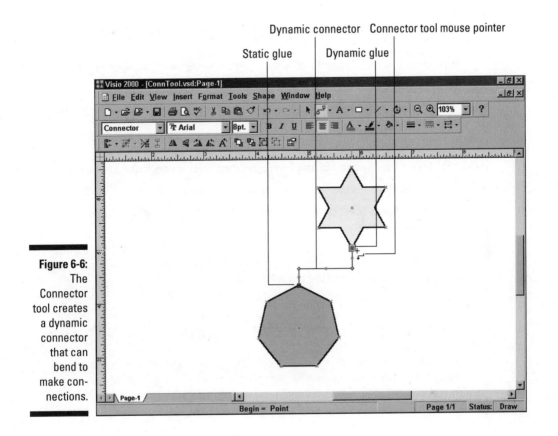

Figure 6-6:
The Connector tool creates a dynamic connector that can bend to make connections.

To use the Connector tool to connect existing shapes with static glue, follow these steps:

1. **Click the Connector Tool button on the Standard toolbar (refer to Table 6-1).**

   The mouse pointer changes to an elbow-shaped arrow.

2. **Move the mouse pointer over a connection point on a shape.**

   You see a bold red border around the connection point.

3. **Click the connection point and then drag the mouse to a connection point on another shape.**

   You see a bold red border around the connection point. After you release the mouse, the connector uses static glue to attach the points.

Connecting shapes with dynamic glue

If you want to use dynamic glue to connect two existing shapes in a drawing, follow these steps:

1. **Click the Connector Tool button on the Standard toolbar (refer to Table 6-1).**

   The mouse pointer changes to an elbow-shaped arrow.

2. **Move the mouse pointer over the first shape you want to connect.**

   You see a bold red border around the entire shape.

3. **Hold down the Ctrl key as you click and then drag the mouse to another shape.**

   When you point to a second shape, you see a bold red border around it. The connector attaches to the most logical point on the second shape automatically by using dynamic glue.

Saving time with the Connect Shapes tool

The Connect Shapes tool is a powerful timesaver. This tool connects two or more 2-D shapes automatically in the order that you want them connected. You can use the Connect Shapes tool to quickly connect a series of shapes that you already placed in a drawing (see Figure 6-7).

To use the Connect Shapes tool, follow these steps:

1. **Click the Pointer Tool button (which looks like an arrow) on the Standard toolbar.**

2. **Hold down the Shift key and click all the shapes in the order that you want to connect them.**

3. **Click the Connect Shapes Tool button on the Action toolbar, or choose Tools⇨Connect Shapes (refer to Table 6-1).**

   Visio connects all the shapes automatically.

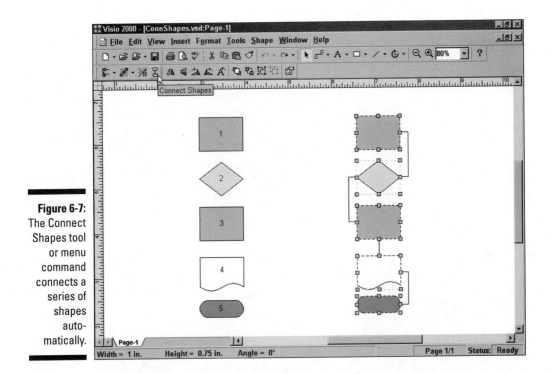

Choosing a "custom" connector to connect shapes

A cool variation of the Connect Shapes tool enables you to connect shapes with the type of connector you choose (something other than a line). Suppose, for example, that you want to connect four boxes with block-style arrows or arrow-tipped lines. (The arrows are examples of 1-D shapes that you can find on the Visio Extras⇨Connectors stencil. The Block Diagram⇨ Blocks, Block Diagram⇨Basic Shapes, and Block Diagram⇨Blocks with Perspective stencils also contain some nifty 1-D shapes to use as connectors.) Figure 6-8 shows the Flow Director 1 shape from the Connectors stencil, which serves as the connector between flowchart shapes.

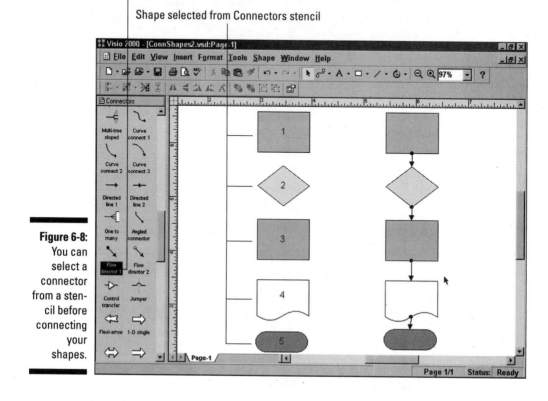

Connector used to connect shapes

Shape selected from Connectors stencil

Figure 6-8:
You can
select a
connector
from a sten-
cil before
connecting
your
shapes.

To connect existing shapes with a connector that you choose, follow these steps:

1. **Click the Pointer Tool button on the Standard toolbar (refer to Table 6-1).**

2. **Choose File⇨Stencils.**

   Open the stencil that contains the 1-D connector that you want to use.

3. **On the stencil that you opened, click the shape that you want to use for a connector.**

4. **In the drawing, hold down the Shift key and click all of the shapes in the order that you want to connect them.**

5. **Click the Connect Shapes Tool button on the Action toolbar (refer to Table 6-1).**

   Visio automatically creates dynamic glue connections between all of the shapes that you selected using the connector you choose.

Dragging connector shapes into your drawing

You can also connect shapes by dragging 1-D connector shapes from stencils onto your drawing. Most stencils usually contain at least one connector shape. You can find connector shapes at the bottom of a stencil, and they are always identified as a connector. If the stencil you're using doesn't contain the connector you want, remember that you can open another stencil by using the File➪Stencils command.

Pulling connectors from shapes

Control handles are those green-shaded square handles on shapes that let you control different aspects and behavior of a shape. (For all the details on control handles, see Chapter 4.) On some shapes, the control handles let you create connectors by "pulling" them out of the control handle.

To find out how you can use a shape's control handle, select the shape, move the mouse pointer over the control handle, and pause for a few seconds. If the control handle is designed for adjusting the connector, Visio displays a tip that says Reposition Connector. (See Figure 6-9.)

Some shapes have more than one control handle, and the one you choose may not be designed for adjusting connectors. Try a different control handle. If you don't find a control handle for adjusting connectors, you can't pull a connector from the shape. You have to use a different method to create connectors.

To pull a connector from a control handle, follow these steps:

1. **Click the Pointer Tool button on the Standard toolbar (refer to Table 6-1).**

2. **Click the shape from which you want to pull a connector.**

3. **Pause the mouse pointer over the control handle to make sure it's for connecting shapes; then drag the mouse to a connection point on the shape where you want to attach the connector.**

4. **Release the mouse button on the connection point.**

   Visio attaches the connector using static glue.

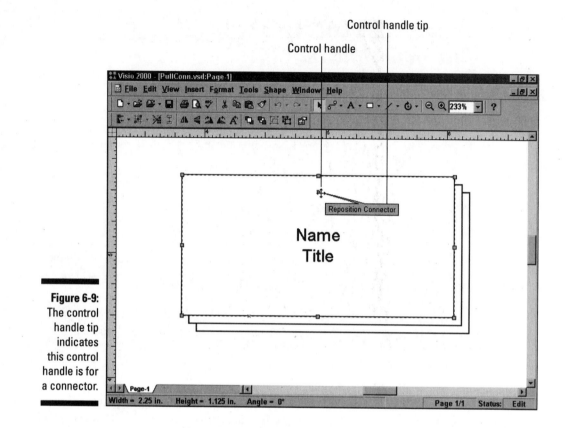

Control handle tip

Control handle

Figure 6-9:
The control
handle tip
indicates
this control
handle is for
a connector.

If you select the first shape again, you can see that, unlike other connectors, this connector is part of the shape. If you move the shape, the connector remains connected to the shape you attached it to. Keep in mind that for most connectors that are part of a shape, you can't switch the glue from static to dynamic.

Managing Your Connectors

Some drawings can become quite complex with connectors running every-where! You need to have some strategies for keeping your drawings clear. This section discusses what to do when connectors cross paths and how to route connectors in the direction you want them to go.

Handling connectors that cross paths

In some drawings, such as flowcharts or network diagrams, you may run into problems when connectors cross each other. In a simple drawing, this may not be an issue. But when a drawing is complex, it may be difficult to follow connectors that cross paths.

To solve this problem, Visio lets you add a *jump* to a connector — sort of a "wrinkle" in a line. The jump makes it easier to see which two shapes are connected. (See Figure 6-10.)

You can choose where you want to add line jumps in a drawing. You also can choose jump *styles*, the way the jump looks. To make these choices, you can use the buttons on the Action toolbar. These are shown in Table 6-2.

Jump on horizontal connector

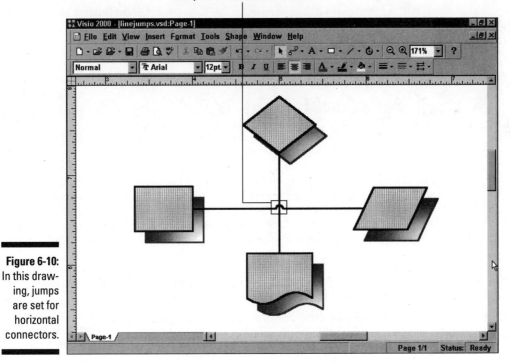

Figure 6-10: In this drawing, jumps are set for horizontal connectors.

Table 6-2	Line Jump Tools on the Layout and Routing Toolbar
Button	*Tool*
⏷	Add Line Jumps To
⏷	Line Jump Style

To add or remove line jumps and choose a line jump style, follow these steps:

1. **Choose View⇨Toolbars⇨Action to display the Action toolbar.**

2. **In the drawing, select the connector or connectors you want to change.**

3. **Click the drop-down arrow on the Add Line Jumps To button; then choose an option (Horizontal Lines, Vertical Lines, and so on). To remove line jumps, choose No Lines.**

4. **Click the drop-down arrow on the Line Jump Style button and then choose a style.**

Using routable connectors and placeable shapes

A *routable connector* is a connector that can change its path so that it doesn't cut across another shape to get to the shape it's connecting to. The connector between the two octagons in Figure 6-11 is routable because it refuses to cut across the upper triangle. The connector between the two triangles *isn't* routable because it plows right through the three-dimensional box in its path.

So, a routable connector is one that can change its path to get out of the way of other shapes. Is *every* connector routable? No. To be routable, a connector must be dynamic. You can determine that a connector is dynamic when you select it, if you see an elbow joint, control points, and vertices — all of which you can manipulate. (In Figure 6-11, notice that the connector between the two octagons is dynamic because it has all of these features.)

A routable connector works only with a *placeable shape.* A placeable shape is any shape that you specify as one that will work with a routable connector. The 3-D box in Figure 6-11 is *not* a placeable shape, so the connector that connects the triangles isn't routable; it runs right through the 3-D box.

Routable connectors and placeable shapes — you have to have one in order to have the other. So how do you get both? Fortunately, Visio does half of the work for you automatically; it sets all shapes to be placeable *if Visio decides they need to be.* That's cool; that way, you don't have to worry about it!

Routable connector   Non-routable connector

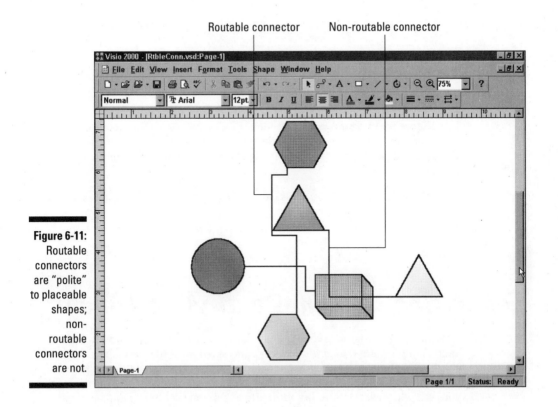

Figure 6-11:
Routable
connectors
are "polite"
to placeable
shapes;
non-
routable
connectors
are not.

When you want to change the routing behavior of a connector, select the connector and then click one of the tools on the Layout and Routing toolbar, shown in Table 6-3.

Table 6-3	Routing Tools on the Layout and Routing Toolbar
Button	**Tool**
	Reroute Freely
	Reroute as Needed
	Reroute on Crossover
	Never Reroute
	Reroute Connector

To make a connector routable, you can do one of the following:

✔ Connect shapes by using the Connect Shapes command.

✔ Use the Dynamic Connector — a shape that appears on many stencils and is always available on the Connectors stencil. (It looks like an elbow-jointed connector with a box at each end.)

✔ Before you begin a drawing, click the Connector Tool button on the Standard toolbar; then drag shapes into the drawing area. (Using the Connector tool, the shapes are automatically connected using a dynamic connector.)

When you use a routable connector, you can "tweak" the path of the connector by moving the control points and vertices that make up the connector's elbow joint. For more details about working with a shape's control points and vertices, see Chapter 8.

Connecting Drawings with Auto Layout

Visio has an automatic layout feature for drawings that typically include connected shapes, such as organization charts, network diagrams, and flowcharts. This feature saves you the trouble of rearranging shapes manually when you revise (add or delete) shapes in a large drawing. In addition, when you're in a hurry, the auto layout feature lets you create rough drawings quickly and have Visio arrange the shapes for you. An example of a messy, hastily drawn organization chart is shown in Figure 6-12.

If you click the Connector tool before you start dragging shapes into your drawing, Visio automatically connects one shape to the next using dynamic connectors. (If you decide not to use the Connector tool, be sure to add dynamic connectors between shapes.) After all the shapes are in the drawing, you're ready to use the auto layout feature.

To use Visio's auto layout feature in a drawing where the shapes are connected, follow these steps:

1. **Drag all the shapes and connectors into the drawing.**

2. **Select all the shapes and connectors.**

3. **Choose Tools⇨Lay Out Shapes.**

   The Lay Out Shapes dialog box appears, as shown in Figure 6-13.

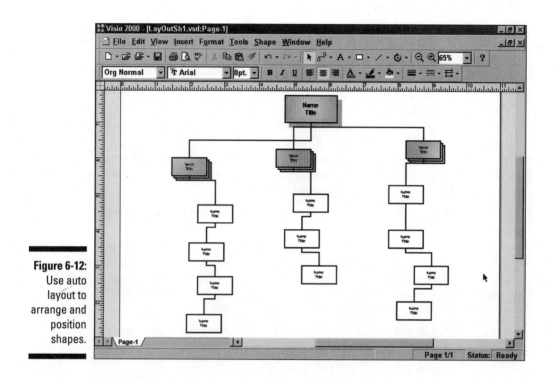

Figure 6-12:
Use auto layout to arrange and position shapes.

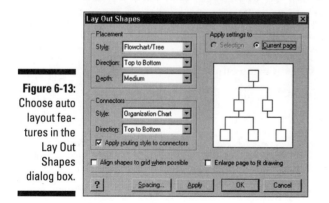

Figure 6-13:
Choose auto layout features in the Lay Out Shapes dialog box.

4. **Click the drop-down arrow for the Placement Style box and then move the up- and down-arrow key to highlight your choice.**

   Visio displays a preview of each style on the right side of the dialog box.

   Choose the style that's most appropriate for your drawing.

   Note: As you work your way through this dialog box, some of the drop-down boxes listed in these steps may become unavailable based on previous choices you make.

5. **Click the drop-down arrow for the Placement Direction box and then move the up- and down-arrow key to highlight your choice. Check the box on the right for a preview.**

6. **In the Placement Depth drop-down list, choose Shallow, Medium, or Deep.**

   In an organization chart, for example, choose Deep if the chart contains more vertical than horizontal shapes — that is, more positions and fewer managers. If the chart contains more horizontal than vertical shapes (more managers than positions) choose Shallow. If the drawing is pretty evenly weighted, choose Medium.

7. **Click the drop-down arrow for the Connectors Style box and then move the up- and down-arrow key to highlight your choice.**

   Visio displays a preview to the right.

8. **Click the drop-down arrow for the Connectors Direction box, move the up- and down-arrow key to highlight your choice, and then preview your selection on the right.**

9. **The dialog box contains the following three check box options. Click those that apply to your drawing.**

   • Apply routing style to connectors

   • Align shapes to grid when possible

   • Enlarge page to fit drawing

10. **In the Apply Settings To box, choose Selection or Current Page.**

11. **Click the OK button.**

If you don't like the way the auto layout feature arranges your drawing, choose Edit➪Undo or press Ctrl+Z. You can always follow the preceding steps again to make different layout choices.

Part III
Customizing Your Work

The 5th Wave   By Rich Tennant

"I used Visio to create this 3-D wallpaper and now half the staff is complaining of headaches. Must be these dang VDT screens!"

In this part . . .

Now you start to get into the nitty-gritty of Visio. Here you read more about positioning shapes precisely, how to draw your own shapes and manipulate them, and how to make more sophisticated drawings by using pages and layers. You also get a brief summary of Visio's wizards and an inkling of what they can do for you.

Chapter 7

Making Your Drawings Precisely Right

*T*his chapter is all about how to measure, place, and line up elements in a drawing by using the tools Visio provides. The tools I show you make these tasks easy and save you time. You don't have to use all these ideas; just pick and choose the ones that make the most sense for your drawings.

Checking Out Your Options

This list gives you a preview of the terms used in this chapter so that you aren't scratching your head and wondering what the heck I'm talking about:

✔ **Alignment and distribution:** Alignment refers to shapes lining up evenly; distribution refers to objects being spaced evenly.

When shapes aren't aligned and distributed evenly in a drawing, your eyes sense that something is wrong. Visio helps you automatically align and distribute shapes.

✔ **Grid lines:** These prominent vertical and horizontal lines make the drawing area look like graph paper.

Many of the figures in this book have the grid turned off. I turned them off so you can focus on the topic at hand. However, the grid is a useful tool for measuring and placing shapes.

✔ **Guides:** You can add guide lines to a drawing to help position and place shapes accurately.

If you draw a person on paper, you may lightly sketch horizontal lines at the shoulder, waist, and knees as guides for helping proportion the figure. You place guides in a Visio drawing for the same purpose.

✔ **Rulers:** These are the objects on the top and left side of the drawing area that look curiously like — well, *rulers!* Rulers, as you may expect, act as measuring devices.

✔ **Scale:** Scale is the ratio of real-life objects to the shapes in your drawing. Remember the last time you looked at a map? The scale was probably 10 miles per 1 inch or something close to that. Unless you can print on life-size paper, you have to scale a drawing when it includes objects that are larger than the paper!

✔ **Snap:** This feature pulls or attracts shapes to any object that you specify: another shape, a grid line, a guide, a connection point. This function helps you place shapes accurately.

As you work through this chapter, it's helpful to have Rulers, Grid, Guides, and Connection Points checkmarked on your View menu. (Just click them.) If they are not checkmarked, they won't show up on your screen, and you'll think I'm just making 'em up (or seeing things)!

You might also find it useful to display the View toolbar (choose View➪ Toolbars➪View). The View toolbar contains the tools listed in Table 7-1. The Grid tool toggles the grid on and off; the Guides tool toggles guides on and off; and the Connection Points tool toggles connection points on and off.

Table 7-1	Tools on the View Toolbar
Button	*Tool*
Rulers	Rulers
Grid	Grid
Guides	Guides
Connection Points	Connection Points

Using the Drawing Grid

Whenever you create a new drawing, Visio automatically displays a *drawing grid* — horizontal and vertical lines that make the drawing area look like graph paper. The grid helps you place shapes where you want them in a drawing.

Just as you can buy graph paper in different grid sizes, you can set the grid *density* (fine, normal, or coarse) for your drawing. Why would you care about density? If you create a drawing with very small shapes that you want to place precisely, you probably want a finer density — say, lines every ⅛ inch or so. On the other hand, if you use very large shapes in your drawing, a ½-inch grid is more than adequate. See Figure 7-1 for an example of a normal density.

Keep in mind that the density that you see on your screen depends on your monitor and the resolution you use. To figure out what fine, normal, and coarse mean on your monitor, experiment with them! Use the steps that appear later in this section to change grid density.

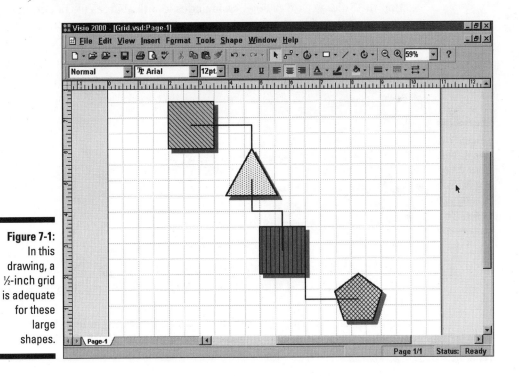

Figure 7-1:
In this drawing, a ½-inch grid is adequate for these large shapes.

The grid in Visio is automatically *variable*. When you zoom in on a drawing, grid lines are closer together; when you zoom out, the grid lines are farther apart. This is a great feature when you want to place shapes right on the money. It doesn't help much to zoom in really close on a shape if the grid doesn't change; that would be like trying to place shapes on paper every ⅛ inch using a ruler that was only marked in ¼-inch intervals. You can place a shape precisely only if the grid gets denser. Of course, like most settings in Visio, you can turn off the variable grid and instead use a fixed grid; see the steps that follow. If you use a fixed grid, the density stays the same, regardless of the zoom percentage you use. Typically, a grid is evenly spaced horizontally and vertically; when horizontal lines occur every ½ inch, vertical lines do, too. However, you can set an uneven grid if you like, with ½-inch horizontal grid lines and ¼-inch vertical grid lines, for example.

To change grid settings or set a fixed grid, follow these steps:

1. **Choose Tools⇨Ruler & Grid.**

   Visio displays the Ruler & Grid dialog box, as shown in Figure 7-2. Notice that the Ruler & Grid dialog box includes identical areas for horizontal and vertical grid lines so that you can set variables independently.

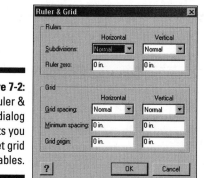

Figure 7-2:
The Ruler & Grid dialog box lets you set grid variables.

2. **Click the drop-down lists for Grid Spacing Horizontal and Grid Spacing Vertical and then click Fine, Normal, or Coarse. To set a fixed grid, click Fixed.**

3. **If you want to get picky about the *minimum* spacing to use (for Fine, Normal, or Coarse), type a number (in inches) in the Minimum Spacing boxes.**

4. **Click the OK button.**

Note: The grid doesn't show when you print your drawing; it's a visual aid only.

If you ever want to turn off the drawing grid, choose View⇨Grid. This command toggles the grid display on and off. Turning off the grid helps you see how the drawing will look when you print it.

Using Dynamic Grid

If you create flowcharts or block diagrams, you should check out the dynamic grid feature. The dynamic grid helps you position new shapes vertically and horizontally relative to shapes you've already placed in the drawing. How does it work? As you drag a flowchart or block diagram shape into your drawing, horizontal and vertical reference lines appear along with the shape. As you move the shape around the drawing, the reference lines "jump" to show you when the shape is in alignment with another shape close by. When the shape is aligned where you want it, release the mouse button; the reference lines disappear.

Dynamic grid is automatically active when you create a new flowchart drawing. To activate dynamic grid for block diagrams or other drawings, use these steps:

1. **Choose⇨Snap & Glue.**

   The Snap & Glue dialog box displays.

2. **Click the Dynamic Grid option in the Currently Active box.**

3. **Click the OK button.**

Alternatively, Visio has a Dynamic Grid toolbar button on the Snap & Glue toolbar. Display the Snap & Glue toolbar by right-clicking on the toolbar area and then clicking the Snap & Glue option. Scan the buttons with your mouse until tool tips reveal the Dynamic Grid button. It looks like a grid with two boxes positioned and a third box moving into place. Click the button to activate it.

Setting Your Scale

When you create a drawing — a flowchart, for instance — that doesn't represent a real-life object, you don't need to worry about scale. Who cares if your "decision" shape is 1⅛-inch wide and your "process" shape is 1¾-inch wide? When you use a template to create a flowchart (or any other type of drawing with abstract shapes), Visio automatically sets the drawing scale to 1:1 (drawing size:actual size).

However, when you create a drawing with shapes that represent any real-life objects larger than a page, the drawing must be *scaled* so that all the objects fit on the page in proper relation to one another. For example, suppose that you want to create an office layout. If you use the Office Layout template, Visio automatically sets the drawing scale to ¼ inch:1 foot. That is, every ¼ inch shown on the printed page represents 1 foot of office space. Terrific — all the work is done for you! An example of a ¼ inch:1 foot office layout is shown in Figure 7-3.

If you're not using a template or if you want to adjust the scale set by a template, you can set a drawing scale yourself — but you'll have to work for it! Well, at the very least, you need to understand the three elements involved:

- ✔ **Page units** represent the measurements on the printed page (like a 6-foot couch that's only ½ inch on the printed page).

- ✔ **Drawing units** represent real-life measurements (like 320 feet for a building landscape plan).

- ✔ **Drawing scale** is the ratio between these two.

To get an accurate scale in your drawing, *you must set all three of these elements.* If you set only the drawing scale, you may end up with inches:inches when you want feet:yards. That's because the default setting for page units and drawing units is typically *inches.* (I say *typically* because many templates define inches as the unit of measure.)

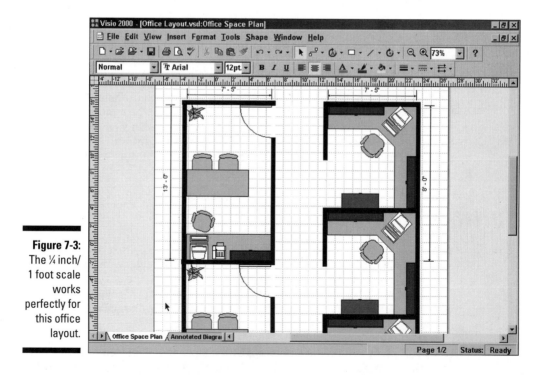

Figure 7-3:
The ¼ inch/ 1 foot scale works perfectly for this office layout.

To set page units, follow these steps:

1. **Choose Tools⇨Options.**

2. **In the Options dialog box, click the Default Units tab.**

3. **In the Page box, choose the unit of measure that you want from the drop-down list.**

4. **Click the OK button.**

To set drawing units, use these steps:

1. **Choose File⇨Page Setup.**

2. **In the Page Setup dialog box, click the Page Properties tab.**

3. **In the Measurement Units box, choose the unit of measure that you want from the drop-down list.**

4. **Click the OK button.**

Use these steps to specify a drawing scale:

1. **Choose File⇨Page Setup.**

2. **In the Page Setup dialog box, click the Drawing Scale tab. (See Figure 7-4.)**

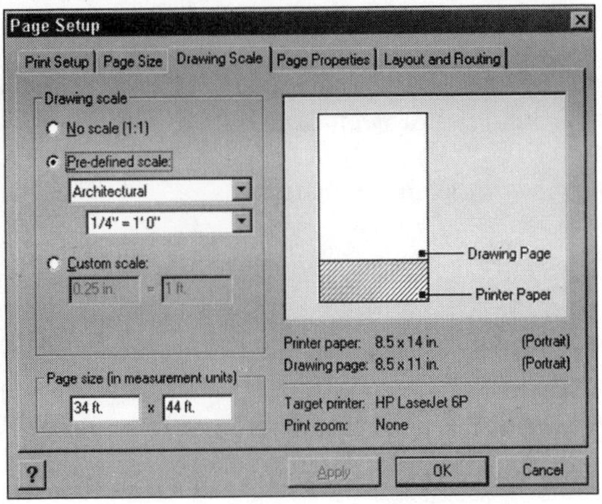

Figure 7-4:
The Drawing Scale tab in the Page Setup dialog box.

3. **Click the Pre-defined Scale radio button, which is in the Drawing Scale area. Choose one of the scale categories — Architectural, Civil Engineering, and so on — from the drop-down list under the radio button.**

4. **Click the drop-down list of measurements to display the preset scales and then click the scale that you want to use.**

   If you don't want to use any of the preset scales listed, go back to Step 3 and choose the Custom Scale radio button instead of the Pre-defined Scale radio button. Enter a scale in the box provided.

5. **Check the Page Size area of the dialog box.**

   It tells you how much "real estate" you can cover on the drawing page with the current settings. If it's too large or too small, go back to Step 4 and choose a scale that fits the page size better. For example, if you need to draw an office plan that's 50 feet x 50 feet and the Scaled Drawing Size shows only 40 feet x 30 feet, you need to adjust.

6. **Click the OK button.**

When you change the scale of a drawing, the change applies only to the drawing's current page. If the drawing has multiple pages, including background pages, you must change the scale separately for each page. For more information about working with multi-page drawings and background pages, see Chapter 10.

Snapping Shapes into Place

Snap is a terrific timesaving Visio feature. You can't imagine how much time that you waste trying to precisely place shapes *without* using snap. The snap feature in Visio works like a magnet. You can attach a shape to one or more elements of your choice. When snap is turned on, a shape jumps to certain points as you drag it around the drawing area.

Shapes snap to any of the following elements:

- ✔ **Alignment box:** A shape's frame (displayed only when a shape is selected).
- ✔ **Connection points:** Blue Xs that appear on shapes when View⇨ Connection Points is checked.
- ✔ **Grid:** Horizontal and vertical graph paper lines in the drawing area.
- ✔ **Guides:** Special lines or points that you add to a drawing to help align shapes.
- ✔ **Ruler subdivisions:** Any mark that appears on the ruler (1 inch, ½ inch, and so on).
- ✔ **Shape geometry:** The outline of a shape.
- ✔ **Shape handles:** The square green points on a selected shape that you use to resize shapes.

✔ **Shape vertices:** The green diamond-shaped points you use to change the angle of a line or to add a new point.

✔ **Shape intersections:** Locations where two shapes intersect.

Snap is automatically turned on for ruler, grid lines, connection points, and guides. This means that whenever you drag a shape around the drawing area, the shape jumps to align itself to ruler subdivisions, grid lines, guides, or connection points on other shapes. For example, suppose you want to place three rectangles 1 inch apart. As you drag the shapes, they jump to the nearest grid line or ruler subdivision, letting you place the rectangles exactly 1 inch apart (see Figure 7-5). Without snap, you could spend a great deal of time shooting in the dark trying to space and line up these suckers! Even with all your effort, they still may not line up correctly.

You can choose to have objects snap to any combination of the elements from the list, or you can have them snap to none. Turning on all snap options at the same time is a little distracting because your shape jumps every time it gets near anything. I recommend that you turn on only those snap options that you really want to use. For instance, you may not want to choose grid and ruler at the same time. Because grid lines rarely correspond to ruler markings, it's not clear where your shape is jumping when both of these options are selected at the same time.

This shape jumps here as you move it.

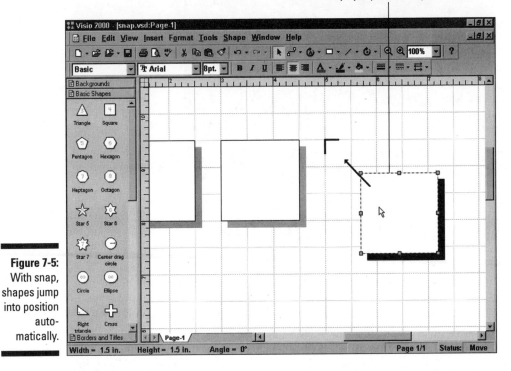

Figure 7-5:
With snap, shapes jump into position automatically.

Along with choosing snap elements, you get to set the *strength* of snap. It's sort of like choosing between a tiny refrigerator magnet and a 10-pound horseshoe magnet. The bigger the magnet, the harder snap pulls. (I doubt you need to set strength; in all my years of working with Visio I've never noticed snap not pulling hard enough!)

To change snap settings or to turn snap off altogether, use these steps:

1. **Choose Tools⇨Snap & Glue.**

   The Snap & Glue dialog box, shown in Figure 7-6, appears.

2. **In the Snap To section, click the check boxes for elements for which you want to activate snap.**

   In the Snap & Glue Strength area on the Advanced tab, adjust the pull by moving the slides along the slide bar.

3. **Click the OK button.**

If you want to turn snap off altogether, choose Tools⇨Snap & Glue. In the Currently Active section of the dialog box, click the Snap check box to remove the check mark and then click the OK button. When you turn snap off, shapes move freely when you drag them around the drawing area (no more Mexican jumping beans).

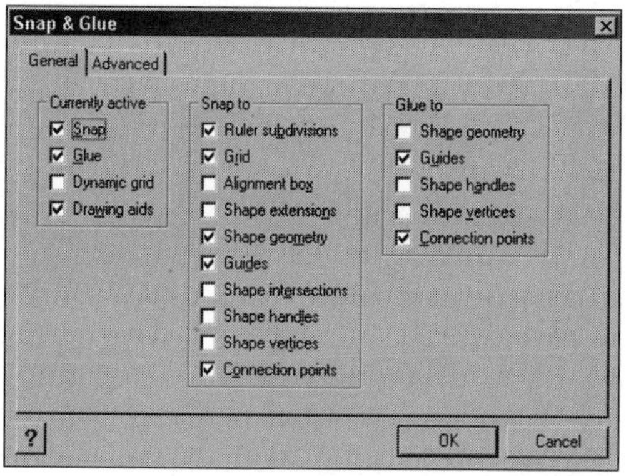

Figure 7-6:
Choose
snap
elements
and strength
in the Snap
& Glue
dialog box.

Measuring Up with Rulers

I don't know about you, but I always feel more comfortable when I know how much space I have to move around in — I like to know what my boundaries are. Rulers tell you just that. Using vertical and horizontal rulers on the drawing page, you can tell exactly how much space you have in a drawing and how big or small elements are.

The rulers in a Visio drawing typically display inch measurements by default, but you have many other choices. For example, you may want to use yards or miles for drawings that represent real-life objects, such as landscape plans. If you use the metric system, you may want to switch ruler units to centimeters or millimeters. To switch default measurement units for the rulers, follow these steps:

1. **Choose File⇨Page Setup.**

   Visio displays the Page Setup dialog box.

2. **Click the Page Properties tab, as shown in Figure 7-7.**

3. **Click the drop-down arrow for Measurement Units; choose the units that you want to use.**

4. **Click the OK button.**

The *zero point* for the rulers (the point where zero appears on a ruler) is generally in the lower-left corner of the drawing page, although you can change this if you want. Why would you want to? Suppose you're drawing an office layout. You may find the drawing easier to work with if you move the zero points to align with the left and upper walls (see Figure 7-8).

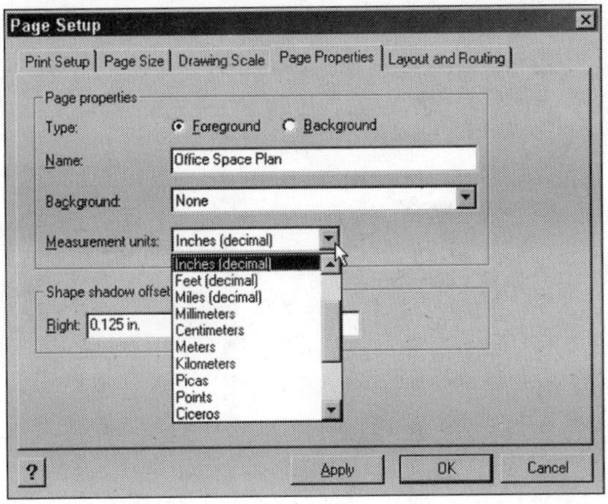

Figure 7-7:
Use the
Page
Properties
dialog box
to set
default ruler
measure-
ment units.

To change the zero point of both rulers, follow these steps:

1. **Move the mouse pointer to the gray square where the vertical ruler and horizontal ruler intersect (in the upper-left corner of the drawing area).**

   The mouse pointer changes to a four-headed arrow.

2. **Hold down the Ctrl key and drag the mouse where you want the zero point of both rulers to be.**

   As you move your mouse, watch the faint dotted line that appears on each ruler, marking the position of the mouse.

3. **Release the mouse button when the zero point is positioned where you want it.**

If you want to change the zero point of just one ruler, use the same basic procedure, but you drag from one ruler only. For example, if you want to place the zero point on the horizontal ruler 2 inches in from the left edge of the paper, follow these steps:

1. **Point to the *vertical* ruler until you see the double-headed arrow mouse pointer.**

2. **Hold the Ctrl key and drag the mouse until the vertical line is positioned where you want the zero point to be on the horizontal ruler.**

New zero points

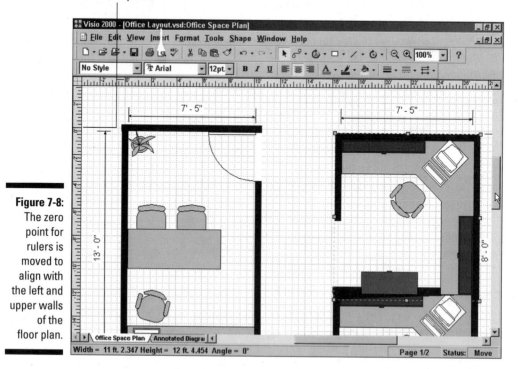

Figure 7-8:
The zero point for rulers is moved to align with the left and upper walls of the floor plan.

If you prefer not to do all this dragging, you can choose Tools⇨Ruler & Grid. When the Ruler & Grid dialog box appears (refer to Figure 7-2), enter zero points (measured in inches) in the Ruler Zero boxes for horizontal, vertical, or both rulers.

TIP

To reset the zero points of both rulers to their default position, just double-click the intersection of the rulers (in the upper-left corner of the drawing area).

TIP

This is a good time to use the snap feature discussed earlier in the chapter. Before you adjust the zero point for your rulers, turn on snap for rulers if it isn't on already. (The steps are detailed in the "Snapping Shapes into Place" section earlier in this chapter.) With ruler snap turned on, your mouse jumps to ruler subdivisions so that you can easily place the zero point.

Using Guides to Guide You

As if you don't already have enough options for positioning shapes in a drawing, Visio gives you two more! *Guide lines* and *guide points* work in combination with snap. Use guide lines when you want a bunch of shapes to stand in a row like soldiers (see Figure 7-9). Use guide points when you want to pinpoint a shape in an exact location.

To make guide lines and guide points work, you have to turn on snap for guides; otherwise, your guides don't do anything except clutter up your drawing. (See the "Snapping Shapes into Place" section earlier in this chapter to set snap elements.) In Figure 7-9, all the shapes are snapped to the guide line because snap is set to work on guides and shape handles. To snap shapes to a guide, drag the shape near the guide. The shape snaps automatically to the guide. When you select the shape, the shape's red selection handles clearly indicate that the shape is glued to the guide. (Visio uses dynamic glue to glue shapes to guides. See Chapter 6 for more information about dynamic glue.)

The useful thing about guide lines and guide points — after you create them — is that you can move them. When you do, all the shapes attached to the guides move right along with them.

Guide line

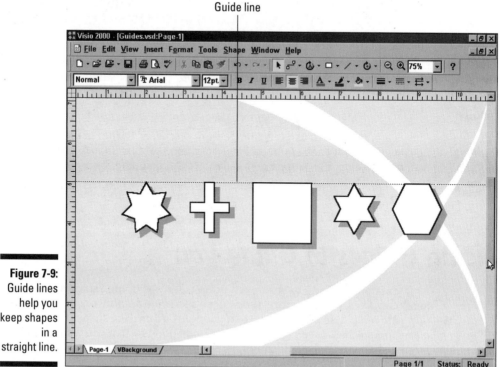

Figure 7-9:
Guide lines
help you
keep shapes
in a
straight line.

Creating guide lines

To create a guide line, use these steps:

1. **Move your mouse pointer over the vertical ruler (to create a vertical guide) or over the horizontal ruler (to create a horizontal guide) until the mouse pointer changes to a double-headed arrow.**

2. **Drag the mouse.**

   As you drag, the guide appears as a blue line that runs back and forth (or up and down) the drawing page.

3. **Stop dragging the guide when it's positioned where you want it.**

   The line turns green because it's selected.

What? Now you want a diagonal guide line? Okay. Just create a horizontal or vertical guide and then rotate it. You can use these steps:

1. **Select the guide line that you want to rotate.**

2. **Choose View⇨Size & Position.**

   The Size & Position window appears near the bottom of your screen.

3. **In the Angle box, type the degree angle of rotation (such as 45).**

   Visio rotates the selected guide to the angle that you specify.

Creating guide points

You can also create *guide points* when you want to pinpoint the corner of a shape in an exact location. On the screen, a guide point looks like a plus symbol (+). To create a guide point, use these steps:

1. **Move your mouse pointer over the intersection of the vertical and horizontal rulers.**

   The mouse pointer changes to a four-headed arrow.

2. **Drag the mouse.**

   Two blue lines — one vertical and one horizontal — follow the movement of your mouse on the drawing page.

3. **Stop dragging the mouse when the intersection of the guides is positioned where you want it.**

   The blue lines disappear, and the guide point (a circle with a cross through it) is displayed on the screen.

In the left-hand side of Figure 7-10, it's clear that the lower-right corner of the square is connected to the guide point, but it's not so clear that the star is connected. That's because each one is connected at a selection handle on the shape's *frame*. Without seeing the star's frame, you'd probably guess that the star *isn't* connected. If you want the tip of the star to touch the guide point, like the star to the right, turn on the snap feature so it snaps to connection points, because the star has a connection point at each tip. (See the "Snapping Shapes into Place" section earlier in this chapter to set snap elements.)

If you want to use multiple guides spaced evenly across your drawing, here is a great way to create them:

1. **Create the first guide.**

2. **Hold down the Ctrl key as you drag a copy of the guide to the next increment you want — say, 1 inch.**

3. **Press the F4 key.**

   Another guide, 1 inch from the last guide, is automatically created.

4. **Press the F4 key as many times as you want to keep creating guides spaced at the same increment you originally chose.**

Guide points

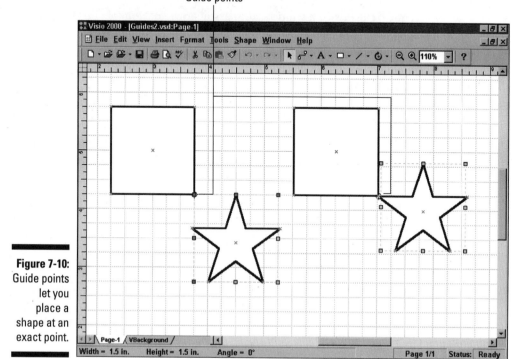

Figure 7-10:
Guide points
let you
place a
shape at an
exact point.

Aligning and Distributing Shapes

Besides using guides, Visio gives you another way to automatically align shapes. Suppose that you create a diagram like the one on the left in Figure 7-11. The shapes aren't lined up, the connectors look goofy, and the whole thing looks like you threw it together in a few seconds! The diagram on the right was aligned with Visio's automatic alignment feature.

With the click of a toolbar button (or via a menu command), you can horizontally align the tops, bottoms, or middles of selected shapes, or vertically align the left edges, right edges, or middles of selected shapes. You first select the shape you want other shapes to align to and then select all the other shapes. The first shape you select becomes the reference point for the alignment of other shapes.

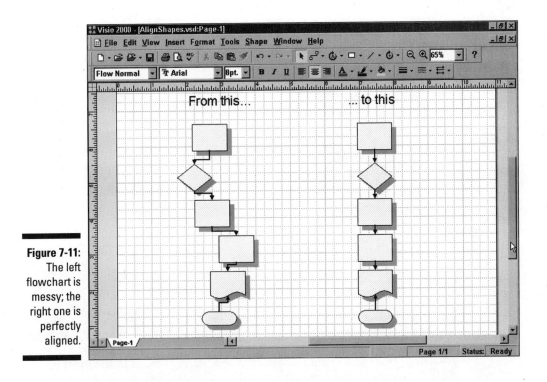

Figure 7-11:
The left
flowchart is
messy; the
right one is
perfectly
aligned.

To align several shapes horizontally, vertically, or both, use these steps:

1. **Select the shape to which you want the other shapes to align.**

2. **Hold the Shift key and at the same time select all other shapes that you want aligned to the first shape.**

3. **Either choose Tools➪Align Shapes or click the Align Shapes Tool button on the Shapes toolbar. (The Align Shapes Tool button looks like a left-aligned box and triangle.)**

    The Align Shapes dialog box appears as shown in Figure 7-12.

Do you notice that the Align Shapes tool on the Action toolbar has a drop-down arrow next to the tool button? If you click the arrow instead of the tool itself, Visio displays a miniature version of the Align Shapes dialog box.

4. **Click the alignment style that you want.**

    If you think you may add more shapes to your drawing that you'll want aligned with these, consider clicking the Create Guide and Glue Shapes to It option, which is at the bottom of the dialog box.

5. **Click the OK button.**

    Visio aligns all shapes to the first shape that you selected.

Align middles horizontally

Align tops | Align bottoms

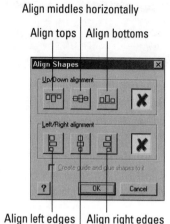

Align left edges | Align right edges

Align middles vertically

Ever try to space several shapes evenly — say, ½ inch apart — across an area? Doing it manually can be very frustrating. Visio refers to evenly spacing shapes as *distributing* shapes, and it is made easy for you: Visio provides a toolbar button (or a menu command, if you prefer) similar to the Align Shapes command. Use these steps to distribute shapes:

1. **Select all the shapes that you want to distribute.**

2. **Choose Tools⇨Distribute Shapes or click the Distribute Shapes Tool button on the Shape toolbar. The Distribute Shapes Tool button looks like three boxes aligned diagonally.**

   The Distribute Shapes dialog box, shown in Figure 7-13, appears.

3. Click the distribution style that you want to use.

If you think that you may add more shapes to your drawing that you'll later want to distribute, consider clicking the Create Guides and Glue Shapes to Them option at the bottom of the dialog box.

4. Click the OK button.

Visio automatically distributes the shapes.

Just like with the Align Shapes toolbar button, the Distribute Shapes tool has a drop-down arrow next to the tool button. You can click the down arrow to reveal a miniature version of the dialog box.

Chapter 8

Creating and Customizing Shapes

. . . .

In This Chapter

▶ Creating shapes by using fun Visio tools

▶ Drawing your own shapes

▶ Manipulating shapes

▶ Adding character to your shapes

▶ Grouping and stacking shapes

. . . .

*B*ecause Visio provides so many shapes in its stencils, you can use Visio quite successfully without ever needing to customize shapes. But if you're really adventurous, you can use Visio to make shapes *your* way. In this chapter, you discover how to get creative with Visio by changing existing shapes and drawing your own shapes.

Creating Unique Shapes the Fun Way

Near the bottom of the Visio Shape menu is a command called Operations. Sounds pretty serious! Well, it's not serious at all. In fact, this command should be called Fun Stuff. After you select this command, Visio gives you a submenu with a list of tools that you can use to create shapes. The following list explains each tool:

- ✔ **Combine:** Creates a new shape from overlapping shapes by cutting out the areas that overlap.

- ✔ **Fragment:** Breaks shapes into separate shapes along the lines where they overlap.

- ✔ **Intersect:** Creates a new shape from *only* the area where two or more shapes overlap (all other areas are deleted).

- ✔ **Subtract:** Cuts away the areas that overlap the first shape that you select.

- ✔ **Union:** Creates a new shape from overlapping shapes by using the perimeter of all the shapes as the new outline.

It may take you awhile to remember exactly what each command does. That's okay, just experiment with them! If you don't like the result, choose Edit⇨Undo and try another one. The following sections illustrate how each of these commands work — they're easier to see than describe.

Uniting shapes

The Union command does as its name suggests — it *unites* two or more overlapping shapes. The Union command combines these shapes by maintaining the perimeters of all the shapes and erasing their inside boundaries (see Figure 8-1).

To use the union feature, follow these steps:

1. **Drag the shapes that you want to unite into the drawing area.**

   If you want to draw shapes, draw them now.

2. **Move the shapes where you want them, making sure each one overlaps at least one other shape.**

3. **Click the Pointer Tool button (see Table 8-1) on the Standard toolbar; then draw a selection box around all the shapes.**

4. **Choose Shapes⇨Operations⇨Union.**

   Visio unites all the shapes.

If some of your shapes aren't overlapped, the Union command doesn't unite them. Although they're treated as one shape, they still appear to be separate.

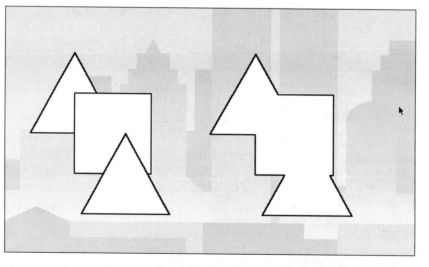

Figure 8-1:
Individual shapes (left) unite to become a single shape (right).

Table 8-1	Tools for Drawing Shapes
Button	*Tool*
	Arc tool
	Ellipse tool
	Format Painter tool
	Freeform tool
	Line tool
	Pencil tool
	Pointer tool
	Rectangle tool
	Rotation tool

Combining shapes

The name of the Combine command is a bit misleading. It may be more accurate to call it the Cutout command. Notice that on the left side of Figure 8-2, two shapes are placed on top of one another. In the shape on the right side, the Combine command uses the outline of the star to cut out the center of the other shape. (You know this is a cutout because you can see the grid through the star.) It's easy to think of the Combine command as the doughnut command.

When you combine shapes that don't overlap, the second shape takes on the attributes of the first shape you select.

Follow these steps to combine shapes:

1. **Draw all the shapes that you want to combine.**

2. **Arrange the shapes so that they overlap.**

3. **Using the Pointer Tool button (refer to Table 8-1) on the Standard toolbar, draw a selection box around all the shapes that you want to combine.**

4. **Choose Shape⇨Operations⇨Combine.**

    Visio creates cutouts where the smaller, fully enclosed shapes overlap the larger ones.

Shape   Cutout

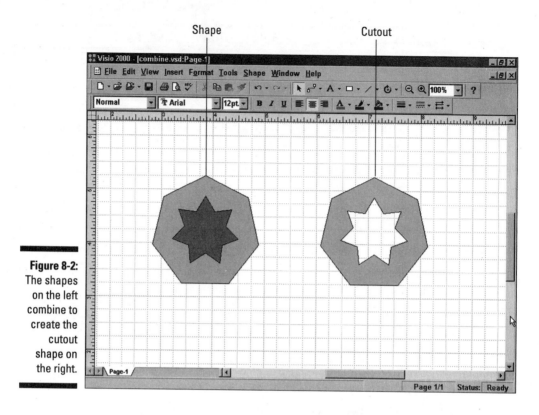

Figure 8-2:
The shapes
on the left
combine to
create the
cutout
shape on
the right.

In Figure 8-3, you see a more complex array of combined shapes. On the left, each shape is a different gray hue. After you combine them into a single shape, all the hues convert to that of the triangle — the shape that's on top of the heap.

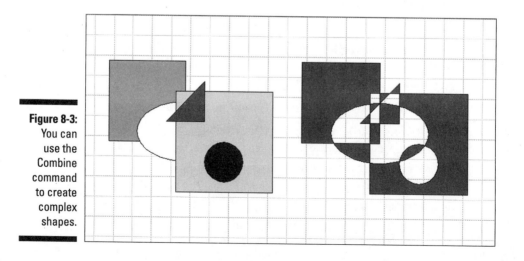

Figure 8-3:
You can
use the
Combine
command
to create
complex
shapes.

Fragmenting shapes

Fragmenting sounds rather dangerous, but no shapes are actually harmed during fragmenting. Fragmenting is fun, and it's a great way to create new shapes from overlapped shapes. The left side of Figure 8-4 shows several overlapped shapes that take on new dimensions when you separate them at their overlap points (right). It's sort of like cutting apart all the pieces where they overlap and making jigsaw puzzle pieces out of them.

To fragment shapes, follow these steps:

1. **Drag all the shapes that you want into the drawing area or draw them.**

2. **Move the shapes so that they overlap.**

3. **Use the Pointer Tool button (refer to Table 8-1) on the Standard toolbar to draw a selection box around the shapes.**

4. **Choose Shape⇨Operations⇨Fragment.**

    Visio breaks all the shapes into separate shapes along their overlapping lines. You can't control the distance Visio uses to separate the shapes, but you can move the shapes individually after they're fragmented.

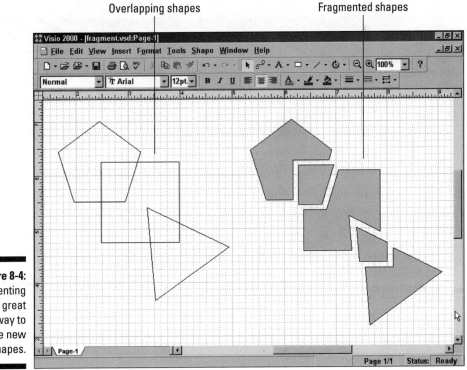

Figure 8-4: Fragmenting is a great way to create new shapes.

Intersecting shapes

Intersecting shapes brings about a radical change. Visio keeps only the parts where *all* the shapes overlap and cuts away the rest. Figure 8-5 shows three overlapping circles. Notice that a part of each circle overlaps the others. After you intersect these shapes, the only thing that's left is the triangular portion from the center where all the circles overlap.

To intersect shapes, follow these steps:

1. **Drag all the shapes that you want into the drawing area or draw them.**

2. **Move the shapes so that they *all* overlap every other shape at some point.**

3. **Use the Pointer Tool button (refer to Table 8-1) on the Standard toolbar to draw a selection box around the shapes.**

4. **Choose Shape⇨Operations⇨Intersect.**

   Visio removes all extraneous parts of the shapes and leaves only the portion where *all* shapes overlap.

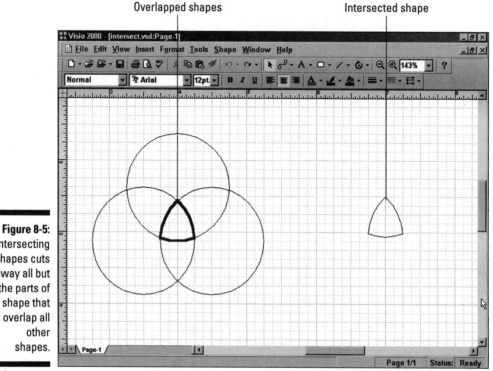

Figure 8-5: Intersecting shapes cuts away all but the parts of a shape that overlap all other shapes.

Subtracting shapes

Subtract is a feature that works just like it sounds: When two shapes overlap, the overlapping part is subtracted — removed — from the first shape that you select. Be careful to remember *the first shape you select;* you need to know which shape you want to leave behind when you finish subtracting. Selecting the wrong shape leaves you with the part that you *don't* want. Figure 8-6 shows the original shapes — the circle and star. The partial star in the center is what's left if you select the star first — before you select the circle and the subtract command. The partial circle on the right is what's left if you select the circle first.

Follow these steps to use the subtract command:

1. **Drag the shapes that you want to work with into the drawing area or draw them.**

2. **Position the shapes so that they overlap.**

3. **Use the Pointer Tool button (refer to Table 8-1) on the Standard toolbar to select the shape that you want to keep.**

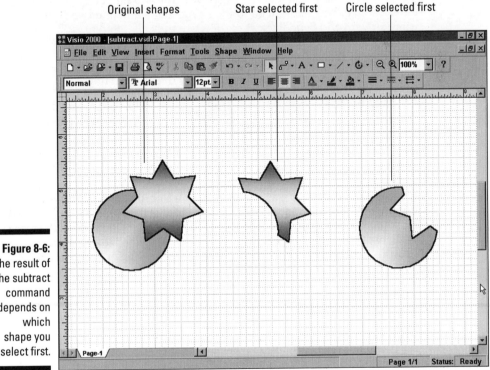

Figure 8-6:
The result of the subtract command depends on which shape you select first.

4. **Select the shape that you want to subtract.**

5. **Choose Shape⇨Operations⇨Subtract.**

   Visio removes the shape that you selected in Step 4 and leaves what remains of the shape that you selected in Step 3.

Restacking shapes

Each time you draw or drag a new shape into the drawing area, Visio places it on top of other, existing shapes. If you don't overlap the shapes, you never notice this, but if you overlap shapes, you notice the overlap immediately — particularly when you want the *first* shape you drew to be on top of the other 50 you drew afterward and it keeps getting covered up — this can be very frustrating if you don't know what's going on! Think of each shape as being drawn on a separate piece of scratch paper. Each time you draw a shape, you drop the paper on your desk. Those that fall on top of others clearly overlap one another. Those that don't *still fall in a stacking order,* whether you're aware of it or not.

Visio provides two commands — Bring to Front and Send to Back — to help you rearrange the stacking order of shapes. You can find both tools on the Action toolbar. You also can go to the Shape menu and find two commands: Bring Forward and Send Backward. How are they all different?

- ✔ **Bring to Front:** Brings a shape to the top of the stack.

- ✔ **Bring Forward:** Brings a shape up only one level in the stack.

- ✔ **Send to Back:** Sends a shape to the bottom of the stack.

- ✔ **Send Backward:** Sends a shape down just one level in the stack.

Bring Forward and Send Backward are found only on the Shape menu; they don't have toolbar buttons.

In Figure 8-7, the triangle was drawn first, so it's on the bottom of the stack. Suppose that you want to move the triangle above the rectangle but below the ellipse. If you try to move the triangle without changing its order in the stack, it's almost completely hidden by the rectangle. You need to use the Bring Forward command several times to raise the triangle's position in the stack.

To rearrange the stacking order of shapes, follow these steps:

1. **Select the shape that you want to move.**

2. **Determine which command or tool you need to use: Bring Forward, Bring to Front, Send Backward, or Send to Back.**

3. **Click the Bring to Front Tool button or the Send to Back Tool button on the Shape toolbar, or choose Shape⇨Bring Forward or Shape⇨ Send Backward.**

4. **Repeat Step 3 if necessary.**

If you prefer using shortcut keys, press Ctrl+F for Bring to Front or Ctrl+B for Send to Back.

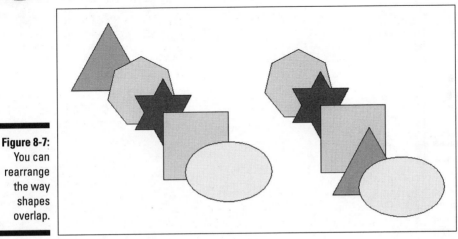

Figure 8-7:
You can rearrange the way shapes overlap.

Drawing Your Own Shapes

As if there weren't enough shapes for you to choose from in Visio, you can make your own, too. Actually, you may find that you often make your own shapes, particularly if you work in a specialized field like architectural design for zoos. Visio gives you many tools for drawing shapes, as shown in Table 8-1.

Drawing with the Line tool

You can use the Line tool on the Standard toolbar to draw lines or shapes that are made up of straight lines. The points where you start drawing a line and where your line stops are endpoints. Visio calls both of these endpoints *vertices* (see Figure 8-8), although your high school geometry book said a vertex is a point at which two lines intersect. Go figure! Between the two vertices is a *control point*, which you use to control the "shape of a shape," as discussed later in this chapter.

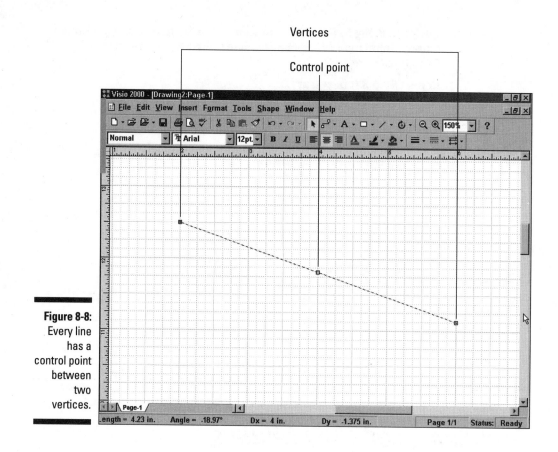

Figure 8-8:
Every line
has a
control point
between
two
vertices.

To draw a simple line, follow these steps:

1. **Click the Line Tool button (refer to Table 8-1) on the Standard toolbar.**

   The mouse pointer changes to a line and a plus (+) symbol.

2. **Place the mouse pointer where you want to begin the line; then drag the mouse where you want the line to end.**

   To draw a line at a 45-degree angle from your starting point, hold down the Shift key as you drag the mouse.

3. **Release the mouse button.**

   The line is selected, and the endpoints appear. (Switch to the Pencil tool — the one that looks like a pencil — on the Standard toolbar if you want to display the control point.)

4. **Click any blank area of the drawing to deselect the line.**

You can also use the Line tool to draw a shape by connecting a series of line segments. To connect segments as you draw, follow these steps:

1. **Click the Line Tool button (refer to Table 8-1) on the Standard toolbar.**

   The mouse pointer changes to a line and a plus (+) symbol.

2. **Draw your first segment by dragging the mouse.**

3. **Point to the endpoint of the first segment; then drag the mouse to draw the second segment of your shape.**

   Repeat Step 3 as many times as you want.

4. **To close the shape, draw another segment from the endpoint of the last segment that you drew to the beginning point of the first segment that you drew, and then release the mouse button.**

   The shape becomes a *closed* shape. You see it fill with white (see Figure 8-9), because the default fill color is white (not transparent).

If your background color is white and your grid is turned off, you can't see the white fill.

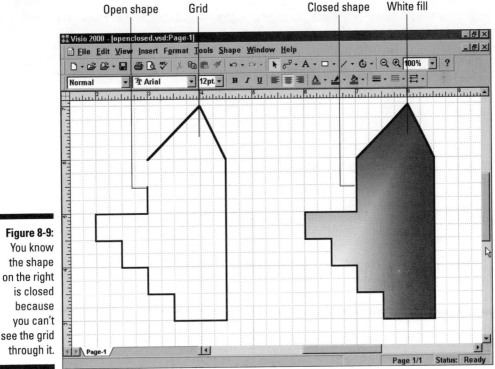

Figure 8-9: You know the shape on the right is closed because you can't see the grid through it.

Whenever you draw shapes by connecting segments, turn on Snap (Tools⇨ Snap & Glue), the feature that pulls shapes into place. Snap helps you connect segments automatically. To find out more about how snap works, see Chapter 7.

If you don't draw all the line segments for a shape consecutively, the shape won't be closed. An open shape isn't filled, although the segments appear to connect.

Drawing with the Pencil and Arc tools

The Pencil tool works almost exactly like the Line tool. If you move the Pencil tool in a straight line, you draw a straight line. If you move the mouse in a curved direction, you draw a portion of a circle. The size and circumference of the circle depend on how far you move the mouse. Use the Pencil tool when you want to draw a shape that includes both curves and lines (see Figure 8-10).

Pencil tool on the Standard toolbar

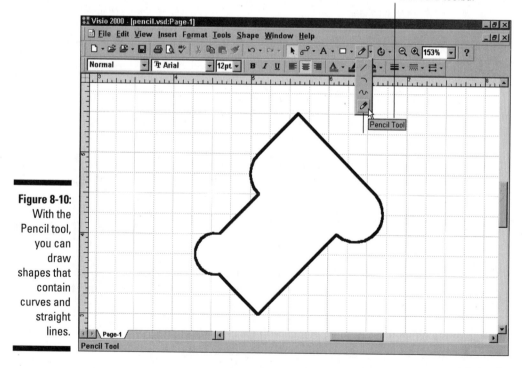

Figure 8-10: With the Pencil tool, you can draw shapes that contain curves and straight lines.

To draw a closed shape by using the Pencil tool, follow these steps:

1. **Click the Pencil Tool button (refer to Table 8-1) on the Standard toolbar.**

2. **Draw the first segment by dragging the mouse and then release the mouse button.**

   Drag in a straight line to create a line; drag in a circular direction to create a curve.

3. **Draw the second segment by pointing to the endpoint of the previous segment, dragging the mouse and then releasing the mouse button.**

   Repeat this motion as many times as you like.

4. **Finish the shape by connecting the endpoint of the last segment to the beginning point of the first segment.**

It may seem obvious that you draw an arc by using the Arc tool, but you may be wondering how the Arc tool differs from the Pencil tool, which also enables you to draw arcs. The Arc tool enables you to draw one quarter of an ellipse, whereas the Pencil tool enables you to draw a portion of a circle (not an ellipse and not limited to one quarter). Use the Arc tool when you want a less-than-circular curve (like an oval). Use the Pencil tool when you want to draw true circular curves. (See the "Creating shapes with the Ellipse and Rectangle tools" section later in this chapter, to find out how to use the Ellipse tool to draw complete circles and ellipses.)

To draw an arc by using the Arc tool, follow these steps:

1. **Click the Arc Tool button (refer to Table 8-1) on the Standard toolbar.**

2. **Place the mouse where you want the arc to begin.**

3. **Drag the mouse in the direction you want the arc to go.**

4. **Release the mouse button where you want the arc to end.**

Creating irregular shapes with the Freeform tool

I call the Freeform tool the doodling tool. You use it the same way you use a pencil when you're doodling. The Freeform tool (it looks like a squiggly line) obediently displays every curve and scribble you make. Just draw with the Freeform tool to create, well — freeform shapes. To create a closed shape like the one shown in Figure 8-11, end your doodling at the point where you began. (The shape in Figure 8-11 is actually a lake drawn for a map!)

Freeform tool on the Standard toolbar

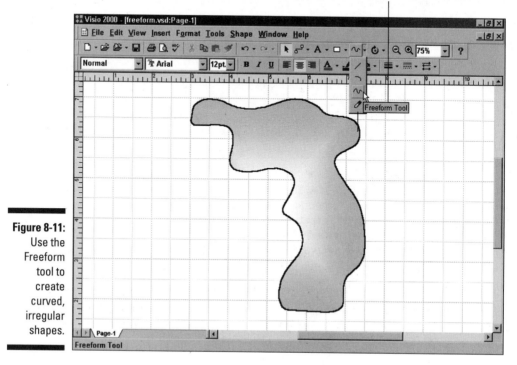

Figure 8-11:
Use the
Freeform
tool to
create
curved,
irregular
shapes.

If your computer includes a drawing tablet, the Freeform tool is great because it's easier to draw with a pen than with a mouse. The Freeform tool also duplicates handwriting quite well when you use a pen.

Creating shapes with the Ellipse and Rectangle tools

You can use the Arc and Pencil tools to draw curves (elliptical or circular). You can use either of these tools to draw four connected segments that form a complete circle or ellipse. But Visio gives you a simpler way by providing the Ellipse tool. The following steps tell you how to use the Ellipse tool:

1. **Click the Ellipse Tool button (refer to Table 8-1) on the Standard toolbar.**

2. **Put the mouse pointer where you want to place the ellipse.**

3. **Drag the mouse in any direction.**

   To draw a perfect circle, hold down the Shift key as you drag the mouse.

4. **Release the mouse button when the ellipse is the size and shape that you want.**

TIP

If you want the ellipse to be a particular size, watch the status bar as you drag the mouse. It tells you the exact width and height of your ellipse as you draw. (If you want to draw a circle, hold down the Shift key as you drag the mouse.) You can also choose Shape➪Size and Position after you draw the shape; then enter exact dimensions in the Height and Width boxes.

The Rectangle tool works exactly the same way as the Ellipse tool. You can use the Line tool to create a rectangle by drawing and connecting four segments. But it's even easier to draw a rectangle by using the Rectangle tool. Follow these four steps to draw a rectangle:

1. **Click the Rectangle Tool button (refer to Table 8-1) on the Standard toolbar.**

2. **Put the mouse pointer where you want to place the rectangle.**

3. **Drag the mouse in any direction. To draw a perfect rectangle, hold down the Shift key as you drag the mouse.**

   To create a rectangle of a specific size, watch the status bar for height and width measurements as you draw.

4. **Release the mouse button when the rectangle is the size and shape that you want.**

Manipulating Shapes

Suppose, for example, that you find a shape in Visio that's almost, but not quite, what you want. You can modify a shape in many ways by tweaking it until it's just what you want.

Moving and adding vertices

With Visio, it's easy to change the form of a shape by dragging part of the shape to a new position. In Figure 8-12, I changed an isosceles triangle by dragging the upper-right *vertex* to a new place. Remember that a vertex appears at the end of every line and at points where lines intersect, which means that you see a vertex at each point of the triangle. Green diamond shapes mark the vertices, but you can only see them when you select the shape by using one of the following tools on the Standard toolbar (just click the tool button and then select the shape):

Vertex   Pencil tool selected from Standard toolbar

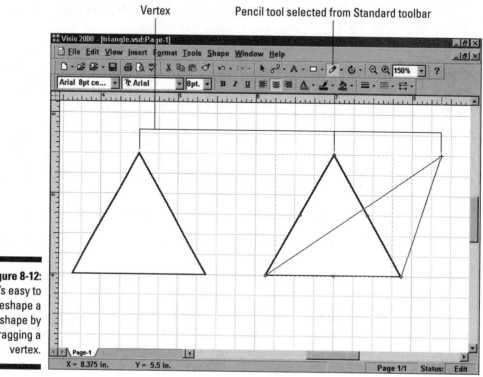

Figure 8-12:
It's easy to reshape a shape by dragging a vertex.

✔ Arc tool

✔ Freeform tool

✔ Line tool

✔ Pencil tool

To move a vertex, follow these steps:

1. **Select the Pencil tool, Freeform tool, Line tool, or Arc tool.**

2. **Point to the vertex that you want to move.**

   When you're within *selection range* of the vertex, the mouse pointer changes to a four-headed arrow.

3. **Click the vertex.**

   The color changes from green to magenta.

4. **Drag the vertex where you want it; then release the mouse button.**

You also can add a vertex to any shape by following these steps:

1. **Select the Pencil tool.**

2. **Select the shape.**

   You see the vertices and control points of the shape.

3. **Hold down the Ctrl key; then click a point where you want to add a vertex.**

   Visio adds the vertex (diamond shape) and a control point (round shape) between the new vertex and the previous one.

4. **Repeat Step 3 for as many vertices as you want to add.**

To be exact, when you add a vertex to a shape, you're actually adding a *segment.* That's because Visio automatically adds a control point between the new vertex and the previous one. Voilà! A new segment. You can use the control point to change the shape of the segment, as I show you in the section, "Moving control points," later in this chapter.

Why would you want to add a vertex to a shape? Check out the five-pointed star in Figure 8-13. It's not bad, but perhaps you want it to look a little snazzier — maybe with five smaller points between the five existing points. To accomplish this task, you need to add some vertices and move others. Currently, vertices appear at the tip of each point on the star and at each inverted angle of the star. (I know they're small and difficult to see in the figure, but you'll see them clearly on your screen!)

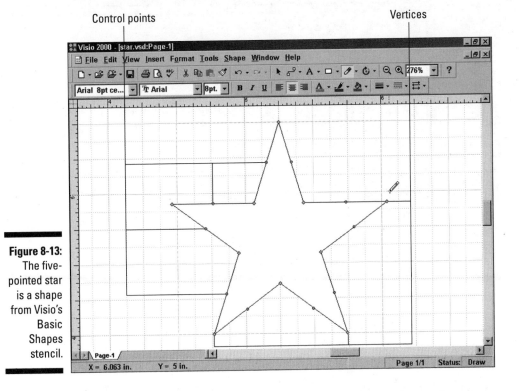

Control points   Vertices

Figure 8-13:
The five-pointed star is a shape from Visio's Basic Shapes stencil.

To create the ten-pointed star (partially shown in Figure 8-14), you pull the inverted angle vertex — let's call it A — out to a point. Before you can do that, though, you need to add new vertices on both sides of A — let's call them B and C. If you pull A without adding B and C, you just make a fatter star with shallower inverted angles. Adding the vertices B and C gives the new tip two new points from which to begin.

Moving control points

Suppose that instead of adding five new points to the star in Figure 8-14, you just want to round out the lines of the star and make it look like one of the stars in Figure 8-15. You use the *control points,* the round shapes that appear between two vertices.

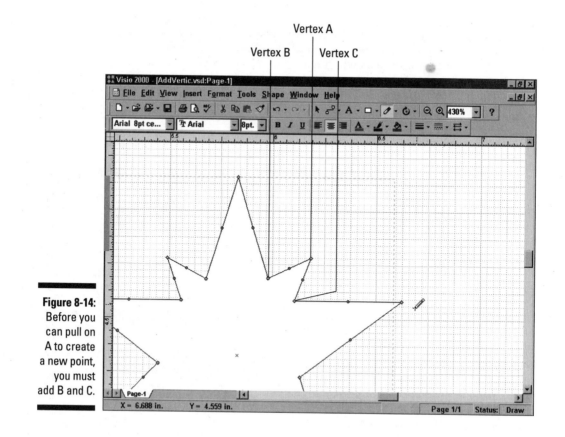

Figure 8-14:
Before you can pull on A to create a new point, you must add B and C.

To move a control point, use these steps:

1. **Select the shape by using the Pointer Tool button (refer to Table 8-1) on the Standard toolbar.**

   You see the selection handles of the shape.

2. **Switch to the Pencil tool.**

   You see the shape's vertices and control points.

3. **Point to the control point that you want to move.**

   The mouse pointer changes to a four-headed arrow.

4. **Click the control point.**

   The selected control point switches from green to magenta.

5. **Drag the control point; then release the mouse button.**

You can make your changes more precise by zooming in on your shape and using the rulers to track the movement of a control point.

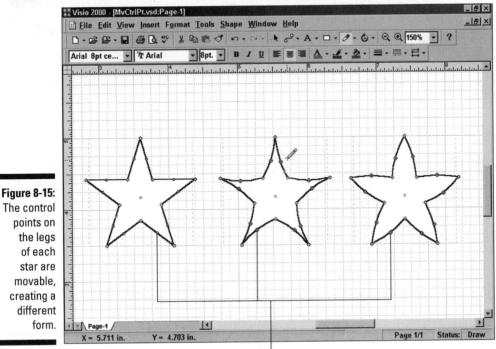

Figure 8-15:
The control points on the legs of each star are movable, creating a different form.

Control points

Rotating shapes

Rotating shapes is something you may need to do frequently. A shape may not be facing the correct angle when you drag it into the drawing. Or it may be easier to draw a shape at one angle and rotate it later.

You can rotate nearly all Visio shapes. You can easily see whether selecting it with the Rotation tool can rotate a shape. If the shape has large, round handles that appear at the corners of the shape's frame, you can rotate it. You also see a *rotation pin* (a round handle with a plus (+) symbol) at the center of the shape. This is the point around which the shape rotates. (If a Visio shape can't rotate, it's for good reason — probably because it doesn't make sense to rotate it.)

Visio provides three ways to rotate a shape:

- ✔ **Rotation handles** on a shape let you drag the shape to rotate it. (Use this method when you want to change a shape's angle quickly but not necessarily precisely.)

- ✔ **Rotate Right and Rotate Left tools** on the Action toolbar let you rotate a shape 90 degrees at a time (clockwise or counterclockwise). (Use this method when you know you want to rotate a shape in 90-degree increments.)

- ✔ **The menu command** (View⇨Windows⇨Size & Position) opens the Size & Position window that enables you to specify a rotation angle. (This is the best method to use when the precise angle of rotation is a priority.)

Rotation handles

To rotate a shape by using the Rotation tool, follow these steps:

1. **Click the Rotation Tool button (refer to Table 8-1) on the Standard toolbar.**

2. **Click the shape that you want to rotate.**

   The rotation handles are visible at the corners of the shape's frame and the rotation pin appears at the center of the shape.

3. **Move the mouse pointer over one of the rotation handles.**

   The pointer changes to the rotation pointer, which looks like a right angle with a curved arrow.

4. **Drag the mouse pointer clockwise or counterclockwise, depending on the direction that you want to rotate the shape.**

   Watch the status bar to see how far (in degrees) the shape is rotating.

5. **Release the mouse button when the shape is in the position that you want it.**

The closer you place the mouse to the rotation pin as you're rotating a shape, the more the rotation angle jumps, sometimes skipping degrees. The farther away you place the mouse pointer from the rotation pin, the more precise the angle of rotation.

Rotation tool

Figure 8-16 shows how you rotate shapes by using the Rotation tool. You can see the rotation symbol in the figure.

Follow these two steps when you want to rotate a shape 90 degrees at a time:

1. **Click the shape that you want to rotate.**

2. **Click the Rotate Right or Rotate Left Tool button on the Action toolbar.**

You can click the Rotate Right or Rotate Left tool repeatedly to continue rotating the same shape in 90-degree increments. This method saves you the trouble of dragging a shape to rotate it or using a menu command.

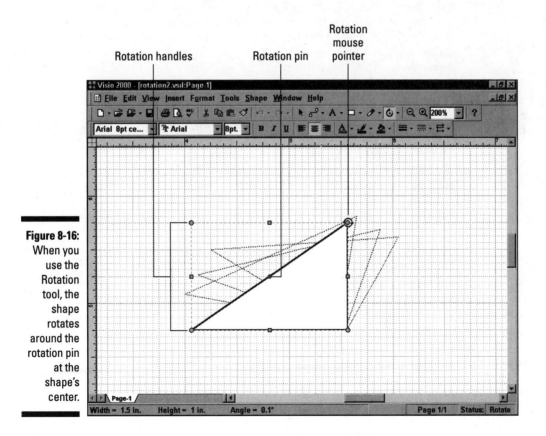

Figure 8-16:
When you use the Rotation tool, the shape rotates around the rotation pin at the shape's center.

Menu command

When precision is really important to you, use the menu command to rotate shapes. You can rotate a shape at a precise angle, as little as .01 degrees. Use these steps to rotate a shape at a precise angle:

1. **Select the shape that you want to rotate.**

2. **Choose View⇨Windows⇨Size & Position.**

   The Size & Position window, shown in Figure 8-17, appears.

3. **In the Angle box, type a positive number for a counterclockwise angle of rotation. Type a negative number for a clockwise angle of rotation.**

4. **Click the OK button.**

   Visio rotates the shape to the angle you specify. Notice that the angle you entered is now reflected on the status bar.

Rotation pin

On most Visio shapes, the rotation pin is right in the center of the shape. If you want a shape to rotate around a different point, you can move the rotation pin. You may need to do this if you want to keep a particular point on the shape anchored. For example, in Figure 8-18, the center of rotation for the triangle moves from the center to the left — outside the triangle. Now the shape rotates around this point.

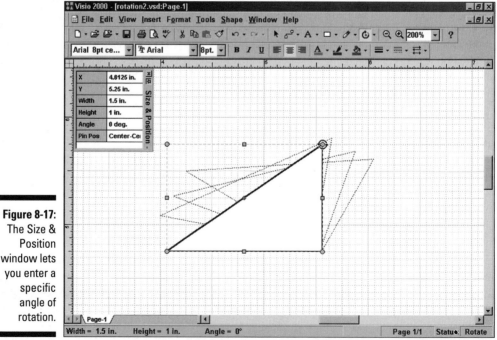

Figure 8-17:
The Size & Position window lets you enter a specific angle of rotation.

Use these steps to move the rotation pin of the shape:

1. **Click the Rotation Tool button (refer to Table 8-1) on the Standard toolbar.**

2. **Select the shape.**

   The shape's rotation handles and rotation pin appear.

3. **Drag the rotation pin to a new position.**

4. **Release the mouse button.**

When you move the rotation pin, it helps to zoom in on the shape. Zooming in enables you to place the pin more precisely, and it also displays a finer grid. If you don't want the rotation pin to snap into place, turn snap off by choosing Tools➪Snap & Glue; then click the Snap check box to remove the check mark.

To easily return a rotation pin to the center of a shape, choose View➪ Windows➪Size & Position. In the Size & Position window, click Pin Pos and then choose Center-Center.

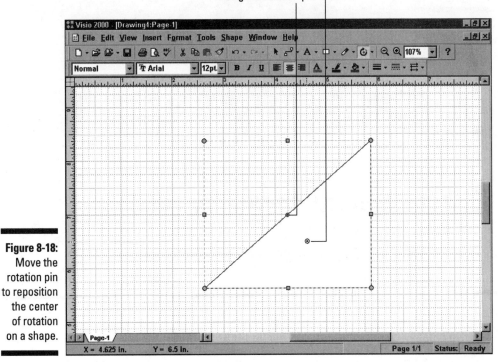

Figure 8-18:
Move the rotation pin to reposition the center of rotation on a shape.

Flipping shapes

Sometimes you may need to *flip* a shape. Flipping is nothing more than taking a shape and turning it over so that it faces the opposite direction. You can flip a shape horizontally or vertically (as shown in Figure 8-19) by using the Flip Horizontal or Flip Vertical tools on the Action toolbar. Select the shape first; then click one of the flip tools.

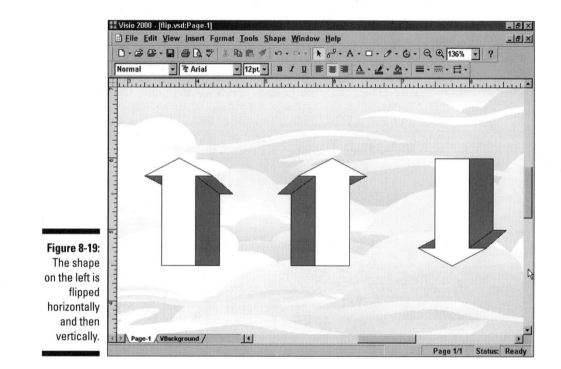

Figure 8-19: The shape on the left is flipped horizontally and then vertically.

Adding Character to Your Shapes

Although many of the Visio shapes are pretty cool, some of them are basic — just an outline of something with no color, weight, pattern, or shadow. Pretty boring, huh? Well, you can jazz up the more basic shapes by adding things like line color and weight, fill color and pattern, and shadowing. These features are typically referred to as *formatting*.

You usually select a shape first and then apply some special type of formatting to it. If you're formatting one shape, why not format a bunch of them at the same time? This saves you a lot of time when you decide that all 382 whatchamacallits in your drawing should be blue and green checkerboards with a purple outline and a magenta shadow. Select all your shapes (no, don't click each one individually, use the Pointer tool to draw a selection box around them) and then apply the formatting that you choose.

If you can't select all the shapes that you want with a selection box, remember that you can hold down the Shift key and click the rest of your stray shapes to add them to the selection.

Changing line style

Every shape has an outline, usually a thin black line. Not only can you change the color of the line, you can change the *weight* (thickness) of it as well as the *pattern*. You can make it fat and green and dash-dash-dashed, or dainty and pink and dot-dot-dotted. You can also decide if you want squared or rounded corners on your shape.

When you work with a 1-D shape like a simple line, you can also add end-points to the beginning or end of the shape, and determine the size of the endpoints.

Follow these steps to make changes to a shape's line:

1. **Select the shape that you want to change.**

2. **Choose Format⇨Line, or right-click and then choose Format⇨Line from the menu that appears.**

   Visio displays the Line dialog box, as shown in Figure 8-20.

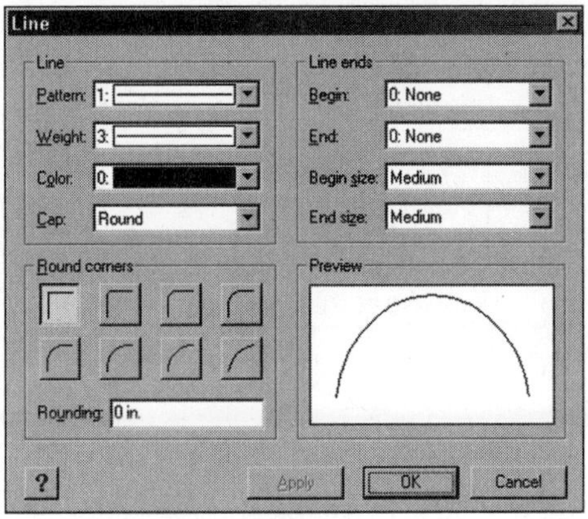

Figure 8-20: Choose a line pattern, color, weight, and style in the Line dialog box.

3. Click the down arrow in the Pattern box to choose a line pattern.

4. Click the down arrow in the Weight box to choose a line thickness.

5. Click the down arrow in the Color box to choose a line color.

6. Click the down arrow in the Cap box to choose blunt lines (square) or soft lines (round).

7. To round the corners of your shape, click one of the rounding styles in the Round Corners box.

   If you want the rounding to be a specific size (such as beginning ⅛ inch from the corner), enter a decimal number in the Rounding box.

8. If your shape is 1-D, choose endpoints and size in the Begin, End, and Size boxes.

9. View all of your choices in the Preview area.

10. Click the OK button.

Visio provides the following five tools that enable you to apply line style changes without opening a menu. When you click the tiny, drop-down arrow next to each tool, Visio gives you a list of choices. These tools, as shown in Table 8-2, appear on the Format and Format Shape toolbars. Choose View⇨Toolbars⇨Format and View⇨Toolbars⇨Format Shape to display these toolbars.

Table 8-2		Line Style Tools on the Format and Format Shape Toolbars	
Button	**Tool**	**Function**	**Toolbar**
	Line Color tool	Lets you choose a line color	Format
	Line Weight tool	Lets you choose a line thickness	Format
	Line Pattern tool	Lets you choose a line pattern	Format
	Line Ends tool	Lets you choose endpoints for a line	Format
	Corner Rounding tool	Lets you choose a line corner style	Format Shape

To use any of these tools, first select the shape and then click one of the tools and select a style.

Adding fill color, pattern, and shadow

White, white, white can become monotonous after awhile. Why not add some excitement to your shapes by making them colorful? Use patterns! Use striking colors! Give them some depth by adding shadows! (Am I too excited about all this?)

Well, maybe you don't want to add *all* of these features. There is such a thing as overkill. . . .

If you want to fill a shape with a solid color, that's cool. Just pick the color and that's that. If you fill a shape with a pattern, however, you have to choose two colors — one for the *foreground* and one for the *background*. The foreground color comprises the pattern — dots, hash marks, stripes, or crisscrosses. The background color is the one that shows through the pattern. Often, patterns show up in black and white, so you don't even think about the possibility of choosing colors for the foreground and background. You can use black and white in Visio as well, but it's good to know what foreground and background colors are so that you get the results you expect.

If you decide to add a shadow to your shape, it doesn't have to be a solid color. You can choose a pattern, foreground color, and background color for it as well. (Now *that's* overkill.)

Follow these steps to accomplish any of these nifty tasks:

1. **Select the shape that you want to change.**

2. **Choose Format⇨Fill, or right-click the mouse and then choose Format⇨Fill from the shortcut menu that appears.**

   Visio displays the Fill dialog box, as shown in Figure 8-21.

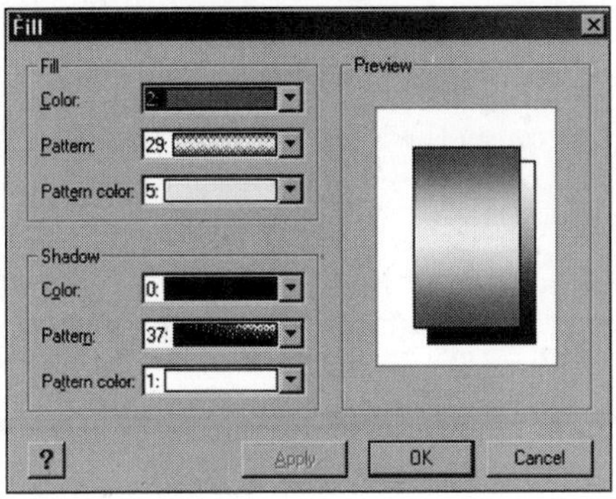

Figure 8-21: Choose a pattern, a foreground color, and a background color for the shape's fill and shadow.

3. **In the Fill box, click the down arrows to choose a pattern, foreground color, and background color.**

4. **In the Shadow box, click the down arrows in each box to choose a pattern, foreground color, and background color.**

   The Preview area shows a sample of the choices that you selected.

5. **Click the OK button.**

   Visio returns to your drawing and reformats the selected shape.

Visio also provides timesaving toolbar buttons for these tools, as shown in Table 8-3. Select a shape that you want to change; then click the down arrow next to the tool to display a drop-down list of choices.

Table 8-3   Fill Tools on the Format and Format Shape Toolbar

Button	*Tool*
Normal ▼	Fill Style tool
🎨 ▼	Fill Color tool
▨ ▼	Fill Pattern tool
◨ ▼	Shadow Color tool

The following list tells you how to use these tools:

✔ **The Fill Style Tool button** on the Shape toolbar lets you choose a fill color.

✔ **The Fill Color Tool button** on the Shape toolbar *also* lets you choose a fill color! Hmm. Why does Visio provide two buttons that do the same thing? Beats me. Choose from the color chips displayed, or click More Fill Colors to display the Fill dialog box (refer to Figure 8-21).

✔ **The Fill Pattern Tool button** on the Shape toolbar lets you choose a pattern style from the list. Or click More Fill Patterns to display the Fill dialog box (refer to Figure 8-21).

✔ **The Shadow Color Tool button** on the Shape toolbar lets you choose a shadow color. To choose a pattern, foreground color, and background color for a shadow, click More Shadow Colors to display the Shadow dialog box.

Copying formats

Suppose that you painstakingly format a shape with a purple and red patterned fill, a burgundy and chartreuse shadow, and a 4-point canary dotted outline (no one ever accused you of having an eye for color!). Now you want to apply those lovely colors and styles to another shape. Do you have to set all of these features by hand again? Nope. Visio makes it easy for you. Ever notice that paint brush tool on your Standard toolbar? It's called the *Format Painter* tool, and it lets you *paint* a format from one shape to another. Follow these steps to copy a format from one shape to another:

1. **Click the shape with the lovely format that you want to copy.**

2. **Click the Format Painter Tool button (refer to Table 8-1) on the Standard toolbar.**

   Your mouse pointer changes to a paint brush.

3. **Click the shape that you want to apply that lovely format to.**

   Presto! All that beautiful color and style is instantly copied to your shape.

Reformatting a shape

So, you decide that you don't like violet polka dots on an orange background with a green frame and a green and purple crisscross shadow pattern. How do you get rid of it? Unfortunately, you can't click a tool that magically removes all the formatting that you add to a shape. You have to reset line, fill, pattern, and shadow features the same way that you added them. But you can reformat one shape and then use the Format Painter tool again to paint a plain style onto other shapes. That's the quickest way to undo what you did.

Managing Shapes by Grouping

Nothing is more frustrating than spending a good deal of time creating a single shape out of many shapes, getting everything perfectly aligned, and then messing it all up when you try to move it or resize it. One way to avoid this is to group shapes so that they behave as a unit.

In Figure 8-22, the knight on the left is a *grouped* shape (it's selected as a unit). The knight in the center is not grouped because you can select all the parts individually. On the right side of the figure, the knight's individual parts are spread out so that you can see how complex the shape is. This figure shows the importance of grouping. Ungrouped, it's easy to accidentally drag the knight off without his shield and horse! Grouped, there's no chance of that happening. Grouping also enables you to size, rotate, and flip the whole shape as a unit.

Creating groups

You can group any set of shapes that you select; their proximity to one another makes no difference! The group you create only has to make sense to you!

To create a group, use these steps:

1. **Select all the shapes that you want to group.**

2. **Choose Shape⇨Grouping⇨Group or click the Group Tool button on the Action toolbar.**

   Visio reframes the shapes with a single frame and handles.

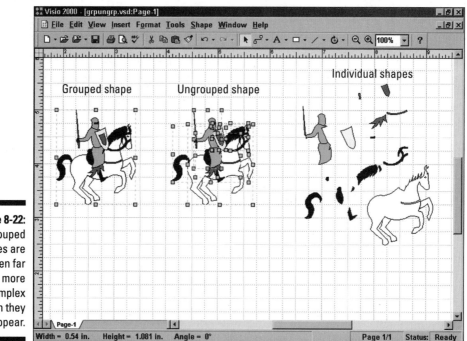

Figure 8-22:
Grouped shapes are often far more complex than they appear.

To ungroup a shape, follow these steps:

1. **Select the grouped shape.**

2. **Choose Shape⇨Grouping⇨Ungroup or click the Ungroup Tool button on the Shape toolbar.**

   Visio separates the grouped shape into its original shapes and selects each one individually.

If you prefer to use shortcut keys, you can press Ctrl+G for Group and Ctrl+U for Ungroup.

Never, never, never create a group, add shapes to it, and then group it again. Adding shapes to a group and regrouping creates what Visio calls a *nested* group. Each time you "group a group," your file size increases exponentially, and your performance (load time and save time) declines significantly. If you want to add shapes to a group, select the group, select the shapes to add, and then choose Shape⇨Grouping⇨Add to Group.

Editing a group

When you click a group, Visio selects the entire group. Clicking a component shape in that group enables you to *subselect* just that component. When you click a group once, you see green selection handles around the entire group. Click again on a member of the group to subselect it. You see green selection handles for only that shape, and the handles that defined the boundaries of the entire group change to a faint line of gray dashes. This feature of subselecting allows you to easily edit a shape in a group (you don't have to ungroup shapes to edit an individual shape). After you subselect a shape, you can move, resize, reshape, fill, change line color, or make any other changes without affecting other shapes in the group. When you finish making changes, click anywhere outside the group or press Esc to deselect the shape.

If you prefer to have Visio select members of a group with the first mouse click and then select the entire group with a second mouse click, you can set Visio to behave this way. Or, maybe you prefer to have Visio select only the group and *never* subselect shapes. This is another option you can set.

To change the way Visio selects groups, use these steps:

1. **Click a grouped shape.**

2. **Choose Format⇨Behavior.**

   Visio displays the Behavior tab in the Behavior dialog box. Look in the Group Behavior area of the dialog box.

3. **Indicate your preference in the Selection drop-down list:**

   - **Choose Members** if you want to select members of a group with a single click and the entire group with a second mouse click.

   - **Choose Group Only** if you want to disable subselecting.

   - **Choose Group First** to change back to Visio's default setting. Choosing Group First selects a group with a single click and individual shapes with a second mouse click.

4. **Click the OK button.**

Adding text to grouped shapes

If a shape is already grouped, you can't display its text block by double-clicking it. To add text to a grouped shape, you use a separate window. Follow these steps:

1. **Select the group.**

2. **Choose Edit⇨Open Group.**

   Visio opens a separate window and zooms in on the group.

3. **In this window, double-click the shape that you want to add text to.**

   Visio zooms in on the shape's text block.

4. **Enter the text you want to add to the shape, then press Esc or click somewhere outside of the text block.**

5. **Click the window's close button.**

   Visio returns to your drawing window, and the text you added appears in the shape.

Chapter 9

Working with Pages

*J*ust about now you may be thinking "A page is a page; what's to know? Pretty boring stuff." There is a lot to know about pages in Visio! Visio files aren't like documents, where text runs smoothly from one page to the next with a few interesting figures thrown in here and there. Some drawings have only one page; others may have multiple pages. And in Visio, pages are independent animals! You can set a different page size, orientation, drawing scale, background, shadow, and even a different header and footer for each page in a single Visio file. You can also rotate a page to make drawing angled lines and shapes easier — and then rotate it again when you're finished drawing. This makes Visio very flexible; it also makes it a little more complex than your average text editor does.

Drawing page refers to the drawing area that you see on the screen, *printed page* refers to the paper you print on, and *printed drawing* refers to the actual drawing as printed on paper. (See Chapter 3 for more details on these printing terms.)

The Role of the Template

Remember that a template is designed to make creating a drawing easier because it sets up a drawing scale (like a typical architectural scale of ¼ inch:1 foot), and it automatically opens the stencils that you may need to create a particular type of drawing (like the Office Layout stencil for creating an office floor plan). See Chapter 2 if you need a refresher on how to start a new Visio file by using a template.

The other important things that a template sets up are the size of the drawing page and the printed page (both usually 8½ x 11 inches) and the orientation of the page (portrait or landscape). You need to be aware of these settings when you work with pages in a drawing. Using a template is a definite advantage because it automatically matches the size and orientation of the drawing page to the size and orientation of the printed page, which ensures that your drawing prints correctly.

Reorienting a Page

Suppose that you're creating a network diagram in portrait orientation, and you realize that the drawing is too wide to fit on 8½-inch-wide paper. You can change the paper orientation to landscape rather than adjust the layout of your drawing. Switching to landscape orientation turns your drawing page 90 degrees so that its width is greater than its length.

When you change the orientation of your drawing page, however, you need to change the printer settings as well. That way your printer expects to print in landscape mode. To change both of these settings, follow these steps:

1. **Choose File⇨Page Setup.**

   The Page Setup dialog box appears.

2. **Click the Page Size tab. (See Figure 9-1.)**

3. **In the Page Orientation area, click either Portrait or Landscape.**

4. **Now click the Print Setup tab (shown in Figure 9-2) and choose the same orientation you chose in Step 2.**

5. **Click the OK button.**

Look closely at the screen sample shown in Figure 9-2. The drawing page and the printer paper shown don't match. This is how the screen sample looks when your drawing page orientation and printer page orientation aren't the same. They should look like the screen sample shown in Figure 9-1. When the pages line up as shown in Figure 9-1, your orientation is set correctly for both the drawing size and the printer page.

When you switch page orientation, the shapes in your drawing don't mysteriously disappear or get erased, but it's likely that some of them are either straddling the page borders or are completely off the page (see Figure 9-3). Remember, you just moved the boundaries of the page, but the shapes are placed where they always were (within the old page boundaries — sort of like the Incredible Hulk bursting out of his shirt). Now that you have new boundaries, you need to move your shapes to get them back onto the drawing page.

Page Orientation area

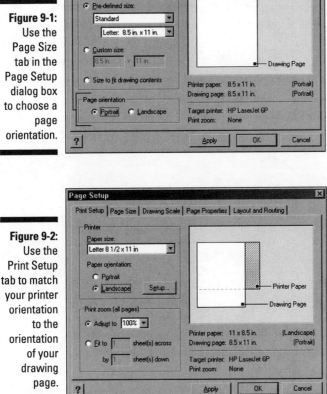

Figure 9-1:
Use the
Page Size
tab in the
Page Setup
dialog box
to choose a
page
orientation.

Figure 9-2:
Use the
Print Setup
tab to match
your printer
orientation
to the
orientation
of your
drawing
page.

Choosing Tools⇨Center Drawing helps you begin rearranging shapes by placing the drawing in the center of the new page boundaries. You may still need
to move some shapes around to fit them on the page, but this tip gives you a
head start.

Shapes off the page

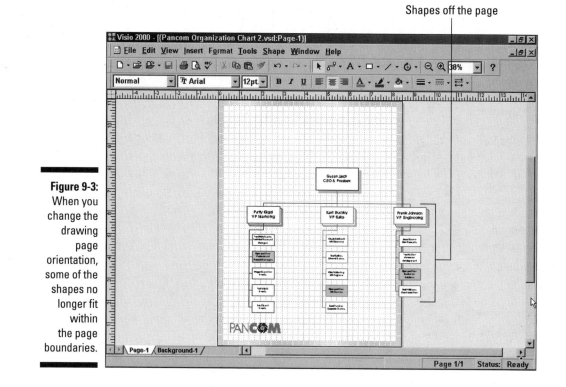

Figure 9-3:
When you change the drawing page orientation, some of the shapes no longer fit within the page boundaries.

Setting a Page Size

Most of us print on standard-sized paper: 8½ x 11 inches. However, you may want to use a different paper size, such as legal (8½ x 14 inches). Visio lets you change your page size settings accordingly. Other common sizes are

- ✔ **Metric:** 148 x 210 millimeters
- ✔ **ANSI Architectural:** 9 x 12 inches
- ✔ **ANSI Engineering:** 8½ x 11 inches

If you prefer, Visio also lets you

- ✔ **Set paper to size currently set for printer.** When you choose this option, you ensure that your drawing page matches the size that's already specified as your printer paper size. In other words, if the paper size defined on the Print Setup tab is set to Legal, choosing this option automatically sets your drawing size to legal size paper.

✔ **Specify a custom size.** This option lets you enter specific dimensions (such as 9 x 12 inches) for custom-sized paper.

✔ **Size the page to fit the drawing contents.** Choose this option if you want the drawing to cover the entire page with no white space surrounding it.

As with page orientation, page size must be the same for the drawing page and the printer setting. Follow these steps to change page size for both:

1. **Display the page for which you want to change the size.**

2. **Choose File⇨Page Setup. If the Page Size tab isn't already selected, click it now.**

   Visio displays the Page Size tab in the Page Setup dialog box. (Refer to Figure 9-1.)

3. **Choose one of the following options from the Page Size area:**

   • Same as Printer Paper Size

   • Pre-defined Size (click the drop-down arrow)

   • Custom Size (enter dimensions in the boxes)

   • Size to Fit Drawing Contents

4. **Click the Print Setup tab.**

   Visio displays the Print Setup tab. (Refer to Figure 9-2.)

5. **Choose a size from the Paper Size drop-down list.**

6. **Click the OK button.**

Some printers can't print on odd-sized or custom-sized paper. Choosing the closest size may work with your printer; but then again, it may not. Be sure to click the Preview Tool button before printing to see exactly how your drawing will look when you print it.

Setting a Unique Page Size

Not only can you set a custom page size by specifying page dimensions, but you can also use the custom page size settings to define unique page dimensions, such as 3 x 5 inches or 6½ x 4 inches. This option isn't just for users who are lucky enough to have a super-duper printer that can print on paper as small as a postage stamp! (Are there any?) It's also a very useful feature for *positioning* or *isolating* a drawing. Let me explain.

Suppose that you want to print a 3-x-5-inch Visio drawing in the upper-left corner of an 8½-x-11-inch piece of paper and leave the remaining white space for reviewers to write comments in (like what is shown in Figure 9-4).

You can try to position the drawing in the right space on the size paper that you're printing on; you also can simply set a custom page size for the drawing. However, you need to keep a couple of things in mind when setting a custom page size:

- ✔ If the drawing already contains shapes, those shapes don't move. If the shapes are outside the new page dimensions, you have to move them inside.

- ✔ The drawing always begins printing in the upper-left corner of your paper. If you want your drawing to print in the lower-right corner (or anywhere else, for that matter), using the Custom Page Size option will not bring the results that you want.

Drawing page   Printed page

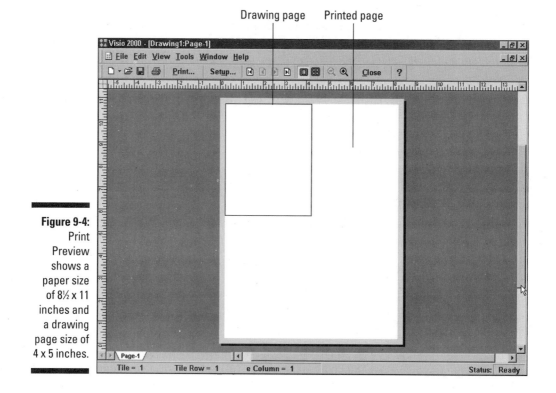

Figure 9-4:
Print
Preview
shows a
paper size
of 8½ x 11
inches and
a drawing
page size of
4 x 5 inches.

To change drawing page and printed page settings by using menu commands, follow these steps:

1. **Display the drawing page that you want to change.**

2. **Choose File⇨Page Setup and then click the Page Size tab.**

   Visio displays the Page Size tab in the Page Setup dialog box. (Refer to Figure 9-1.)

3. **In the Page Size area, select the Custom Size radio button.**

4. **In the boxes below the Custom Size option, type the page dimensions that you want.**

5. **Click the Print Setup tab.**

   Refer to Figure 9-2.

6. **From the drop-down list for Paper Size, choose the paper size that you're *printing on*.**

   In this case, the drawing page size and paper size *don't* match.

7. **In the Paper Orientation area, choose the orientation that best accommodates the custom drawing page size that you specified in Step 4.**

8. **Click the OK button.**

You can also size your drawing page with your mouse. (This method is actually more fun!) Here's how:

1. **Display the drawing page that you want to change.**

2. **Click the Pointer Tool button (which looks like an arrow) on the Standard toolbar.**

3. **Press and hold down the Ctrl key and move the mouse pointer over the edge of the drawing page that you want to drag.**

   To resize the page's height and width at the same time, move the mouse pointer over one of the page's corners. The mouse pointer changes to a double-headed arrow.

4. **Drag the mouse until the page is the size that you want, noting the page dimensions on the status bar.**

   The result is the same as with the menu commands. When you preview your drawing, you can clearly see that your drawing size is different from your paper size. (Refer to Figure 9-4.)

Another Page, Please. . . .

When you create a new Visio drawing, it includes only one page. You can add pages to a drawing, and of course, you have many good reasons for doing so! Try some of these ideas:

- ✔ **Keep a set of related drawings,** such as a collection of maps with driving directions for your city, on separate pages in one Visio file.

- ✔ **Use pages to create overview drawings and detail drawings** of your corporate, regional, and branch organization charts, for example. You can even add *jumps,* similar to links between Web sites, from one page to another. (See Chapter 14 for more on adding jumps.)

- ✔ **Use pages to keep track of the history and revisions of a drawing,** which can work something like this: Page 1 is the original draft, Page 2 is the second draft, Page 3 is the review drawing, Page 4 is the revised drawing, Page 5 is the second review drawing, and Page 6 is the final drawing.

- ✔ **Create a mini–slide show** with a series of drawings on separate pages and present them in full-screen view.

- ✔ **Include your company name and logo on background pages** so that the logo shows through on every page without being part of your drawing. The icing on the cake is that each page in your drawing can have its own background page, so you can vary the content from page to page.

Adding and deleting pages

You can add as many pages to a drawing as you like. Pages are always added at the end of the drawing — in other words, you can't *insert* pages between other pages. (You can, however, reorder pages, as I show you later in the "Reordering pages" section.) The new page that you add takes on all the attributes of the page that's currently displayed. If you want to change some of these attributes, you can do so at the time that you create the page, or later, by using the File➪Page Setup command.

Use these steps to add a page to a drawing:

1. **In your drawing, display the page with the attributes that you want the new page to have.**

   Of course, that would be the *only* page in your drawing if you haven't added a page yet!

2. **Choose Insert➪Page.**

   Visio displays the Page Properties tab in the Page Setup dialog box, as shown in Figure 9-5. A name for the new page is suggested in the Name field.

3. **You can see that the Foreground radio button is already selected as Type. To create a background page, click the Background radio button.**

4. **Either enter a new name in the Name field or use the suggested name (Page-2, Page-3, and so on).**

   At this point, you're free to click the Page Size or Drawing Scale tab to change settings for the new page. However, this isn't necessary if you want the new page to take on the attributes of the page that you displayed in Step 1.

5. **Click the OK button.**

The new page appears after all the other pages in the drawing; if you have five already, the new page is number six. If you later decide to change the page size, refer to the "Setting a Unique Page Size" section earlier in this chapter. To change drawing scale attributes, see Chapter 7.

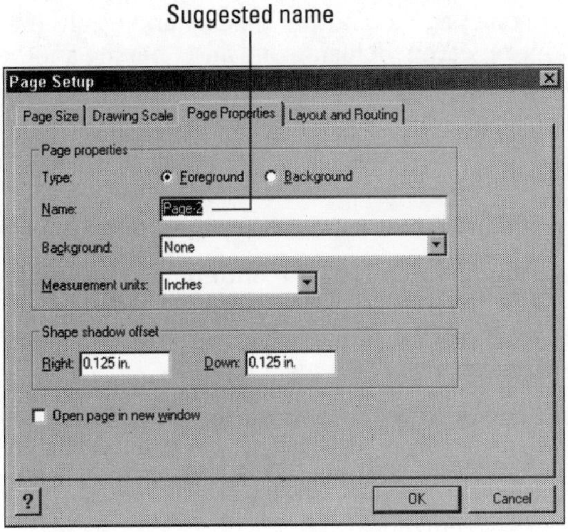

Suggested name

Figure 9-5:
Use the
Page
Properties
tab to set
attributes
for a new
page.

To delete a page, use these steps:

1. **Choose Edit➪Drawing Page➪Delete Pages.**

   The Delete Pages dialog box appears and lists all the pages in the drawing by name.

2. **Click the page that you want to delete.**

3. **Click the OK button.**

   Visio removes the page from the drawing.

The Delete Pages dialog box doesn't let you select more than one page at a time, so if you want to delete other pages, you need to repeat the steps given earlier in this chapter.

Getting from one page to another

Visio 2000 has several new features that make it compatible with Microsoft Office. The page tabs at the bottom of each drawing are one such feature. To move from one page to another, just click the page tab — it's as simple as that! Refer to Chapter 2 for more information on page navigation.

Show me all your pages!

When your drawing contains multiple pages, viewing more than one page at a time lets you compare one page to another quickly and easily. It also lets you edit each page without repeatedly closing one and opening another. Visio opens the new page in a separate window. Use these steps to open additional page windows:

1. **Choose Edit⇨Go To.**

   Visio displays a submenu that lists all the pages in the drawing.

2. **Click the Page option, which is at the bottom of the submenu.**

   Visio displays the Page dialog box, which lists all the pages in the drawing.

3. **Click the page that you want to view.**

4. **Click the Open Page in New Window option, which is at the bottom of the dialog box.**

5. **Click the OK button.**

   Visio opens the page in a new window.

6. **Repeat Steps 1 through 5 to open additional pages in a new window.**

   Each time you open a new page, it becomes the current page on your screen.

7. **Choose either Window⇨Tile or Window⇨Cascade to arrange all the open windows on your screen.**

Reordering pages

When you add pages to a drawing, Visio automatically adds them to the end of the drawing (although the menu name is Insert — go figure!). Because Visio doesn't let you insert pages in a drawing (such as between Pages 3 and 4), the only way to put additional pages in the order that you want them is to *reorder* them.

Reordering pages in Visio 2000 couldn't be easier! Just drag the page tab and drop it in the spot you want. If you use the default page names (Page-2, Page-3, and so on) when you add the page, Visio automatically updates the page names when you reorder pages. If you named a page with your own title when you created it, you may want to change the title after reordering. If so, choose File⇨Page Setup and then click the Page Properties tab. Type the page's new title in the Name box and then click the OK button.

Viewing on the Big Screen

You can use the Preview Tool button to see how your drawing will look on the printed page. (If you don't remember how, see Chapter 3!) Did you know that you can use your *entire* screen to display a drawing, without title bars, menu bars, status bars, scroll bars, or any other Windows trimmings? If your drawing has multiple pages, you can move from page to page on the big screen. This is a great way to create a mini–slide show for a small group of viewers — and because you don't need a slide projector, you won't have to sign over your firstborn child and your mortgage to the AV department!

Use these steps to view pages in full-screen mode:

1. **Display the first page of your drawing on the screen.**

2. **Choose View⇨Full Screen.**

   Visio switches to full-screen mode and displays the first page of your drawing.

3. **To move to another page, press one of these options according to your intended direction:**

   • N (for next page), Page Down, right-arrow key

   • P (for previous page), Page Up, or left-arrow key

   If you prefer to use the mouse, click the left mouse button to move forward from page to page.

4. **Click the right mouse button to bring up a shortcut menu with Previous, Next, and Go To options.** (Right-clicking is an important method to remember if you're on Page 3 and you want to go quickly to Page 42!)

5. **Press Esc to return to the Visio screen.**

Hyperlinks — shapes that you click to go to another page — are a really cool Visio feature. If your drawing contains hyperlinks, click the hyperlink shape to leap to the link. For detailed steps about adding hyperlinks to a drawing, see Chapter 14.

What's in a Background?

As if you didn't have enough pages in your drawing already, now you can add *background* pages! Why would you want to do that? The best answer is that they offer flexibility. If you want to show a filename, date, company name, logo, page number, or any other information about a drawing — but you don't want it on your drawing page — you can put all that information on a background page. Using a background page is sort of like printing your drawing on a transparency and slipping the background page underneath. The information on the background page shows through the transparency — visible and printable — but the drawing itself doesn't get mucked up with all sorts of extraneous information. (It also keeps other users from changing its content.)

The technical term for a drawing page is *foreground page*. The foreground page gets its name because it appears on top of a background page.

You can create as many background pages as you want in a drawing file. What can you do with them?

✔ Assign a single background page to a single foreground page.

✔ Assign a single background to several foreground pages.

✔ Assign a different background page to each foreground page.

✔ Assign a background page to another background page.

The most important thing to realize is that you *can't* assign more than one background page to any one page. So what do you do if you want a foreground page to have more than one background? You can piggyback background pages on a foreground page by assigning a background to a background and then assigning that background to a foreground. Clear as mud? Figure 9-6 illustrates how pages can be assigned to one another.

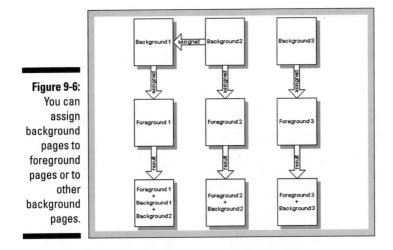

Figure 9-6:
You can
assign
background
pages to
foreground
pages or to
other
background
pages.

Creating and assigning a background page

Background pages aren't very useful by themselves. To use a background page, you must create it and then *assign* it to another page. Unassigned, you can still print a background page, but it prints entirely by itself (without any foreground information).

To create a background page, follow these steps:

1. **Display the page in your drawing with the attributes that you want the background page to have.**

2. **Choose Insert⇨Page.**

   Visio displays the Page Properties tab in the Page Setup dialog box. (See Figure 9-7.)

3. **For Type, click the Background radio button.**

4. **Either use the default name given in the Name field (Background-1, Background-2, and so on) or enter a new name.**

   You can now click the Page Size or Drawing Scale tab in this dialog box if you want to change any page size or drawing scale attributes.

5. **Click the OK button.**

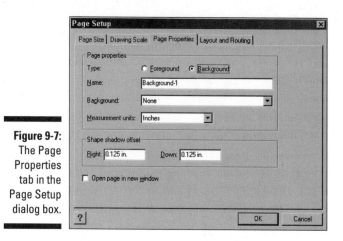

Figure 9-7:
The Page
Properties
tab in the
Page Setup
dialog box.

You just created a background page! Now you need to assign it to the page (foreground or background) that you want it to go with. To assign the background to another page, follow these steps:

1. **Display the page that you want to assign the background page to. (Think of this as the parent page.)**

2. **Choose File⇨Page Setup.**

   The Page Setup dialog box comes up.

3. **Click the Page Properties tab. (Refer to Figure 9-7.)**

   The Name field displays the name of the current page.

4. **Click the Background drop-down arrow.**

   All background pages that you created are listed here. Click the one that you want to assign to the page you selected in Step 1.

5. **Click the OK button.**

Displaying a background page

After you assign a background page to another page, the shapes of the background page are visible on the screen whenever its foreground page displays. If you don't want the background page shapes to display when the foreground page displays, you must unassign the background from the foreground. Remember that *unassigning* doesn't delete the background page; it just leaves it sitting unassigned until you choose to assign it. Sort of like the last kid picked to be on the kickball team, except the background page doesn't smell like peanut butter.

Editing a background page

Because a background page is just a type of page, you edit it just as you do a foreground page. Display the background page by clicking the page tab at the bottom of the drawing.

Are you driving yourself crazy trying to select a shape on a page that refuses to select? That's because the shape is on the *background* page assigned to your foreground page. It just *appears* to be on the foreground page. The only page that it can possibly belong to is the background page. It's hard to tell between to the two because Visio makes no distinction between them on the screen.

Rotating Pages

The best computer software program is one designed to work the way you worked before you had the program. Think about the following example: If you draw, with pencil and paper, a map of a city where streets fall at odd angles, you probably draw all the streets that run parallel to the edges of your paper and then *turn the paper at an angle* and draw in the angular streets. Right? That's exactly what happens when you rotate a drawing page in Visio: The program thinks the way you think when you're working on paper. Scary thought, huh?

When you rotate a page, all the shapes in the drawing rotate along with it. That includes *guides,* those vertical and horizontal lines you drag into your drawing from the rulers to help you position shapes. (To review creating and using guides, see Chapter 7.) When you know that you're going to rotate a page, you can use guides sort of like a custom grid.

Rulers and the drawing page grid *do not* rotate when you turn a page. This is a good thing — you can always maintain a horizontal and vertical baseline from which to work, regardless of the angle of the paper.

Figure 9-8 shows a city map. The angled streets were drawn after rotating the page 45 degrees.

In Figure 9-9, you see the same city map rotated 60 degrees. You can also see the *guides* that were drawn to make it easy to lay out the streets. Notice that the *grid* remains parallel to the rulers bordering the drawing area. The guides are pulled from the vertical ruler to set them at a 60-degree angle to the grid.

To rotate a page, you must first enable page rotation (unless you're using Visio Technical, in which case page rotation is automatically enabled) by following these steps:

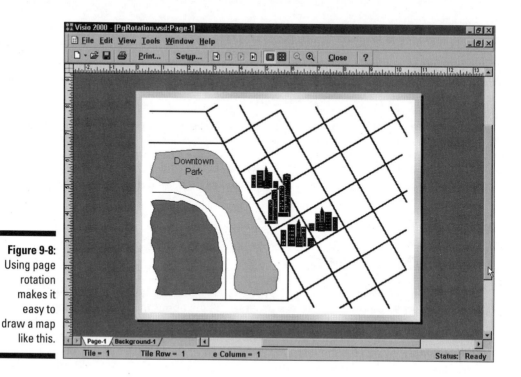

Figure 9-8:
Using page
rotation
makes it
easy to
draw a map
like this.

1. Choose Tools⇨Options.

Visio displays the Options dialog box.

2. Click the Drawing tab.

3. Click the Enable Page Rotation check box.

4. Click the OK button.

To rotate a page, drag it from one corner either clockwise or counterclockwise. If you want to rotate to a specific angle, watch the status bar as you drag the page; it tells you the exact angle (in degrees) of the page as you rotate it. Use these steps to rotate a page:

1. Click the Rotation Tool button on the Standard toolbar.

The Rotation Tool button looks like a dot with an arrow circling it.

2. Move the mouse pointer over any corner of the page.

The pointer changes to a round rotation pointer.

3. **Drag the mouse either clockwise or counterclockwise, depending on the direction that you want to rotate the page.**

   The farther you move the mouse pointer away from the page corner, the more precise the angle you can choose.

4. **Release the mouse button when the page rotates to the angle that you want.**

Grid parallel to rulers   Guide lines

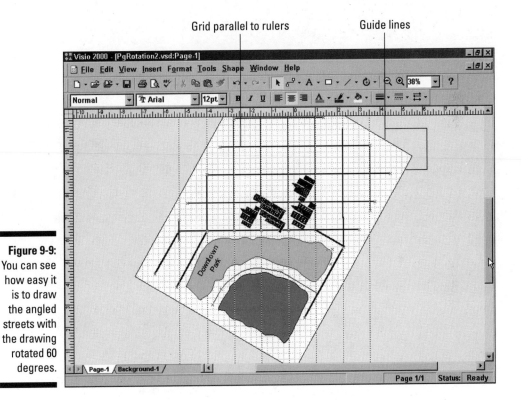

Figure 9-9:
You can see
how easy it
is to draw
the angled
streets with
the drawing
rotated 60
degrees.

Chapter 10

Love That Layered Look

. . . .

In This Chapter

▶ Discovering what layers are and why you may want them

▶ Creating, removing, renaming, and hiding layers

▶ Assigning (and reassigning) shapes to layers

▶ Creating layers on background pages

▶ Protecting shapes on a layer from changes

▶ Changing the color of shapes on a layer

▶ Printing layers — only the ones you want!

. . . .

*V*isio defines a *layer* as a named category of shapes. Huh? How about a more vivid description? When you were a kid, did you ever have one of those cool anatomy books with the transparent sheets? The bottom sheet had the skeletal structure, the next sheet had internal organs, and then you added the nervous system, the muscular structure, and finally the skin? Well, the layer system in Visio works in much the same way. You can create layers in a Visio drawing for the same purpose as your old anatomy book: to show groups or categories of shapes independently of others or as part of the whole. Think of layers in a Visio drawing as being transparent, just like the transparent sheets in an anatomy book.

How can you use layers? In a landscape drawing, you may want to include structural walls and pathways on one layer; grass, ground cover, and small shrubs on another; trees on a separate layer; and ornamental flowers on another layer. Another example is a layout for a building or home in which the walls, doors, and windows appear on one layer, and the wiring, electrical system, plumbing, and HVAC system (heating, ventilation, and air conditioning) appear on individual layers. You can display just one layer to view the shapes in a particular group or display all layers to view the complete plan.

Getting the Essential Facts on Layers

You need to know the essential facts about layers so that you can make decisions about how and when you want to use them. Don't let all of these facts scare you off! As you read the following list, try to form a mental picture of what's going on.

- A Visio drawing can have more than one page.

- Each page can have its own set of layers.

- Visio automatically assigns some shapes to predefined layers (based on the template that you choose).

- A shape can be assigned to (and therefore, appear on) one or more layers. (This is the only point for which our anatomy book example doesn't hold true: A liver or spleen appears only on the internal organs sheet; you don't find it duplicated on the skeletal structure sheet or the nervous system sheet.)

- A Visio page (with or without layers) can have one or more background pages.

- Although similar in behavior, a background page is not the same as a layer! A background page can have its own layers.

Confused yet? It becomes clearer if you keep in mind an image of one transparent sheet as a *layer,* a stack of transparent sheets as a *page,* and multiple stacks as separate pages in a drawing. Although a Visio background page is also transparent, its purpose is to display repetitive information (such as a company logo or document title and date) rather than a category of shapes, as a layer does. If the bottom transparent sheet of the anatomy book had only a title, such as "The Human Body," it would be analogous to a Visio background page (see Figure 10-1). Check out Chapter 9 to find out how to create multiple pages and background pages in a Visio drawing.

The bottom line is that when you want to group and display categories of shapes in a drawing, use layers. When you want repetitive information to appear on each page of a drawing, use a background page.

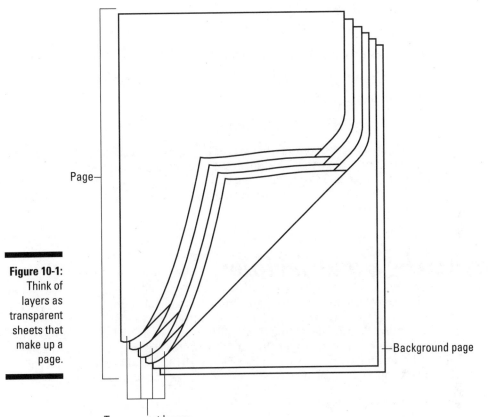

Figure 10-1:
Think of
layers as
transparent
sheets that
make up a
page.

Page

Background page

Transparent layers

Discovering How Layering Works

In general, you *assign* shapes to a specific layer or to more than one layer. However, some Visio templates include predefined layers. In these cases, the shapes in the template's stencils are preassigned to a particular layer. This means that Visio has done some of the work for you already; you don't have to create layers for your drawing. When you drag a shape onto the drawing page, Visio automatically creates the layer to which that shape is preassigned. When you drag another shape that is preassigned to a different layer, Visio adds that layer to the drawing. However, the layers aren't added to your drawing until you use the shapes in your drawing. The Office Layout template is a good example of a template with predefined layers. Some layers on the Office Layout template include:

✔ **The building envelope** (walls, doors, windows)

✔ **Equipment** (computers, copy machines)

✔ **Movable furnishings** (desks, chairs)

✔ **Nonmovable furnishings** (corner work surfaces, panels)

✔ **Spaces** (shapes that delineate floor space)

✔ **Power/communications** (telephone jacks, power outlets)

A layer (preassigned, or one that you add) applies to a single page in a drawing. If you add a page to your drawing, it doesn't contain any layers until you either drag a shape into the drawing that's preassigned to a layer, or create a new layer, as I describe in the "Adding a layer or removing one" section later in this chapter.

Using the View Toolbar

Visio's View toolbar contains many buttons that enable you to control your view of a drawing (for example, the Grid button, the Guides button, the Connection Points button, the Ruler button, and so on). The last button on the View toolbar is the Layer Properties button. Click this button to display the Layer Properties dialog box (see Figure 10-2). You also can choose View➪ Layer Properties to display the Layer Properties dialog box.

If you prefer using toolbar buttons, I suggest displaying the View toolbar. To display the View toolbar, right-click in the toolbar area and choose View from the pop-up menu. Or, choose View➪Toolbars➪View.

Working with Layers

As you may suspect, there are a few things that you must know about working with layers. In this section, you discover how to add, name, and remove layers, as necessary; place shapes onto a layer; make a layer active or inactive; and hide layers.

Adding a layer or removing one

When the template you're using doesn't include predefined layers (or if you're not using a template at all), you can create layers of your own to help you organize your shapes. Even if you are using a template that includes layers, you can add to them if you need to.

Follow these steps to add a layer:

1. **Choose View⇨Layer Properties or click the Layer Properties Tool button on the View toolbar.**

   Visio displays the Layer Properties dialog box, showing a list of layers for the current page (see Figure 10-2).

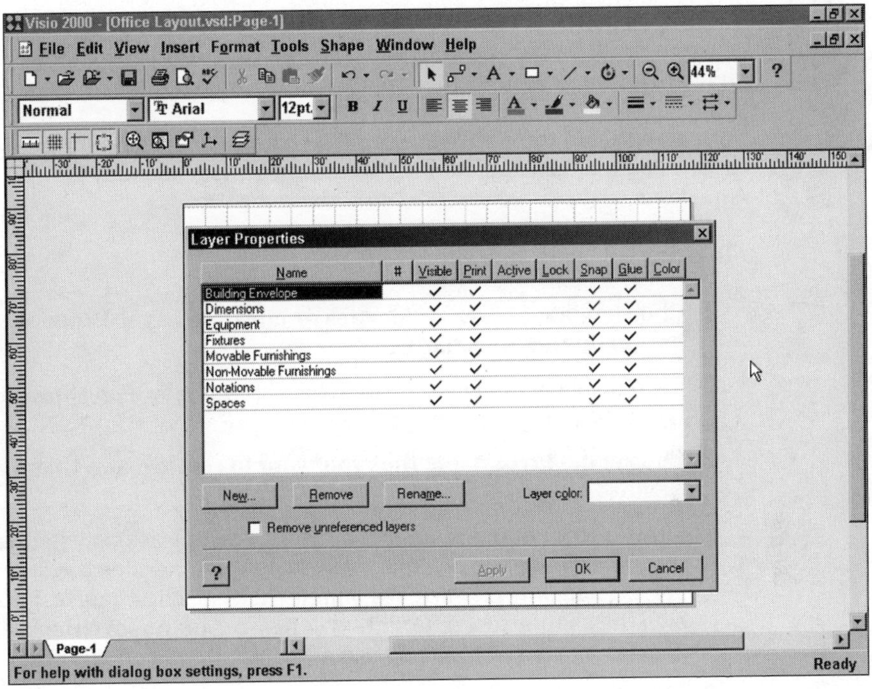

Figure 10-2:
The Layer Properties dialog box lists all layers on the current page of the drawing by name.

If your Layer Properties dialog box is empty, it doesn't necessarily mean that the template you're using doesn't include predefined layers. The layers show up in this dialog box only after you've dragged preassigned shapes onto your drawing page.

2. **Click the New button.**

   Visio displays the New Layer dialog box (see Figure 10-3).

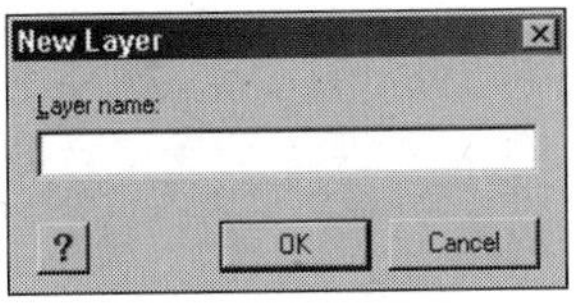

Figure 10-3:
Type a name for the new layer in the Layer Name box.

3. **In the Layer Name box, type the name that you want for a new layer and then click the OK button.**

   Your new layer is added to the list in the Layer Properties dialog box.

4. **If you want to add more layers, click the Apply button and then repeat Steps 2 and 3.**

5. **Click the OK button to close the Layer Properties dialog box.**

When you add or remove layers, Visio adds or removes them from only the current page. If your drawing has multiple pages and you want to add or remove layers, you need to add or remove for each page.

You may decide to remove a layer. If so, make sure that you reassign all shapes on that layer to another layer. Otherwise, you may lose all shapes on that layer.

To remove a layer, follow these steps:

1. **Choose View⇨Layer Properties or click the Layer Properties Tool button on the View toolbar.**

   Visio displays the Layer Properties dialog box, which shows a list of layers for the current page.

2. **Choose the layer name that you want to remove and then click Remove.**

   If the layer contains shapes, you see a warning asking whether you really want to remove the layer. If you're willing to sacrifice the shapes on the layer, go ahead and click Yes. If not, click No, click Cancel, and then reassign the shapes to a different layer before you remove the layer. (See the "Assigning shapes to layers" section later in this chapter.)

3. **Click the OK button.**

If you respond "No" to the warning message and then immediately try to remove another layer, beware, Visio will not display the warning message again! Visio deletes the layer, even though it contains shapes. You can restore the layer by clicking the Cancel button.

Renaming a layer

You may want to change the name of a layer to something that better describes the shapes that you use, or just because you feel like it. It's best to use this option when you're working with layers that you create.

I don't recommend renaming a predefined Visio layer. Here's why: As soon as you drag another shape into a drawing that's preassigned to the Visio layer, the Visio layer name appears on the list again in the Layer Properties dialog box, and your drawing includes both the Visio layer and the layer you renamed. This can be confusing if you want all your shapes to appear on a single layer.

To rename a layer, follow these easy steps:

1. **Choose View⇨Layer Properties or click the Layer Properties Tool button on the View toolbar.**

   Visio displays the Layer Properties dialog box.

2. **Choose the layer that you want to rename and then click Rename.**

   Visio displays the Rename Layer dialog box.

3. **Type the new name in the Layer Name box and then click the OK button.**

   Visio displays the new layer name in the Layer Properties dialog box.

4. **Click the OK button.**

Hiding a layer

One of the big advantages of using layers in a drawing is that you can turn them off when you don't want to display their shapes. Consider the building layout example I talked about earlier in the chapter. If you want to work on the plumbing layer of the building, you also want to display the layer that contains the building walls (that is, the Building Envelope), but you don't need furniture cluttering your view. Or, if you want to distribute the drawing to employees so that they can decide how they want their furniture arranged in their offices, it's not important for them to see the plumbing and HVAC layers. They do, however, need to see the Building Envelope and Electrical layers so that they know where walls and electrical outlets are located in their offices.

To hide a layer, follow these steps:

1. **Choose View⇨Layer Properties or click the Layer Properties Tool button on the View toolbar.**

   The Layer Properties dialog box appears (refer to Figure 10-2).

2. **Find the name of the layer that you want to hide. Click on the check mark that appears in the Visible column.**

   The check mark is removed, making the layer invisible.

To display or hide all layers at the same time, click the Visible button (the column header is a button). This button toggles every item in the column on and off.

3. **Click the OK or the Apply button.**

If you want to hide just one layer, click the OK button. If you want to hide other layers, click Apply; then repeat Step 2 until all the layers that you want hidden are hidden.

To redisplay a hidden layer, follow the same steps and add a check mark to the Visible column in the Layer Properties dialog box.

Assigning shapes to layers

Some templates automatically assign some shapes to predefined layers, but what happens when you use a template that doesn't have predefined layers? If you create your own layers, you assign shapes to the layers you choose. (Yes, it's more work than using a template with predefined layers, but think of the fun you'll have!)

Follow these steps to assign a shape to a layer:

1. **Select the shape to assign.**

If the shape is part of a group, click the group and then click the shape to select it by itself (it displays gray handles).

2. **Choose Format⇨Layer.**

The Layer dialog box appears, as shown in Figure 10-4.

Figure 10-4:
The Layer dialog box lists all layers for the drawing on the current page.

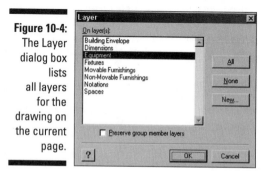

3. **Click the layer that you want to assign the shape to.**

Sometimes you may want a shape to appear on two or more layers so it's always visible, even when other layers are hidden. To assign a shape to more than one layer, go back to Steps 1 and 2. For Step 3, hold down the Ctrl key as you click on all the layers you want to assign the shape to.

4. **Click the OK button.**

Are you curious which layer a particular shape is assigned to? To find out, select the shape and then choose Format➪Layer. The Layer dialog box appears and the layer the shape belongs to is highlighted.

You can move a shape from one layer to another by following these steps:

1. **Select the shape you want to move.**

2. **Choose Format➪Layer.**

3. **In the Layer dialog box, click on the layer you want to move the shape to.**

4. **Click the OK button.**

Activating layers

When you drag a shape that isn't preassigned to a layer into your drawing, or when you create a new shape, the shape goes unassigned. When you *activate* a layer, all unassigned shapes you use in your drawing are automatically assigned to the active layer. You can activate a single layer, or you can activate multiple layers. The advantage of activating multiple layers is that the unassigned shapes you use in your drawing are automatically assigned to *all* of the active layers.

To activate a layer or layers, follow these steps:

1. **Choose View➪Layer Properties or click the Layer Properties Tool button on the View toolbar.**

   The Layer Properties dialog box appears (refer to Figure 10-2).

2. **In the Active column, click the layer or layers that you want to make active.**

3. **Click the OK button.**

Using shapes on many layers

Why would you want a shape to appear on more than one layer? One reason is that when a particular layer is hidden, the shape is still visible on other layers. Another reason is that you can track a group of shapes on one layer and component shapes on individual layers. For example, suppose that you're diagramming a computer network that contains components from multiple manufacturers. You would have an IBM layer, an HP layer, a Dell layer, a Compaq layer, and so on. But you would also have a layer called Network Components, which would include shapes from *all* of the manufacturer layers. This gives you an easy way to track all network shapes or shapes by manufacturer.

Using Layers on Background Pages

A background page appears behind another page; its contents "show through" the page to which it is assigned. Background pages are designed to contain repetitive information — text or graphics that you want to appear on one or more pages in a drawing. A company name, logo, or document name are examples of information that you may want to put on a background page. Individual pages in a drawing can have their own or the same background page; you determine to which page (or pages) a background is assigned. See Chapter 9 for information on creating and assigning background pages.

Just as pages can have layers, so can background pages. To create layers on a background page, you first need to create the background page. See Chapter 9 to find out how to create the background page.

After you create a background page, follow these steps to create layers for your background page:

1. **Display your background page by clicking on the Background Page tab at the bottom of the drawing area.**

2. **Choose View➪Layer Properties or click the Layer Properties Tool button on the View toolbar.**

3. **Click New to display the New Layer dialog box (refer to Figure 10-3).**

4. **In the Layer Name box, type a new name and then click the OK button.**

   Visio adds the name to the Layer Properties list.

5. **Click the OK or the Apply button.**

   If you want to add other layers, click Apply and then repeat Steps 3, 4, and this step. If you want to add just one layer, click the OK button.

Protecting Layers from Changes

After you go to all the trouble of defining layers and adding shapes to them, nothing is worse than another user (or yourself) accidentally deleting or changing them. How can you avoid this? You can protect a layer from changes by *locking* it. When a layer is locked, you can't move, change, or delete shapes. You also can't add shapes to the layer.

To lock a layer, follow these steps:

1. **Choose View⇨Layer Properties or click the Layer Properties Tool button on the View toolbar.**

   Visio displays the Layer Properties dialog box (refer to Figure 10-2).

2. **Locate the layer that you want to lock and then click in the Lock column across from the layer name.**

   A check mark appears in the column. This shows that the layer as locked.

   If you want to lock all layers quickly, click the Lock button (the column header for the Lock column is a button.) To unlock all layers at the same time, click the Lock button again.

3. **Click the OK or the Apply button.**

   To lock just one layer, click the OK button. To lock other layers, click Apply and then repeat Step 2 and this step for each layer that you want to lock. When you finish, click the OK button.

If you're not sure that this method works, you can test it easily. Just try to move, delete, or copy a shape on the locked layer. You can't do any of these things because Visio doesn't even let you *select* the shape. When you're ready to work on the layer again, you can unlock it easily by removing the check mark from the Lock column.

For obvious reasons, you can't lock an active layer that's marked as an active layer. Not so obvious? Remember that all unassigned shapes are automatically assigned to the active layer or layers. If you could lock the active layers, your shapes wouldn't be assigned to any layer. When you try to lock an active layer, Visio automatically makes the layer inactive.

Locking a layer isn't foolproof protection from changes. After all, you can unlock a layer just as easily as you can lock one. Think of a locked layer as an alert or a reminder — to yourself or other users — that shapes on a locked layer *shouldn't* be changed. If you want a file to be fully protected from changes, open it or distribute it to other users as a read-only file. For more information on read-only files, see Chapter 13.

Assigning a Color to a Layer

Why would you want to assign a color to a layer, you ask? Suppose that your drawing has a half dozen layers and you're beginning to get confused about which shapes belong to what layer. Assigning a color to each layer lets you determine quickly which shapes belong to a particular layer. You can also assign a color to all locked layers. This reminds you immediately which shapes you can't alter. Or, if you're distributing the drawing to other users for review and comment, you may want to assign a color to the layer that each user may change. Get the idea?

To assign a color to a layer, follow these steps:

1. **Choose View⇨Layer Properties or click the Layer Properties Tool button on the View toolbar.**

   Visio displays the Layer Properties dialog box (refer to Figure 10-2).

2. **Find the layer that you want to assign a color to and then click in the Color column across from the layer name.**

   A check mark appears in the column.

3. **At the bottom of the dialog box, choose a layer color from the Layer Color drop-down list or click Custom.**

   Visio offers a dozen or so colors and ten shades of gray. If these aren't enough options, you can create a custom color by clicking Custom at the bottom of the list. After you click Custom, the Edit Color dialog box, shown in Figure 10-5, appears.

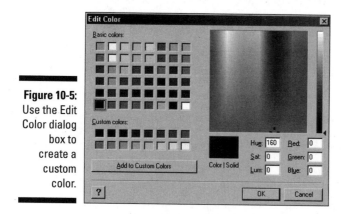

Figure 10-5: Use the Edit Color dialog box to create a custom color.

To create a custom color, follow these steps:

1. **Find the layer that you want to assign a color to and then click in the Color column across from the layer name.**

   A check mark appears in the column.

2. **At the bottom of the dialog box, click Custom.**

   The Color dialog box appears (refer to Figure 10-5).

3. **Click an empty Custom Colors dialog box (in the lower-left part of the dialog box).**

4. **On the left side of the dialog box, click one of the Basic Colors closest to the color that you want to create.**

5. **Move the pointer in any direction in the large color box area on the right side of the dialog box to customize the color.**

   - **To change the intensity of the color:** Move the small, black arrow up and down the vertical slide bar at the far right of the dialog box.

   - **To adjust the Hue, Sat (Saturation), and Lum (Luminosity) of a color:** Enter a number in one of these boxes.

   - **To adjust the amount of Red, Green, or Blue in a color:** Enter a number in one of these boxes.

6. **Click the Add to Custom Colors button.**

To create more custom colors, repeat Steps 1 through 4. To use one of your custom colors for the selected layer:

1. **Click your custom color in the Custom Colors box (refer to Figure 10-5) and then click the OK button.**

   The Color dialog box closes. The Layer Properties dialog box is still open. Your custom color now appears at the bottom of the list.

2. **Click your custom color to apply it to the layer that you want to add the color to.**

3. **Click the OK or the Apply button.**

   Visio displays all the shapes on the layer in the color you chose.

4. **To remove the color, choose View⇨Layer Properties again or click the Layer Properties Tool button on the View toolbar. Remove the check mark from the Color column.**

Removing a color from a layer doesn't remove any custom colors that you created. They are still available in the Color dialog box.

If you have a color printer and you assigned colors to layers, the layers print in their designated colors.

Selecting Layers to Print

What good are layers if you can't print them selectively? In a building layout, for example, you probably want to print only the Building Envelope (walls) and Plumbing layers for the plumber. The plumber doesn't want or need to see the wiring, HVAC, and furniture layouts. And your employees, who need to place their furniture in their offices, certainly don't need to see the technical parts of your drawing. The only layers they need to see are the walls, non-movable furniture, and the electrical outlets.

Visio automatically assumes that you want to print all layers, but you can change this easily by following these steps:

1. **Choose View⇨Layer Properties or click the Layer Properties Tool button on the View toolbar.**

2. **For the layers that you don't want to print, remove the check mark in the Print column by clicking it.**

3. **Click the OK button.**

Don't be deceived by the Visible column in the Layer Properties dialog box! You can't keep a layer from printing by making it invisible. The Print column is the only setting that affects printing; the Visible column affects only what you see on the screen. If a layer isn't visible, but a check mark appears in the Print column, it prints!

Snap and Glue Options for Layers

If you followed some of the steps in this chapter, you've seen the Layer Properties dialog box, and you're probably wondering what the Snap and Glue columns are for. What are snap and glue, you ask? *Snap* is a feature that works like a magnet to let you align and position shapes accurately in a drawing. You can specify that shapes automatically snap to other shapes, to grid lines, to guide lines, ruler divisions, and so on. *Glue* is a feature that keeps shapes connected even when you move them. Connection lines between shapes either stay connected at the same point on the shape, or move to a more convenient connection point, depending on the glue options that you specify. See Chapter 6 for more information about Glue and Chapter 6 for more about Snap.

The following rules apply to the Snap and Glue options in the Layer Properties dialog box:

✔ **Snap:** When Snap is checked for a particular layer, shapes on that layer can snap to shapes on other layers and vice versa. (In other words, Snap is enabled in both directions.) When Snap is not checked for a particular layer, shapes on that layer can still snap to shapes on other layers, but not vice versa.

✔ **Glue:** When Glue is checked for a particular layer, shapes on that layer can glue to shapes on other layers and vice versa. (In other words, Glue is enabled in both directions.) When Glue is not checked for a particular layer, shapes on that layer can still glue to shapes on other layers, but not vice versa.

If you want shapes on other layers to steer clear of shapes on a particular layer, uncheck both options (snap and glue) for that layer.

Chapter 11

Saving Time with Visio Wizards

....

....

*I*f you're like me, you always appreciate some extra help anytime you're learning a new application. A little magic here and there can't hurt. Well, wizards aren't exactly magic, but they're the next best thing.

A wizard is something that understands the task you need to accomplish — maybe even better than you do. A wizard picks your brain. A wizard asks you important questions about the task and makes you think. A wizard is logical, organized, and objective. A wizard is a dutiful and obedient servant; it does exactly what you tell it to do. Although mysterious, a wizard is your loyal and faithful assistant.

What's a Wizard and Why Do I Want One?

Okay, okay! What's a wizard, really? A *wizard* is a *macro,* a kind of mini pro-gram that leads you through the steps of accomplishing a specific task, such as creating an organization chart, an office layout, or a project timeline. A wizard displays dialog boxes that ask you a series of questions, each designed to lead you one step closer to your goal. The wizard records all the information that you give it and, after asking its last question, does what it was designed to do, whether that's creating a drawing or compiling a report.

Why would you want to use a wizard? Because wizards make things quick and easy for you. They are especially helpful if you're trying to accomplish a particular task for the first time. A wizard can also ensure accuracy and con-sistency in a drawing, leaving you to worry about other details. Before you get too excited about wizards, though, let me make it clear that some wizards accomplish very simple tasks, whereas others accomplish complex ones. Sometimes a wizard is nice to use just because you're feeling lazy. Feel free to avoid hunting through menu commands and dialog boxes; sit back and have a wizard ask you all the questions — that's what they're there for. The best way to discover wizards is to experiment with them.

Visio contains some additional tools that perform tasks for you as well. They're included throughout this chapter although they're technically not wizards. You can think of them as wizards, however, because they are mini programs that perform a task for you.

Discovering What Wizards Can Really Do

In Visio, you have specific tasks that wizards can help you accomplish. Here are some of the basic wizards found in all Visio products:

- ✔ **Build Region:** This tool gathers shapes (like states, provinces, and countries) that you drag into your drawing, pulling them together into a geographically correct map. For example, you can drag Washington, Oregon, Idaho, California, and Utah shapes (from the Maps of the U.S. stencil) onto the drawing page and place them anywhere. Build Region positions them correctly in relation to one another.

- ✔ **Chart Shape Wizard:** When you create a chart and want to use multiple shapes to depict quantity, this wizard creates the additional shapes for you and stacks them (horizontally or vertically). For example, if you're creating a bar chart to show numbers of people who own personal computers, you can choose a personal computer shape to represent quantity. The higher the quantity, the more shapes the wizard adds to the chart. You can also use this wizard to stretch 2-D shapes to represent increasing or decreasing quantity. For example, a stretchable pencil is a great shape for a teacher's chart that shows average hours of homework for each grade in school.

- ✔ **Page Layout Wizard:** If you're not using a template, this wizard is good for helping you set up your drawing page size, orientation (landscape or portrait), and drawing scale. The wizard also prompts you for information about adding a title or page border to your drawing. For more information about using templates, refer to Chapter 2.

- ✔ **Organization Chart Wizard:** This wizard lets you create a generic organization chart (to which you can later add data) and create an organization chart based on data that you have in a Microsoft Excel file (.XLS), an Org Plus (.TXT) file, a text file (comma-delimited or tab-delimited), or an *Open Database Connectivity*-compliant (ODBC-compliant) database table. See Chapter 14 for examples and more details on this wizard.

✔ **Shape Explorer:** Looking for a particular shape but don't remember which stencil it's on? Shape Explorer helps you find it. You don't even have to know the name of the shape; just type in a description of the shape, and Shape Explorer searches for it.

✔ **Stencil Report Wizard:** Want a Visio drawing of all the shapes on a stencil? This wizard gives you an example of every shape on a stencil, as well as its name and description. If a shape is a simple star, the description "six-pointed star" may seem rather obvious. But what if the shape is a Catalyst 3000B Switch with the description "Cisco – 16-Port Catalyst 3000 Switch w/10K addr, SNMP, Address Filter, Spanning-Tree Protocol w/VLAN suppt, Full Duplex"? This description isn't so obvious. A stencil report serves as a great reference guide for a stencil. For a quick glance at the shapes in many of Visio's stencils, see Appendix A.

✔ **Print ShapeSheet:** The ShapeSheet spreadsheet describes Visio shapes in every way imaginable. The ShapeSheet contains mathematical and geometric information about the shape, as well as the x, y coordinates of its vertices and connection points; text box characteristics; line and fill characteristics; protection, glue, and layer characteristics; and much more. The Print ShapeSheet tool displays a Print dialog box in which you can select the ShapeSheet characteristics that you want to print. You can print to your printer, to a file, or to the Windows Clipboard.

Some of the more advanced wizards include the following:

✔ **Custom Properties Editor:** Use this tool to edit the data stored in shapes by adding data fields or deleting existing data fields. Now you can get rid of data fields that you don't use and add data fields that are particularly important to you.

✔ **Database Export:** This tool lets you *export* (transfer out of Visio) data that is stored in a drawing's shapes. Where do you export it to? An ODBC-compliant database file, which saves you from re-creating a database table from data that already exists in the Visio Custom Properties and ShapeSheet spreadsheets.

✔ **Database Wizard:** Want to link to a database the data stored in your shapes? Use the Database Wizard to do it. This wizard links data to ODBC-compliant databases like Microsoft Access and Oracle SQL Server. (*Linking* makes a connection between the data stored in Visio shapes and the data stored in a database so that when one is changed, the other is updated.)

✔ **Property Reporting Wizard:** A shape in Visio is much more than just a shape. A shape is not only *smart* (its behavior changes based on the circumstances in which you use it), but it stores data such as inventory numbers or cost data. The Property Reporting Wizard compiles data from the shapes that you select. The data is turned into a report that you can store in a spreadsheet.

✓ **SmartShape Wizard:** This is one of Visio's coolest wizards because it lets you change the way a shape looks and behaves. For example, you can reposition a shape's text box, add a hidden note to a shape, or change the attributes of a *locked* (protected from change) shape.

TIP

Visio Standard, Visio Technical, and Visio Professional all include wizards. Technical and Professional include all the wizards that Standard offers, in addition to some specialized wizards.

Finding the Wizard That You Want

Because a wizard is a macro, you can always find wizards listed under Tools⇨Macros. This command leads to a submenu that then lists categories of macros, and finally, the names of individual wizards and tools. (See Figure 11-1.)

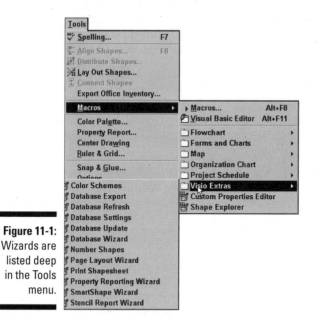

Figure 11-1:
Wizards are listed deep in the Tools menu.

WARNING!

The list shown in Figure 11-1 is from Visio Standard. If you're using Visio Professional or Technical, you may see additional wizards on your screen.

If you're not sure in which category a wizard is listed, you can always choose Tools⇨Macros⇨Macros (or click Alt+F8), which displays a dialog box that lists all tools and wizards in alphabetic order. To use one of these wizards, click the wizard that you want and click Run.

Visio lists wizards in other locations as well. For example, suppose you start Visio using the Charts and Graphs template and then decide that you want to use the Chart Shape Wizard. When you open the Tools menu, the Chart Shape Wizard appears on the Tools menu. This is true when you use other templates as well. Keep in mind, though, that not every template has a wizard associated with it.

Some wizards are also listed when you start Visio. From the Welcome to Visio 2000 dialog box, click Choose Drawing Type to display the Choose Drawing Type dialog box shown in Figure 11-2. When you choose a template category, wizards are listed along with templates.

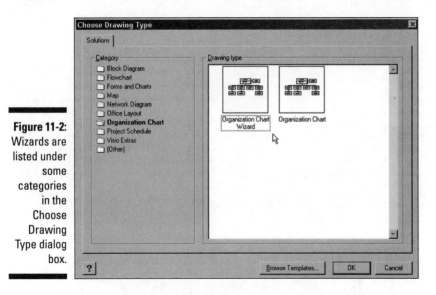

Figure 11-2: Wizards are listed under some categories in the Choose Drawing Type dialog box.

Using a Wizard

Wizards are probably one of the easiest tools to use. When you start a wizard, a special dialog box comes up and describes what the wizard does and the tasks that you can perform by using it. The Back, Next, and Cancel buttons are at the bottom of the box. Each of these buttons performs a different task:

- ✓ **Back:** Cancels the changes you made and refreshes the screen.
- ✓ **Next:** Takes you to the next screen in the wizard script, which presents you with more questions or choices.
- ✓ **Cancel:** Exits the wizard without completing the task.

Some wizards have a More Info button like the one shown in Figure 11-3. When you click this button, the wizard displays helpful hints or information that may help you run the wizard.

Not all the wizard's screens are shown here because they are self-explanatory and incredibly easy to follow — really, they are — they're nothing like that gas station attendant's directions! A Finish button appears in the place of the Next button on the wizard's last screen. After you click Finish, the wizard returns to your Visio drawing page and completes the task that it was designed for.

Figure 11-3:
Click the
More Info
button to
bring up a
separate
window
about the
wizard.

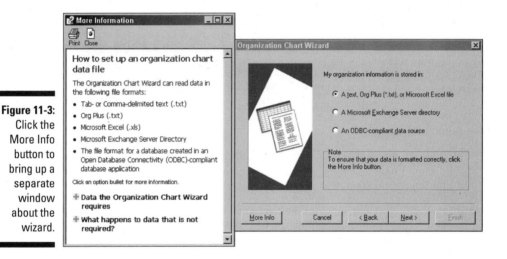

Finding more help on the Web

Wizards are great helpers for particular tasks, but sometimes you have questions or problems that even a mighty wizard can't handle. You can find more help at the Visio Corporation Web site. You can access the Web site from Visio by choosing Help➪Visio on the Web. Visio dials out and goes directly to its Visio on the Web page.

✔ **To find out about Visio support and service:** Click the Support tab and then select one of Visio's support resources (such as Technical Support, Support Forums, or Y2K Information).

✔ **For help learning Visio or learning about Visio:** Click the Learning tab for Training, White Papers, Case Studies, SmartPages Magazine, and more.

✔ **To find out about add-on products, consulting services, and more:** Click the Extras tab and choose a category.

✔ **To find out about downloads available from Visio and third parties:** Click the Downloads tab.

Part IV

For the Die-Hard Visio Junkie: Using More Advanced Stuff

In this part . . .

*I*f you're a die-hard Visio user, you're still hanging in there! See how to go one step beyond using Visio shapes, stencils, and templates, and find out how to create your own. Discover how storing information in shapes can help you create reports and learn about protecting your work from changes. If that's not enough, see how to incorporate elements of Visio into other programs, use Visio drawings on the Net, and add hyperlinks to drawings.

Chapter 12

Creating Stencils, Master Shapes, Templates, and Styles

Y ou're ready to start customizing Visio by creating your own Visio stencils, master shapes, templates, and styles. The flexibility that Visio offers is a great asset, and it also makes Visio that much more useful to you because you can tailor it to suit your unique needs.

If the template that you're using doesn't contain all the shapes that you need, choose File➪Stencils to open additional stencils.

Working with Stencils

Chapters 1 and 2 cover the basics of opening and using stencils. This chapter goes beyond the basics and tells you about document stencils, how to customize existing stencils, and how to create new ones.

Using the Stencil toolbar

As you work with stencils, you can use the buttons on the Stencil toolbar if you want. Table 12-1 shows you the Stencil toolbar buttons and their functions. To display the Stencil toolbar, right-click on the toolbar area and choose Stencil, or choose View➪Toolbars➪Stencil.

Table 12-1	Tools on the Stencil Toolbar
Button	*Function or Tool*
	Creates a new stencil
	Displays a document stencil
	Displays icons and names only for current stencil
	Displays icons only for current stencil
	Displays shape names only for current stencil

Using a document stencil

Whenever you create a new drawing, Visio automatically creates a document stencil. You may not have been aware of it until now (unless you discovered it on your own by looking at the Window menu!). If you're working on a drawing, choose Window⇨Show Document Stencil and see what happens. Visio opens a stencil called Document Stencil. It includes all the shapes that you've used so far in the current drawing (see Figure 12-1). Each time you add a shape from a stencil to your drawing, it's automatically added to the document stencil.

So what's the point of a document stencil? It acts sort of as a shape history log for your drawing. Suppose that you had to open 15 different stencils to find all the shapes you need for your drawing. At some point, you'll probably close some of those stencils when you don't need them anymore. If you want to reuse any of those shapes, you can drag them from the document stencil onto your drawing instead of hunting down the original stencil and reopening it.

The document stencil is always there with a drawing, regardless of whether you display it. To display it, choose Window⇨Show Document Stencil. To close it, click the stencil's icon and then choose Close.

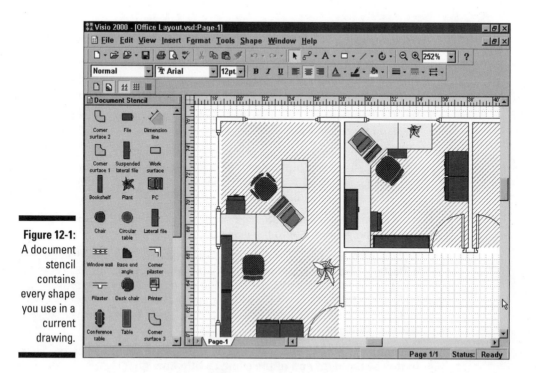

Figure 12-1:
A document
stencil
contains
every shape
you use in a
current
drawing.

Creating a custom stencil

If you find yourself using the same shapes over and over again from several different stencils, why not create a custom stencil? You can use a custom stencil to store your most frequently used shapes and avoid having to open multiple stencils every time you create a new drawing.

The quickest way to create a custom stencil is to base it on an existing stencil or drawing. These steps describe how to create a custom stencil:

1. Do one or both of the following:

- Open a drawing that already contains most of the shapes you want to include. If you don't have one, open the next closest thing, or just create a sample drawing and drag all the shapes you want on your custom stencil into the drawing. (If you make a sample drawing, the order and arrangement of the shapes doesn't matter. You don't really care about the drawing; it's the stencil you want to save.)

- Open a Visio stencil that you want to copy shapes from, or open the document stencil (choose Window⇨Show Document Stencil). Arrange the stencils on the screen so you can see all of them.

2. **Choose File⇨Stencils⇨New Stencil or click the New Stencil button on the Stencil toolbar.**

   Visio opens a new stencil named Stencilx on the left side of your screen, where x is a number. If you create more new stencils, the number is incremented each time. (Don't worry, you'll rename it soon enough.)

3. **Drag a shape onto the custom stencil (see Figure 12-2) by using one of these methods:**

   • From the drawing page, press and hold down the Ctrl key (so the shape is *copied*, not *moved*) as you drag a shape onto the new stencil. (If you hold down the Ctrl key as you drag the shape, you see a plus (+) symbol next to your mouse pointer.)

   • From the document stencil or from a Visio stencil, simply drag the shape you want onto the new stencil.

   What's the difference? If you drag a shape from the drawing, Visio names it Master .0 (and names subsequent shapes Master .1, Master .2, Master .3, and so on). If you drag a shape from the document stencil or from a Visio stencil onto the new stencil, it is automatically *copied* (not *moved*), and it keeps its Visio name (like "Rectangle," or "Terminal Server" or "External Interactor").

4. **When all the shapes you want are on the custom stencil, click the Save button at the right end of the stencil's title bar.**

   Visio displays the Save As dialog box.

5. **Navigate to the C:\Program Files\Visio2000\Solutions folder, where stencils are stored.**

   If you installed Visio in a different directory, locate that directory.

6. **Either click the Create New Folder icon to create a new folder or choose a folder that's appropriate for the category of your new stencil.**

   You can always store a miscellaneous stencil in the Visio Extras folder.

7. **In the File Name box, type a name for the stencil.**

   The name will appear on the Stencils submenu.

8. **In the Save As Type box, choose Stencil (*.vss).**

9. **Be sure the Workspace and Read Only check boxes are unchecked.**

10. **Click the Save button.**

    Visio displays the Properties dialog box, as shown in Figure 12-3.

Shape dragged from drawing

Shape dragged from document stencil

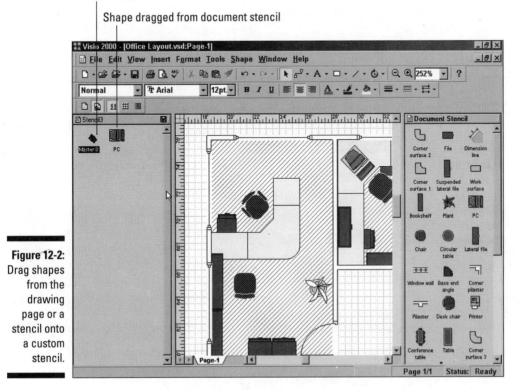

Figure 12-2:
Drag shapes
from the
drawing
page or a
stencil onto
a custom
stencil.

11. **In the Properties dialog box, enter any information about the file that you want to store.**

See Chapter 2 for information on saving files.

12. **Click the OK button.**

Now when you choose File⇨Stencils, your custom stencil is listed in the category you chose when you saved it (see Figure 12-4).

In Step 3, you see that shapes you drag from a drawing are given a temporary name such as Master .0 or Master .1. (See the next section, "Adding master shapes to stencils," to find out how to rename shapes on a stencil.)

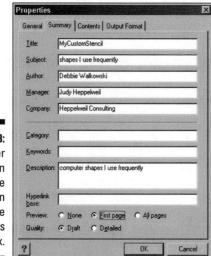

Figure 12-3:
Enter
information
about the
stencil in
the
Properties
dialog box.

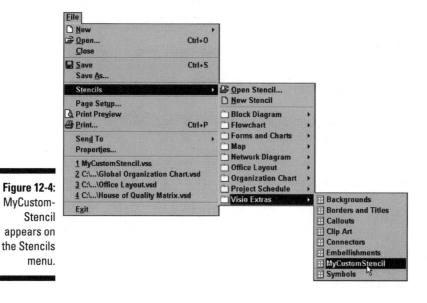

Figure 12-4:
MyCustom-
Stencil
appears on
the Stencils
menu.

Adding master shapes to stencils

Part of the process of creating a stencil involves adding master shapes to the stencil. If you want to add more shapes to a stencil later — any stencil — you can do so easily. Here's how:

1. **Open the drawing that contains the shape you want to add to a stencil.**

2. **Open the stencil to which you want to add shapes.**

3. **Drag a shape from the drawing onto the stencil.**

   Visio displays a message saying the stencil is currently open as read-only.

4. **Click the Yes button to be able to edit the stencil.**

   Visio adds the shape to the stencil with the name *Master .x* where .x is a number.

5. **Right-click on the shape in the stencil and choose Master Properties from the shortcut menu.**

   Visio displays the Master Properties dialog box (see Figure 12-5).

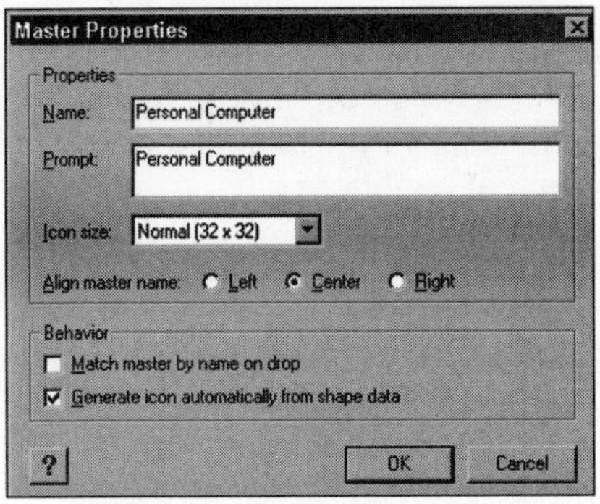

Figure 12-5:
Use the
Master
Properties
dialog box
to give a
shape a
unique
name.

6. **In the Name field, type a name for the shape.**

7. **(Optional) In the Prompt field, type the description or instruction that you want to appear on the status line when you point to the shape in the stencil.**

8. **Click the OK button.**

   Visio updates the name of the shape on the stencil.

9. **Repeat Steps 3 through 8 to add more shapes to the stencil.**

10. **Click the Save icon at the right end of the stencil's title bar.**

Deleting master shapes from custom stencils

Visio protects its stencils so that you don't accidentally wipe out shapes you need! However, you can delete master shapes from a custom stencil anytime you like because you created the stencil yourself. You may find yourself adding and deleting shapes often. Follow these steps to delete a shape:

1. **Open the custom stencil.**

2. **Right-click on the shape you want to delete.**

3. **From the shortcut menu, choose Delete.**

It's as simple as that. If you change your mind right away, you're in luck, because you can choose Edit⇨Undo after you delete a shape to bring it back. However, if you do anything else before you choose Edit⇨Undo, you lose your shape. Undo reverses only the most recent action taken.

Creating Custom Templates

A template is like a model for a drawing; it sets up the page size, orientation, drawing scale, grid, and text and font styles for your drawing area. Then a template opens up appropriate stencils for the type of drawing that you're creating. The biggest advantages that templates offer are consistency and efficiency. That's why creating and saving custom templates is a good idea.

If you create a series of related drawings, you want them to be consistent from the first to the last. It's possible that none of the Visio templates meet your needs exactly, but you can create a custom template that does. You can base your custom template on an existing Visio template or drawing and then change it, or you can create the custom template from scratch.

To create a custom template from a Visio template or an existing drawing, follow these steps:

1. **Start Visio and select the drawing type that you want to use.**

   If Visio is already running, choose File⇨New⇨Choose Drawing Type. If you want to base your new template on an existing drawing, choose File⇨Open.

2. **Choose File⇨Stencils to open any other stencils that you want to include in your new template.**

3. **Choose File⇨Page Setup.**

   Visio displays the Page Setup dialog box.

4. **Click the appropriate tab to change anything about the template (page size and orientation, drawing scale, page properties, and so on).**

5. **If you want your template to include a background page, create it now (see Chapter 9 for details).**

6. **Choose File⇨Save As.**

   Visio displays the Save As dialog box.

7. **In the Save In box, choose the folder that you want to save your new template in.**

   Choose the Visio Solutions folder if you want the template to appear in the Choose Drawing Type dialog box when you start up Visio or when you choose File⇨New⇨Choose Drawing Type.

8. **In the File Name box, type a name for your new template.**

9. **In the Save As Type box, choose Template (*.vst).**

10. **In the Save area of the dialog box, make sure the Workspace option is checked.**

11. **Click the Save button.**

The best way to create a custom template from scratch is to set up a drawing with all the settings you want the template to have. Choose File⇨Page Setup to set the page size, drawing scale, and page property settings that you want for the new template. And don't forget about background pages (see Chapter 9) and layers (see Chapter 10). When the drawing is the way you want it, repeat Steps 6 through 11.

Working with Styles

A *style* is a collection of attributes that apply to a shape, such as a green and yellow striped fill, a purple outline, and bold orange text in the Haettenschweiler font. The style has a name (such as Tasteless) and is saved along with a template or a drawing file. (Chapters 4 and 7 talk about working with components of a style.)

What's the point of having a style? A style saves you the time of applying all of Tasteless's attributes individually to a shape. You simply apply the style to as many shapes as you want, and — voilà! — you have multiple Tasteless shapes. Using styles not only saves you time but also ensures consistency when you want shapes to be formatted exactly alike.

A style can contain just one attribute or dozens of attributes. It can contain text attributes, line attributes, or fill attributes, or any combination of the three. Most Visio templates contain at least a few predefined styles (with one, two, or all three attributes). To see examples of styles, open any sample Visio file from the Visio/Samples folder. Make sure that the Format Text and Format Shape toolbars show up on your screen. (If you don't see the toolbars, right-click anywhere in the toolbar area to select these toolbars.)

The Format Text toolbar contains a Text style box; the Format Shape toolbar contains Line and Fill style boxes. To see how different styles are applied in the drawing, click a shape and look at the style boxes on the toolbar. Now click several other shapes and watch the style boxes each time you click another shape. You see that some shapes have a style assigned to them, whereas others don't. In Figure 12-6, you can see that the selected shape (floor space) uses the Space line style, Space text style, and Space fill style, all of which are predefined by the Office Layout template.

Text style box

Line style box   Fill style box

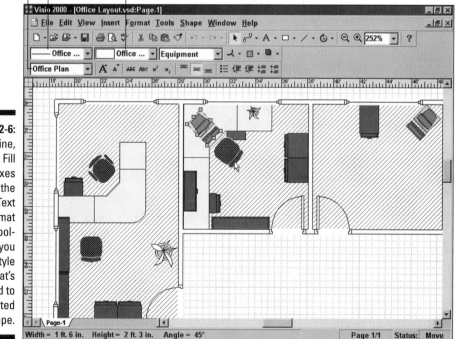

Figure 12-6:
The Line, Text, and Fill style boxes on the Format Text and Format Shape tool-bars tell you the style that's applied to the selected shape.

Creating and saving a style

You can base a new style on an existing one or create it from scratch. If the style that you want to create is similar to another style, begin with the existing style, make the changes that you want, and then save the new style under a different name.

Use these steps to create a style:

1. **Choose Format⇨Define Styles.**

   Visio displays the Define Styles dialog box, as shown in Figure 12-7.

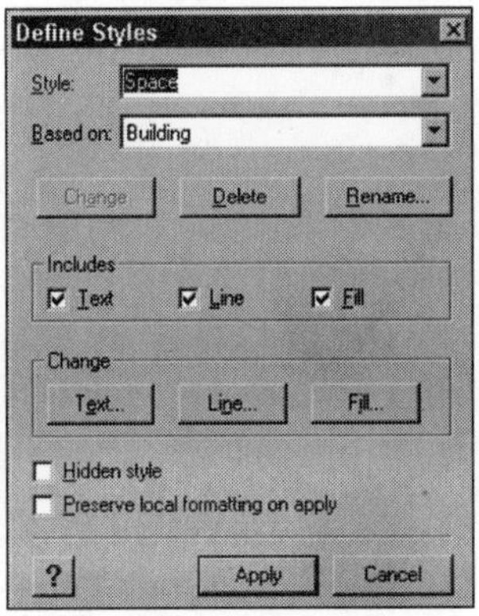

Figure 12-7:
The Define
Styles
dialog box.

2. **In the Style box, type a name for the new style.**

   If you're basing the new style on an existing one, choose it in the Based On box.

3. **In the Includes area, check all the characteristics that your new style includes (Text, Line, or Fill).**

4. **For each option you chose in Step 3, click the appropriate button in the Change box (Text, Line, or Fill).**

   In the dialog box that appears, choose the attributes that you want and then click the OK button to close the box.

5. **In the Define Styles dialog box, click the Apply button.**

You can also use the Define Styles dialog box to rename existing styles or delete styles you don't want to use anymore (refer to Figure 12-7).

Typically when you define a style, that style is available only to the current drawing. However, if you save the style with your template, the style is available in all drawings you create by using that template.

Applying a style to a shape

After you create a style, you simply apply it to a shape to assign all the style's attributes to the shape at once. If you want to apply the style to more than one shape, you can save yourself some time by applying the style to all the shapes at once. Follow these steps to apply a style to all shapes:

1. **Select the shape that you want to apply a style to.**

   To select more than one shape, press and hold down the Shift key as you click several shapes.

2. **Apply text, line, and fill styles.**

   To apply styles individually, click the down arrow for the style box on the appropriate toolbar (for example, the Fill style box on the Shape toolbar).

   To change several styles at the same time, choose Format⇨Style. In the Style box that appears, choose the appropriate styles from the drop-down boxes by clicking the down arrows; then click the OK button.

Copying a style from one drawing to another

If you've spent a lot of time creating and applying styles to different shapes in a drawing, you may want to use those styles in a different drawing. To copy styles to another drawing follow these steps:

1. **Open the drawing that contains the styles you created.**

2. **Create a new drawing and arrange the two drawings side by side.**

3. **Select a shape whose style you want to use in the new drawing and choose Edit⇨Copy or click the Copy button on the Standard toolbar.**

4. **Go to the new drawing page and choose Edit⇨Paste or click the Paste button on the Standard toolbar.**

Remember that if you want a style to be available to new drawings, you can define it as part of a template. See the "Creating Custom Templates" section earlier in this chapter.

Chapter 13

Managing Information in Your Shapes

. . . .

In This Chapter

▶ Storing information in a shape

▶ Creating reports from stored data

▶ Customizing the behavior of a shape

▶ Adding protection to your shapes and drawings

. . . .

*V*isio is far more sophisticated than it might appear at a quick glance. You might never guess that a Visio diagram or drawing could have all sorts of data stored with it. It might be an even further leap to assume that you could run reports on that stored data — but you could. Or how about the idea that you can *program* Visio shapes to behave or appear in a particular way? These are not trivial features. They greatly enhance your ability to use Visio in many creative ways, as you see throughout this chapter.

Storing Data in Visio Shapes

Shapes are more than what they appear to be. Some are *smart* — their behavior changes depending on the circumstances in which they're used. Others have very sophisticated geometry. All shapes can store data.

Why would you want to store data in a shape? You might not if your drawing illustrates a simple workflow process like Get bills⇨Enter payables⇨Pay bills⇨ Record in register⇨File paperwork. However, perhaps your process is more complex, and there are costs associated with each task. You may want to store cost data, resources required to complete the task, and the duration of time involved in each task.

Now, pretend you are a property manager in charge of distributing and tracking computer equipment for your company. (It may not sound as exciting as whale watching, but it pays!) In an office layout plan, you can store inventory numbers and owner information for each computer component shape shown in a drawing. You may want to store additional information, such as serial numbers, acquisition dates, manufacturer names, or model numbers.

Visio calls any type of custom data you store in a shape *custom properties data.* The data is entered in a shape's custom property *fields* under field names like Inventory Number or Owner. Many Visio shapes have built-in fields for entering custom property data. For example, all office layout shapes include inventory number and owner fields. Flowchart shapes contain fields for recording cost, duration, and resources.

Surprise! Some Visio shapes don't have custom properties fields. (Some shapes are too ordinary for you to care about storing data in them.) To find out if a shape has custom property fields, select the shape and choose Shape➪Custom Properties; alternatively, you can right-click on the shape and then choose Shape➪Custom Properties. If the shape contains custom property fields, Visio displays a Custom Properties dialog box like the one shown in Figure 13-1. If the shape does not have custom shapes, a message tells you so.

Figure 13-1: When a shape has custom properties, the data appears in the Custom Properties dialog box.

Field names   Data

Custom Properties

Inventory Number: 4982-1C

Owner: Stanley Walters

Prompt

Enter the person or group responsible for this item.

?   Define...   OK   Cancel

Another way to display custom properties data is with the Custom Properties window. (See Figure 13-2.) The nice thing about this window is that it stays on the screen so you can constantly monitor custom properties data as you click different shapes in a drawing. Each time you click a shape, that shape's data is shown. If a selected shape doesn't contain data, the box simply says No Custom Properties. But the Custom Properties window isn't just a display box; you can use it to edit data as well. Just click a field and start typing to enter or change data.

You can float the Custom Properties window by dragging it anywhere on the screen, and you can dock it along any edge of the drawing area. Like the Pan and Zoom window, when the Custom Properties window is docked, you can roll it up like a window shade — click the thumbtack icon and then move the mouse away from the window. To make the window reappear, move the mouse over the title bar. For more details, see Chapter 2.

Custom Properties window   Selected shape

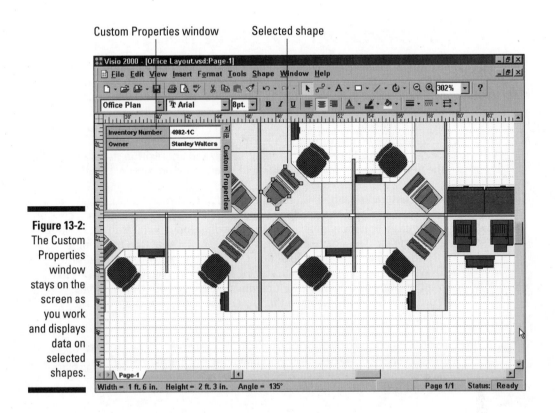

Figure 13-2:
The Custom
Properties
window
stays on the
screen as
you work
and displays
data on
selected
shapes.

Entering custom properties data

When a Visio shape contains custom properties fields, entering the data is easy:

1. **Open the drawing that has the shape you want to store data in.**

2. **Click the shape for which you want to store data.**

3. **Choose Shape⇨Custom Properties or right-click the shape and then choose Shape⇨Custom Properties.**

   Visio displays a Custom Properties dialog box like the one shown in Figure 13-1. The fields that appear in the box depend on the shape you selected in Step 1.

4. **In each field, enter the data you want to store.**

5. **Click the OK button.**

Editing custom properties fields

The custom properties fields for Visio's shapes are predefined, but that doesn't mean they're inflexible — you can change them with the Custom Properties Editor. Visio lets you do this so that the fields are meaningful to your particular situation. If Materials better describes what you want to track than Resources does, why not change the field name? Suppose you want to create an office layout drawing, but for each equipment shape, you want to store data on serial numbers, manufacturers, and acquisition dates in addition to the fields already provided. You need to add custom property fields.

Use the Custom Properties Editor to change, add, or delete fields in a Visio shape. You can also use the editor to add fields to a custom shape you created. In either case, you individually edit the custom property fields for each shape in either the local stencil or the standalone stencil. (Aha! Don't remember what local and standalone stencils are? Refer to Chapter 12.) When you edit the fields of shapes in the standalone stencil, the changes affect the shapes in the current drawing and every other drawing you create with that stencil. If you edit property fields of shapes in the local stencil, only the shapes in the current drawing are affected.

Although deleting custom property fields is possible, it's best not to do so with Visio-created shapes. Doing so may affect other aspects of the shape's behavior that you're not aware of. Feel free, however, to add, change, or delete fields that you have created.

The Custom Properties Editor is actually a wizard, so using it is very easy. (Refer to Chapter 11 for more information on using wizards.) Follow these steps:

1. **Choose Tools⇨Macros⇨Custom Properties Editor.**

   Visio displays the first screen of the Custom Properties Editor Wizard as shown in Figure 13-3.

2. **In the first screen, choose the stencil or drawing for which you want to edit custom properties; then click the Next button.**

   The choice you make determines which wizard screens you see next.

3. **Follow the instructions on the rest of the screens and then click the Finish button when the instructions are complete.**

As you work through the stencil screens, be prepared to provide the name of the drawing or stencil whose shapes you want to edit. When adding custom properties fields to a shape, choose names for the fields before you start the wizard. Be sure to click the More Info buttons in the wizard if you want details about information the wizard is asking for.

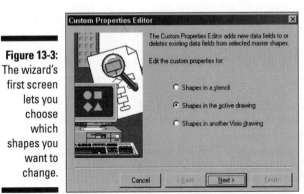

Figure 13-3:
The wizard's first screen lets you choose which shapes you want to change.

Want to test whether your custom property fields have really changed? Drag a shape onto your drawing from the stencil you edited. Right-click on the shape and then choose Shape⇨Custom Properties. The Custom Properties dialog box appears, and the changes you made to the field names are shown. Now you can enter the data to be stored.

Reporting on Data Stored in Visio Shapes

Why store data in shapes unless you can report on it? Data sitting in a shape is of limited use as reference information; it's much more useful as a report. Visio provides the tools you need to generate inventory and numeric reports from the data stored in your shapes. An *inventory report* typically counts items (or counts duplicate items). A *numeric report* typically calculates (totals, averages, maximums, minimums, and the like), though you can include more complex calculations by using spreadsheet formulas.

Now add one more dimension to the picture. When you use layers in your drawing, you can report more precisely on the data stored in shapes. For example, in a space-plan drawing, you may have plumbing on one layer, electrical on another, structural walls on another, and cubicle walls, dividers, and fixed furniture on another. Now you have the flexibility to create reports for one layer at a time, a combination of layers, or all layers.

Creating a report

When you're ready to create an inventory or numeric report from data stored in shapes, choose Tools⇨Property Report. This command starts the Property Reporting Wizard, which guides you through the process of creating a report.

Wondering how to specify mathematical calculations for a report? Don't worry, the wizard asks you. Do you want to know how to select shapes to report on? The wizard asks you this, too. I encourage you to experiment with the wizard until you get the results you want. Remember that each screen in a wizard has a Back button in case you change your mind about any choices you make.

Midway through the wizard screen journey, Visio creates and displays the report in a spreadsheet-type format. Think of it as a trial report — you can always change it. If you're happy with the report and want to save it outside Visio, you can save it as a spreadsheet as a Microsoft Excel file (.XLS) or as a text file (.TXT) by clicking the Save tool just above the spreadsheet grid on the wizard screen. If you want to change anything about the report, click the Back button to return to the wizard and make changes to the spreadsheet/report data.

When the report is the way you want it, the wizard asks you how you want the report formatted: You can add a title, column headings, or perhaps a file-name. When you click Finish on the last wizard screen, the data is pasted into your drawing but not as a spreadsheet. The data is pasted in a special report shape that looks similar to the table shown in Figure 13-4.

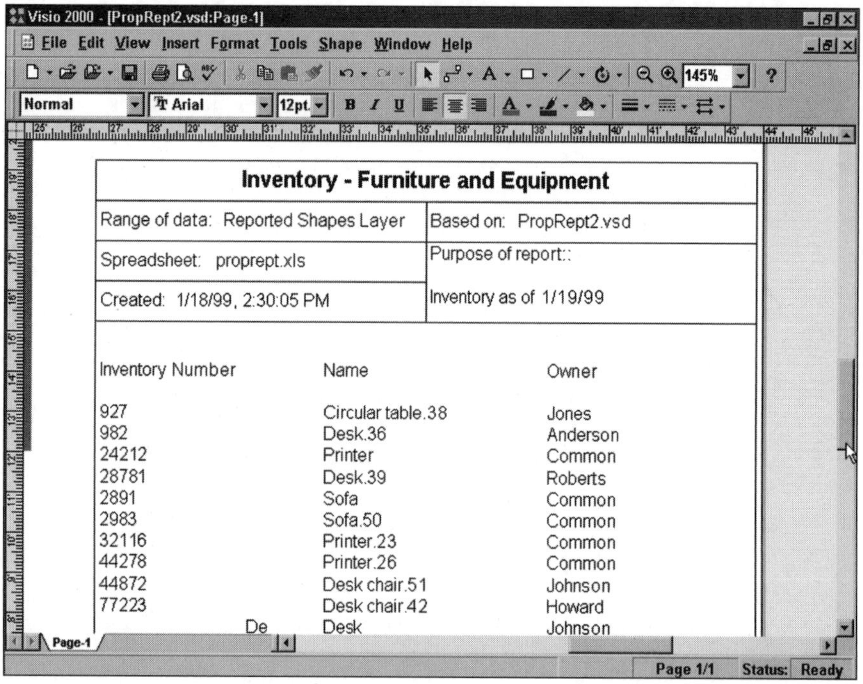

Figure 13-4: This furniture and equipment inventory was generated by the Property Reporting Wizard.

Updating reports

After you spend time creating reports, do you want to re-create them every time your data changes? You probably want to do that about as much as you want a root canal. Fortunately, Visio understands this, so it lets you update existing reports with new data by using — you guessed it — the Property Reporting Wizard. The wizard can update the data as long as the report is complete and pasted into your drawing in a report shape like the one shown in Figure 13-4. If you saved the report data as a spreadsheet when you originally created the report, the Property Reporting Wizard generates a new spreadsheet when you update the report. When the new spreadsheet appears, you can save it under a new name or overwrite the previous file.

To update a report, use these steps:

1. **In your drawing, right-click the report shape.**

   The shortcut menu appears.

2. **Choose Update Property Report.**

   The Property Reporting Wizard loads and updates your report data.

3. **If you originally saved the report data as a spreadsheet, the wizard displays a new spreadsheet reflecting the updated data. To save the spreadsheet, click the Save tool above the spreadsheet.**

   Voilà! The wizard finishes its task and updates the report shape in the drawing.

Customizing Shape Behavior

Are you tired yet of hearing about how smart Visio's shapes are? Don't go to sleep on me yet — there's more. Visio lets you set a shape's *behavior,* as discussed later in this chapter. You can pick and choose the characteristics you want a shape to have.

You can define the behavior and attributes of any shape — a Visio shape or a shape of your creation. After you change a shape's behavior on a drawing, the *document stencil* (a sort of history log stencil that's stored with your drawing) contains the shape so you can use it again and again in that drawing. If you want to use the shape in other drawings, save the shape as a master on a custom or Visio stencil. (For details on saving a shape as a master, refer to Chapter 12.)

Using the SmartShape Wizard

If you want to change several shape attributes all in one place, using the SmartShape Wizard is the best way to do it. This wizard addresses four major areas of shape behavior and appearance:

- **Built-in connectors.** You can add connectors to those shapes that don't have any built in so you can pull a connector from a shape.

- **Hidden note.** You can add a note or comment to a shape that you can show or hide by using a command on the shortcut menu.

- **Protect shape attributes.** You can lock certain attributes — such as size, position, or formatting style — to prevent them from being changed.

- **Text.** You can place a shape's text box, decide whether text rotates when you rotate the shape, and determine whether the font size automatically adjusts based on the amount of text in the text box.

In the following section, "Setting shape behavior with a menu command," you see that Visio's Format menu has commands for controlling shape behavior, shape protection, and double-click behavior. If you compare the options available there to the SmartShape Wizard, you notice that some of the options are the same and some are different. How do you know whether to use the SmartShape Wizard or the menu commands? As a general guideline, using the SmartShape Wizard is best when you want to make more global changes — changes you may want to save and apply to a master shape that you can use in many drawings. Use the commands on the Format menu when you want to make changes to selected shapes.

To use the SmartShape Wizard, follow these steps:

1. **Open the drawing that contains the shape you want to change.**

2. **Click the shape whose behavior you want to define.**

3. **Choose Tools⇨Macros⇨Visio Extras⇨SmartShape Wizard.**

   The SmartShape Wizard screen, shown in Figure 13-5, appears on your screen. All your options are shown on the bottom-left side of the first wizard screen.

4. **Click all the options that you want to change.**

5. **Click the Change Option button.**

   Visio displays a screen with questions about the first option that you checked.

6. **Click the Next button.**

   When you answer all the questions for the first option that you checked, the wizard returns to the first screen. (For some options, the wizard may display two or three screens' worth of questions.)

7. **Repeat Steps 5 and 6 until you complete all the options that you checked.**

8. **Click the Finish button.**

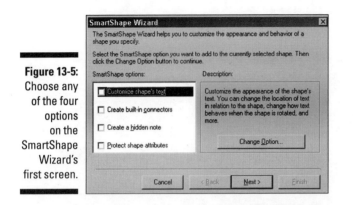

Figure 13-5:
Choose any
of the four
options
on the
SmartShape
Wizard's
first screen.

Setting shape behavior with a menu command

The Visio Format menu also has a command for changing shape behavior. Choosing Format⇨Behavior displays the Behavior dialog box. This lets you decide how a shape behaves, how a shape displays on-screen, how the shape resizes when it's part of a group, and how its connectors behave (whether its connectors are routable; refer to Chapter 6 for more information). The Behavior dialog box also lets you define what happens when you double-click a shape.

If these are the attributes you want to set, use the Format⇨Behavior command rather than the SmartShape Wizard.

Here's how to use the Format⇨Behavior command:

1. **In your drawing, select the shape or shapes you want to change.**

2. **Choose Format⇨Behavior.**

   The Behavior tab is already selected. Visio displays the Behavior tab in the Behavior dialog box, as shown in Figure 13-6.

3. **In the Interaction Style area, choose whether you want the selected shape to behave as a 1-D or 2-D shape.**

4. **In the Selection Highlighting area, choose the shape attributes you want to be visible when the shape is selected in the drawing.**

5. **In the Resize Behavior area, choose how you want the selected shape to behave if it's grouped with other shapes.**

6. **Click the Placement tab. Choose an option for Placement Behavior from the drop-down list.**

   Depending on the option you choose, other settings in the dialog box are either available or grayed out.

7. **Click the OK button.**

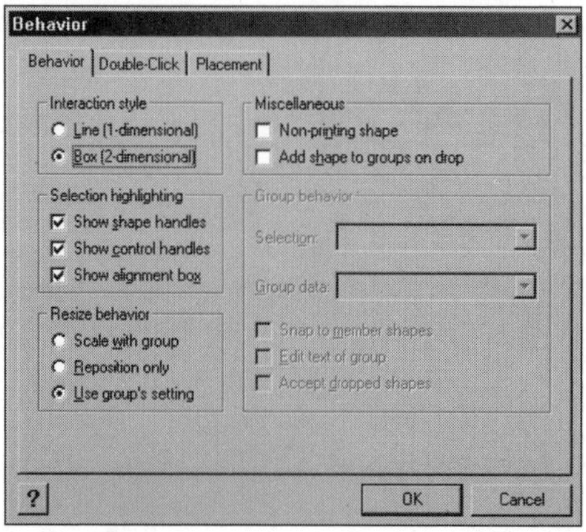

Figure 13-6:
Use the
Behavior
dialog box
to change
the behavior
of selected
shapes.

Setting a shape's double-click behavior

One of the coolest Visio features is the capability to set how a shape behaves when you double-click it. By default, a shape's text box opens when the shape is double-clicked, but a bunch of other choices are available. You can set a shape's double-click behavior to open a grouped shape, display a help screen, run a macro, jump to another page in the drawing, or do nothing at all (sort of like a pet rock).

Jumping to another page is a way to create a *drill-down drawing*. Figure 13-7 shows an overview diagram of a *wide area network* (WAN) covering China, Taiwan, and Japan. The map is impressive enough on its own, but the truly slick feature is that you can drill down to another page of the drawing that shows a detail map.

When you double-click the Bridge shape (about in the middle of China), Visio switches to the drawing called China LAN, as shown in Figure 13-8. This map is the second page of the same drawing shown in Figure 13-7. Now that you're here, how do you get back? Check out the callout in the upper-right corner of the drawing. When you double-click it, Visio returns to Page 1.

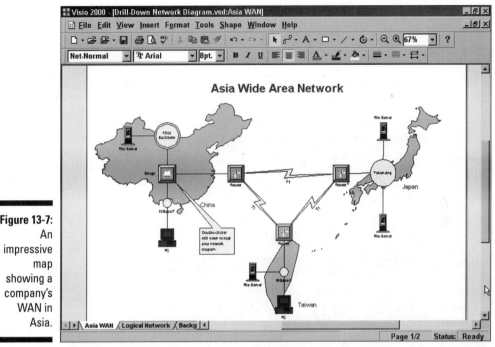

Figure 13-7:
An
impressive
map
showing a
company's
WAN in
Asia.

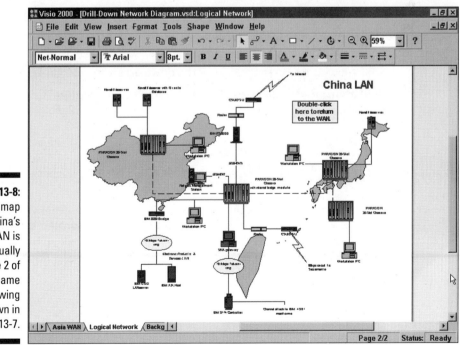

Figure 13-8:
A detail map
of China's
LAN is
actually
Page 2 of
the same
drawing
shown in
Figure 13-7.

Use these steps to set a shape's double-click behavior:

1. **In your drawing, select the shape that you want to change.**

2. **Choose Format⇨Behavior and then choose the Double-Click tab.**

   Visio displays the Double-Click tab of the Behavior dialog box, as shown in Figure 13-9.

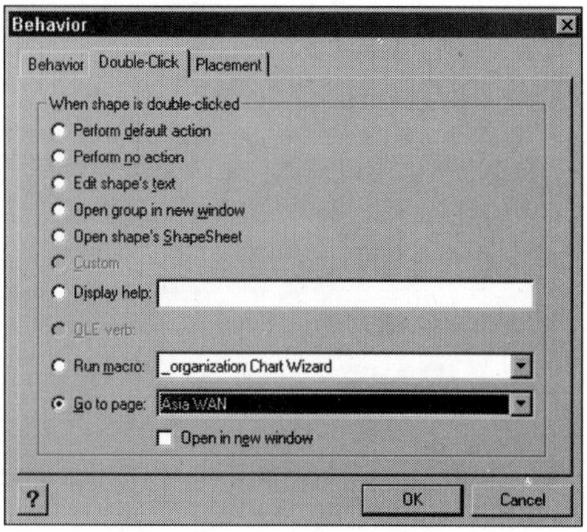

Figure 13-9:
Use the
Double-
Click tab
in the
Behavior
dialog box
to set a
shape's
double-click
behavior.

3. **Choose one of the options listed.**

   If you choose Run Macro, click the down-arrow to select a macro from the list.

   If you choose Go to Page, click the down-arrow to select a drawing page.

4. **If appropriate, check the Open in New Window option.**

5. **Click the OK button.**

Protecting Your Work

When you create drawings that you're going to share with others, you want to protect your work from unwitting destroyers. You can protect entire drawings from being changed or you can protect selected aspects of a shape from being changed. The following sections discuss the several methods available for helping you protect your work.

Keeping shapes from being changed

Using either the SmartShape Wizard or a menu command, you can keep shapes in a drawing from being changed. When you use the wizard, you have more locking options than you have with the menu command. Both of these options are described in this section.

Securing with the SmartShape Wizard

The SmartShape Wizard can change many aspects of a shape, one of which is its *protection*. You protect a shape either by locking certain aspects of it or by locking the entire shape. When you run the SmartShape Wizard and choose the Protect Shape Attributes option, the wizard displays the screen shown in Figure 13-10. You can use the SmartShape Wizard to set protection on any of the attributes, as shown in Figure 13-10.

Figure 13-10: Use the SmartShape Wizard to set protection on one or more shape attributes.

The lock options listed in Figure 13-10 are self-explanatory. When an option is grayed out, it doesn't apply to the shape that's currently selected. For example, the Prevent Ungrouping option doesn't apply when you select a single, ungrouped shape to lock, so the option is grayed in the dialog box.

To run the SmartShape Wizard for shape protection, use these steps:

1. **Open the drawing that contains the shape that you want to protect.**

2. **Select the shape or shapes you want to protect.**

   To select more than one shape, hold down the Shift key as you click shapes.

3. **Choose Tools⇨Visio Extras⇨SmartShape Wizard. (Refer to Figure 13-5.)**

4. **Click the Protect Shape Attributes option.**

5. **Click the Change Option button. Visio displays the SmartShape Wizard Protection screen (refer to Figure 13-10).**

6. **Click Next and then click Finish.**

If you want the protection to apply to the shape every time you use the shape, add it to a custom or Visio stencil. (See Chapter 12 for more information about stencils.)

Using a menu command to lock your shape

Another way to lock a shape's aspect is by choosing Format⇨Protection. This brings up the dialog box, as shown in Figure 13-11. Like the SmartShape Wizard, this command lets you lock aspects of a shape to prevent them from being changed. Notice that all of the options listed in the Protection dialog box are also available using the SmartShape Wizard. If you want to lock only one aspect of a shape, using this command is quicker than using the wizard. Also, when you want to unlock an aspect, using the Format⇨Protection command may be quicker than using the wizard.

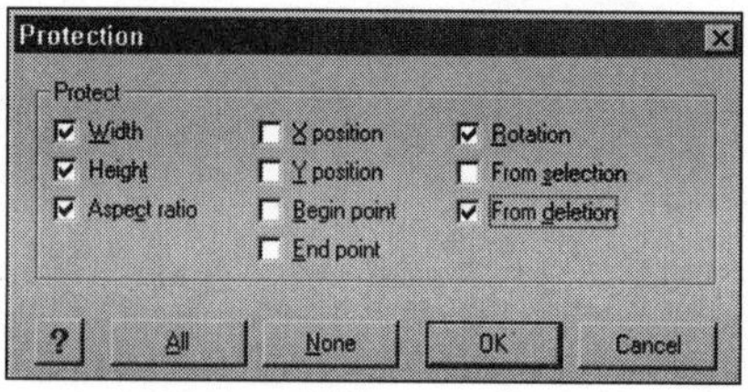

Figure 13-11: Choose Format⇨ Protection to display this dialog box.

To lock selected aspects of a shape using the Format⇨Protection command, follow these steps:

1. **Open the drawing that contains the shape that you want to protect.**

2. **Select the shape or shapes you want to protect.**

To select more than one shape, hold down the Shift key as you click the shapes.

3. **Choose Format⇨Protection.**

The Protection dialog box comes up (refer to Figure 13-11).

4. **Click each shape aspect that you want to lock.**

5. **Click the OK button.**

If you choose to protect a shape from selection, be aware that you must use the Tools⇨Protect Document command and then choose the Shapes option. This makes a shape unselectable. The Tools⇨Protect Document command is described in the following section.

Keeping drawings secure

You have several options for protecting drawings from change. The method you choose depends on the results you want to achieve. All the methods make a drawing readable by others, but not changeable (to whatever degree you define).

Password-protecting a drawing

Password protection in Visio probably isn't what you expect it to be. Password protection does *not* prevent a drawing from being opened without a password; rather, it protects certain *aspects* of the drawing from being changed. For example, when you password-protect a drawing, you can choose to protect styles, backgrounds, shapes, and master shapes, which means other users can't change these aspects of the file without knowing the password and exposing the file.

The Backgrounds option is a good solution for partially locking a drawing. For example, if you want other users to be able to edit the actual drawing but not the shapes on the background page, protect only the background. You can also protect shapes from being changed, but *beware!* To protect shapes, you must password-protect the drawing *in addition to* using the Format⇨ Protection command to protect shapes from selection. If you do one without the other, shapes are *not* protected from change.

Use these steps to password-protect a drawing from specific changes:

1. **Open the drawing that you want to protect.**

2. **Choose View⇨Window⇨Drawing Explorer.**

   Visio opens the Drawing Explorer window, as shown in Figure 13-12.

3. **Right-click the icon that is to the left of the drawing's filename. Select Protect Document from the shortcut menu that appears.**

   Visio displays the Protect Document dialog box, as shown in Figure 13-13.

4. **Enter a password in the Password box.**

   Don't forget your password and don't forget whether you used uppercase or lowercase characters!

5. **Check any or all of the drawing aspects (styles, shapes, previews, backgrounds, or master shapes) that you want to protect.**

6. **Click the OK button.**

Current filename and icon

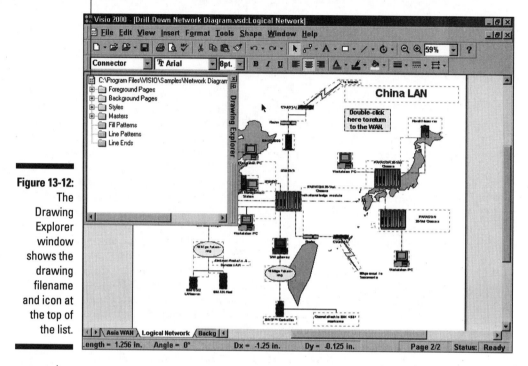

Figure 13-12:
The Drawing Explorer window shows the drawing filename and icon at the top of the list.

When you want to make changes to the drawing again, choose Tools⇨ Unprotect Document and enter your password. This unlocks the file.

Figure 13-13:
Enter a password in the Protect Document dialog box.

Locking layers

Locking layers protects parts. Now say that five times really fast. If you want other users to be able to edit some but not other layers, *locking layers* is a perfect solution. When a layer is locked, shapes on that layer can't be selected or changed in any way. Be aware, however, that if the user knows how to unlock the layer, shapes on that layer can be changed. You can't password-protect a layer.

To lock one or more layers of a drawing, do this:

1. **Open the drawing whose layers you want to protect.**

2. **Right-click the toolbar area and select the View toolbar from the drop-down menu.**

3. **Click the Layer Properties tool (it looks like a stack of pages) on the View toolbar to display the Layer Properties dialog box.**

4. **In the dialog box, put a check mark in the Lock column for each layer you want to lock.**

5. **Click the OK button.**

Saving files as read-only

If you truly want to keep other users from changing a drawing, the best way to protect the drawing is to save it as a read-only file. The file can't be changed no matter what other protections are set in the drawing or file. The only way another user can work around changing the file is to save a writable version of the file under a different name and then change that file. Your file is still protected in that case.

To save a file as read-only, follow these steps:

1. **Open the drawing that you want to save as a read-only file.**

2. **Choose File⇨Save As.**

   Visio displays the Save As dialog box shown in Figure 13-14.

3. **Click the drop-down arrow on the Save In box. Select from the list the folder you want to save the file in.**

4. **In the File Name box, type the name you want to save the file as.**

5. **In the Save box, click the Read Only check box.**

6. **Click the Save button.**

Check the Read Only option

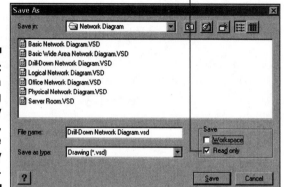

Figure 13-14:
To protect a
drawing
from any
changes,
choose the
Read Only
option.

Chapter 14

Using Visio with Other Programs

In This Chapter

▶ Generating drawings from data stored in other programs

▶ Incorporating drawings into non-Visio programs

▶ Linking and embedding drawings in other documents

▶ E-mailing drawings

▶ Using drawings on the Internet

I rarely use files from one computer program all by themselves. Programs these days are not islands unto themselves. This chapter shows you how to incorporate Visio drawings in other programs and how to create Visio drawings using data, which includes text, shapes, or drawings stored in other programs. I also show you how to e-mail Visio drawings and use them on the Internet.

Creating Drawings from Data in Other Programs

Want to save yourself some work? If you have data stored in places other than Visio, such as Microsoft Excel, Microsoft Project, a database, or a simple text file, you can create drawings from your stored data. Why would you want to do that? Check out these three good reasons:

✔ **You can avoid re-entering data.** Maybe you have a lot of data that already exists in another program, such as Excel. Do you want to take the time to re-enter the entire database in Visio — just so that you can create a drawing? Probably not — and you shouldn't have to. (If only your Mom had said that when you sat facing your green beans.) If the data already exists, you can save yourself a lot of time by saving the file in a format that Visio can use to create a drawing for you.

✔ **You can enter the data in the program in which you use it most.** If your data doesn't already exist, sometimes it can be faster to enter the raw data in another program — the program where you really need the data — and have Visio do the work of creating a drawing for you.

✔ **You can share drawings with other Visio users who may not have the same applications that you use to store and compile data.** Suppose that you're a project manager and rely on Microsoft Project to schedule and track large projects. Your site managers, however, don't have Project on site. They do, however, have Visio. You can use Project to generate daily or weekly *Gantt charts* (which maps project tasks on a timeline) in Visio and e-mail them to your site managers. The managers don't need to have Project or know how to use it. (If only your Dad had said that when you stood facing the lawnmower.) All they need to do is open a Visio drawing.

Creating organization charts

It's easy to create Visio organization charts from employee data stored in a database, in Excel, and in comma-separated variable (.CSV) and text (.TXT) files. (You can create comma-separated variable files and text files using any text editor or word processing program.) The data must be set up in a format that Visio can work with.

In database and spreadsheet files:

✔ Columns represent fields

✔ The first row represents column headings

✔ Remaining rows represent records

In a .TXT or .CSV file:

✔ The first row represents column headings

✔ Remaining rows represent records

Because a .CSV file has no columns, individual fields are separated by a comma. (This is known as a *comma-delimited file;* the comma is a *delimiter.*) Text files typically separate individual fields with a tab.

In order to generate a Visio organization chart from a data file, the file must include three fields:

✔ Employee name

✔ A unique identifier for each employee, whether a name or number

✔ The person the employee reports to

Take a gander at Figure 14-1, which illustrates a .CSV file that's used as input for generating an organization chart. This is how the file should look.

The fields don't have to appear in any particular order; the wizard finds the data it needs based on the column headings. To leave a field blank, enter a comma between the two commas used to separate entries. (In an Excel file, leave the cell blank.) Notice in Figure 14-1 that a final field, Master_Shape, is added to the data file. This is not required, but you can use it if you want to choose a specific Visio shape for your data. You also can include more data fields in the organization chart, such as the employee's phone number or physical location.

A comprehensive database compiled by a large corporation's Human Resources department may include 30 or more fields of data on each employee. If your data file is this large, just generate a subset composed of the data that you want to use and then use that file as input for Visio.

To create an organization chart from an existing data file, use these steps:

1. **Start with a blank drawing in Visio.**

2. **Choose Tools⇨Macros⇨Organization Chart⇨Organization Chart Wizard.**

   Visio displays the first screen of the wizard.

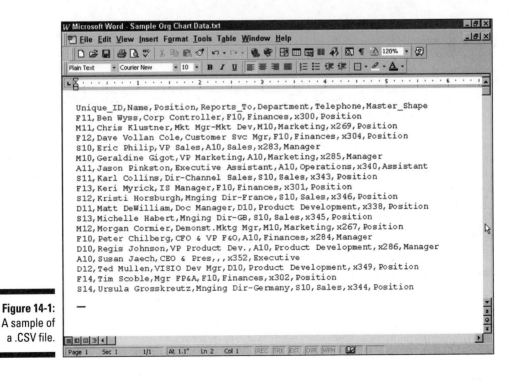

Figure 14-1:
A sample of a .CSV file.

3. **Click the Next button to go to the second screen of the wizard (see Figure 14-2).**

4. **Choose one of the following sources of your data and then click the Next button.**

   • A text, Org Plus (*.txt), or Microsoft Excel file

   • A Microsoft Exchange Server directory

   • An ODBC-compliant data source

5. **Follow the wizard (which asks questions about the design and layout of the organization chart) through to the last screen.**

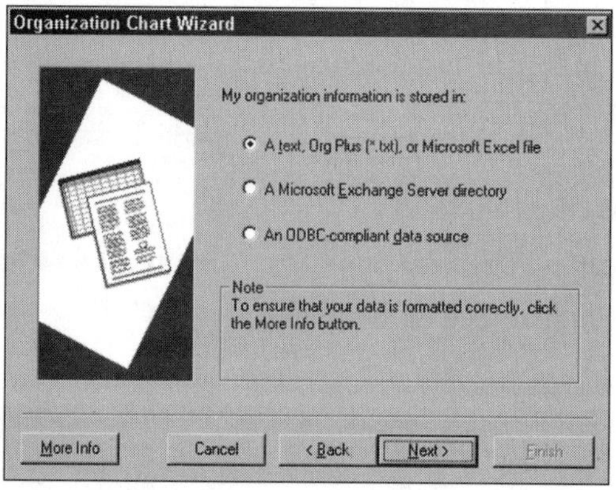

Figure 14-2:
This screen
asks you to
choose the
source of
your data.

> **Organization Chart Wizard**
>
> My organization information is stored in:
>
> ○ A text, Org Plus (*.txt), or Microsoft Excel file
>
> ○ A Microsoft Exchange Server directory
>
> ○ An ODBC-compliant data source
>
> Note
> To ensure that your data is formatted correctly, click the More Info button.
>
> More Info   Cancel   < Back   Next >   Finish

Visio creates the organization chart based on your data file, the fields that you choose to include, and the format you specify. If the chart has some unexpected results, go back, check the format and content of your input file, and then run the wizard again. The wizard creates a new file each time it's run.

If you choose an option in Step 4 for creating new data, create and save the data. Then run the wizard again, choosing Read Data From Existing File in Step 4.

The More Info button on most wizard screens is very helpful! If you ever need an explanation of the information the wizard's looking for, click this button to display a More Information dialog box.

Creating project timelines (aka Gantt charts)

A project timeline, or *Gantt chart,* includes information about the tasks that you need to complete to accomplish a goal, the duration of each task, their dependent tasks, and the resources required to complete each task. If the data that you want to use exists in a .TXT or .CSV file, fields must be separated by a tab or a comma, respectively. You can also either use data from Microsoft Excel in .XLS format or data from Microsoft Project in exchange format (.MPX). The data must include at least the following fields for each task:

- ✔ **Unique task number or identifier:** Any number or name that you give to a task to identify it uniquely.

- ✔ **Task name:** The name that you give to a task that's part of a project.

- ✔ **Duration:** The time allowed to complete a task.

- ✔ **Start date:** The date that you want a task to begin.

- ✔ **End date:** The date that you want a task to be completed.

- ✔ **Dependent task:** A task that can't be started until another task is completed. If the first task slips, the entire list of dependent tasks slips.

- ✔ **Resource:** The human resources or materials needed to complete a task.

The Gantt Chart Wizard can create a .TXT or .XLS template if your data doesn't exist yet. This saves you the time of setting up your text or Excel file with the required fields. Just use the template and fill in the data as described in the following steps.

To create a project timeline Gantt chart, use these steps:

1. **Start Visio, using the Timeline drawing type.**

2. **Choose Tools⇨Macros⇨Project Schedule⇨Gantt Chart.**

   Visio displays the Gantt Chart Options dialog box.

3. **Enter the tasks options, duration options, time units, and timescale range that apply to your project and then click the OK button.**

   Visio creates a Gantt chart placeholder in your Visio drawing.

4. **Now choose Tools⇨Macros⇨Project Schedule⇨Import Project Data.**

   Visio displays the Import Project Data dialog box.

5. **Choose the source of your data and then click the OK button.**

   - Choose the Enter Data in New Text File or Enter Data in New Excel Workbook option if you want to create the data.

   - Choose the Enter Data in New Microsoft Excel Workbook option if you want to create new data in an Excel spreadsheet.

   - Choose the Read Data From Existing File option if your data exists in a .TXT, .CSV, or spreadsheet file (like Excel). (Click the Browse button if you need to search for the file's location.)

   Depending on the data source you choose in Step 5, the wizard may display additional dialog boxes. If you are creating new data in a text or Excel file, the wizard tells you step-by-step what to do next. Enter the data for your chart in a text file or Excel file and then save the file. Now that you have existing data, you must rerun the Import Project Data macro (Step 4) and choose the Read Data From Existing File option.

Using Visio in Non-Visio Documents

The Windows *object linking and embedding* (OLE) feature makes it possible to share many different types of data and graphic images between Windows-compatible applications. You can link an entire Visio drawing or selected shapes from a Visio drawing to a document in any program that supports OLE. Most Windows programs support OLE.

For instance, you can insert Visio shapes or drawings into a Word document. You also can do the opposite — insert data or images from another application into Visio. This section describes the different methods for sharing data and images between programs.

Dragging or pasting shapes

If you want to use one of the Visio shapes in another document, the easiest way is to drag it right in! If both programs support Windows OLE (object linking and embedding is discussed in this chapter's later sections, "Linking shapes and drawings" and "Embedding shapes and drawings"), you can drag shapes from Visio into the program. Use these steps to copy a shape or an entire drawing to another document:

1. **Open the Visio drawing or stencil that holds the shape that you want to use.**

2. **Open the other application (such as Word or Excel) and the file where you want to insert a Visio shape.**

3. **Click the Maximize/Restore button (which looks just like the one in Windows) in Visio to make the Visio window smaller than full screen.**

4. **Click the Maximize/Restore button in the other application to make the window smaller than full screen.**

5. **Arrange the windows on the screen so that you can see the shape that you want to drag and a blank portion of the other document window.**

6. **To copy a shape (rather than just move it), press and hold the Ctrl key while you drag the shape from Visio into the other application's document area.**

   If you want to insert an entire Visio drawing in another document, choose Edit⇨Select All, press and hold the Ctrl key, and drag so that the shapes are copied instead of moved.

When you release the mouse button, the shape or shapes are pasted into your document.

You can also use the Cut, Copy, and Paste commands to accomplish the task of including a Visio shape in another document. The following steps show you how:

1. **Open the Visio drawing or stencil that holds the shape that you want to use.**

2. **Open the other application (such as Word or Excel) and the file where you want to insert a Visio shape.**

3. **Click the Maximize/Restore button (which looks just like the one in Windows) in Visio to make the Visio window smaller than full screen.**

4. **Click the Maximize/Restore button in the other application to make the window smaller than full screen.**

5. **Arrange the windows on the screen so that you can see the shape that you want to drag and a blank portion of the other document window.**

6. **In your drawing, select the shape or shapes that you want to paste in the other document.**

7. **To cut the shape(s) from Visio, choose Edit⇨Cut or press Ctrl+X. To copy the shape(s) from Visio, choose Edit⇨Copy or press Ctrl+C.**

8. **Click the other document where you want to paste the shape or shapes and choose Edit⇨Paste or press Ctrl+V.**

   The shape or shapes are pasted into the other document.

Neither of the methods just described (dragging or pasting shapes) makes any connection between the two files; these steps are similar to dropping a clip art image into a document. No association or connection between the two files or the data in each file is formed.

Linking shapes and drawings

Another way to share data between programs is to *link* data from one file to another. I can show you how to link Visio data to other files and be done with it, but an understanding of the difference between linking and embedding is essential. That is tackled later in this chapter's "Embedding shapes and drawings" section.

Linking creates a special connection between two files: the *source file* (where the data is created and displayed) and the *destination file* (where the data is displayed only). When you link data to a destination file, the original data stays in the source file where you created it. It's sort of like your Uncle Eddie after Thanksgiving dinner; it never really moves anywhere. The destination file makes a note of the data's *location* and looks to that location to display a *representation of the data.*

Still scratching your head? Think of it like this: Suppose you link a Visio drawing (the source file) to an Excel spreadsheet (the destination file). When you open your Excel spreadsheet, you see the Visio drawing displayed right before your eyes — like magic! But like the magician's sawed-in-half woman, it isn't really there. It's as if Excel opened up a door in the spreadsheet and moved your drawing right into the doorway. You see the drawing, but it isn't part of your Excel file. You still have only one drawing, and it's located in Visio.

Why do you care if the drawing is part of your destination file? Several reasons. When you update the drawing in Visio, the drawing is automatically updated in the other program, too. And, because the drawing isn't really part of the destination file, it doesn't increase your file size at all. One more thing: You can double-click the drawing in the other program and update it there. How is that possible, since the drawing isn't really in the other program? More magic. When you double-click the drawing, Visio actually starts and opens your drawing in its own window so that you can update the drawing using Visio menus and toolbars. When you finish updating the drawing and save it, close Visio. Your screen returns to the other program, where the file is automatically updated if you saved the changes in Visio.

All of these reasons make linking a good option to choose when you want to use a drawing in several different files and keep it updated in all its locations. To link data from a Visio drawing to another file, follow these steps:

1. **In Visio, open the drawing that you want to link to another file.**

   Note that the file must be saved before it can be linked.

2. **To link the entire drawing, choose Edit⇨Copy Drawing. To link a portion of the drawing, select the shapes that you want to link and choose Edit⇨Copy.**

3. **Open the document in the other program where you want to link the Visio drawing.**

4. **Choose Edit⇨Paste Special.**

   Some programs may use a different command for linking files. If this command is not on your menu, check the online help or user documentation for the program that you're using.

5. **In the Paste Special dialog box, choose Visio 5 Drawing Object from the list box.**

6. **Click the Paste Link radio button and then click the OK button.**

   The drawing or shapes that you linked are now displayed in the non-Visio program's document.

Embedding shapes and drawings

Embedding offers a way to share data between files that is different from linking. In fact, in some ways you can think of it as the opposite of linking. When you *embed* data in another file, it actually becomes part of the destination file, which means that the size of the destination file increases. If you update the data in the source file, the data in the destination file is *not* automatically updated. (Likewise, if you change the data in the destination file, the data in the source file remains unchanged.) Embedding is a good option to use when you definitely want the data to be part of your destination file, when you know the data doesn't need to be updated, or if you aren't storing a copy of the source file on your computer.

You can embed a new file that you create or you can embed an existing file. Use these steps to do either:

1. **Open the document in the program where you want to link the Visio drawing.**

2. **Choose Insert⇨Object.**

   The Object dialog box appears, as shown in Figure 14-3. Notice that the Create New tab is selected.

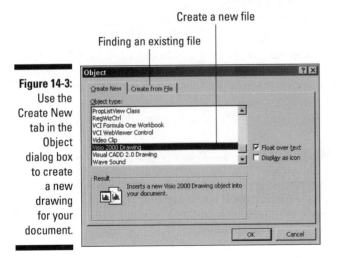

Create a new file

Finding an existing file

Figure 14-3:
Use the
Create New
tab in the
Object
dialog box
to create
a new
drawing
for your
document.

3. **Embed your drawing in one of the following ways:**

   • **To create a new Visio drawing:** Choose Visio 2000 Drawing from the list and click the OK button.

Visio starts in its own window. Create your drawing. Now click in the document window of the program that you're using. Visio automatically embeds the drawing in your document and closes the Visio window.

- **To embed an existing drawing:** Click the Create from File tab in the dialog box, enter the filename, and click the OK button. (If you don't know the filename, click the Browse button to find the file, as shown in Figure 14-4.)

Visio embeds the drawing in your document.

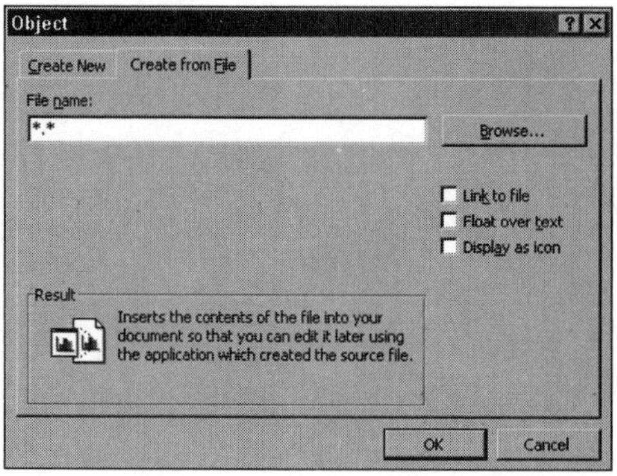

Figure 14-4:
On the Create from File tab in the Object dialog box, choose an existing drawing.

Object	? X
Create New	Create from File

File name:
`*.*`   Browse...

☐ Link to file
☐ Float over text
☐ Display as icon

Result
Inserts the contents of the file into your document so that you can edit it later using the application which created the source file.

OK   Cancel

When you use the Create New tab in the Object dialog box to create a new Visio drawing for your document, be aware that you can't save the drawing as a Visio file. If you want to save the drawing in Visio, create it first in Visio and then use the Create from File tab in the Object dialog box to embed the saved file.

Exporting shapes and drawings

When you want to use a Visio shape or drawing in a program that doesn't support OLE, your option is to *export* the file. Exporting converts the data in a Visio file to a non-Visio file format — one that you choose. In the other program, you then *import* the file as a picture.

The file type that you choose for exporting depends on two things: the program that you want to use the drawing in and how you're going to use the drawing. For example, if you're creating a PostScript document, you may want to export the Visio drawing in .ps format. If you want to make changes to the drawing using Adobe Illustrator, save the drawing in .ai format. If you just want to insert the drawing into another file as a picture without editing it, use one of the more common graphics formats, such as *.bmp, .tif, or .gif. If you want to give the drawing to a friend who uses a Mac, save the drawing in .pct format. Table 14-1 lists all the file types that you can use to export a Visio drawing.

Table 14-1	File Formats for Exporting Visio Drawings
Format	**File Extension**
HTML	.htm, .html
Adobe Illustrator	.ai
Computer graphics metafile	.cgm
Encapsulated PostScript	.eps
Enhanced metafile	.emf
Graphics interchange format	.gif
IGES drawing file format	.igs
JPEG	.jpg
Macintosh PICT format	.pct
Portable network graphics format	.png
PostScript file	.ps
Tag image file format	.tif
Vector markup	.vml
Windows bitmap	.bmp, .dib
Windows metafile	.wmf
Zsoft PC Paintbrush bitmap	.pcx

To export a Visio drawing (or selected shapes from a drawing), follow these steps:

1. **Start Visio and open the drawing that you want to export.**

   If you want to export a few shapes rather than the whole drawing, hold down the Shift key as you click the shapes that you want to export.

2. **Choose File⇨Save As to display the Save As dialog box.**

3. **Choose from the Save In drop-down menu the folder where you want to save the drawing.**

4. In the File Name box, type a name for the file.

5. Choose a file format from the Save As Type drop-down menu.

6. Click the Save button.

In the other program, use the program's Import command to bring the Visio drawing into the document.

Sending drawings via e-mail

If you use electronic mail and want to e-mail drawings to other Visio users, you can do so as long as your e-mail program supports the *Messaging Application Program Interface* (MAPI) protocol. (Check with your network administrator to see if your program supports MAPI protocol.) The message recipient must also have Visio running on his or her computer in order to view the Visio drawing.

To e-mail a drawing to another Visio user, use these steps:

1. **Start Visio and open the drawing that you want to send via e-mail.**

2. **Choose File⇨Send To⇨Mail Recipient.**

   Visio displays the Mail Profile dialog box. Your mail profile (such as Microsoft Outlook) is specified in the Profile Name box.

3. **Click the OK button or click the drop-down arrow to select a different mail profile.**

4. **Click the OK button again.**

   If your mail program isn't already running, it starts automatically. A new e-mail message is created with a Visio icon and the Visio filename already placed in the file.

5. **Enter the recipient's e-mail address, the subject, and any message that you want to appear with the file.**

6. **Send the message as you normally would.**

How do you view a Visio drawing sent to you by e-mail? Just start your e-mail program and display the e-mail message. The message contains a Visio icon for the drawing file. Double-click the icon to view the drawing.

If you're running Microsoft Office 2000 or 97, you can use the Office features that let you route an e-mail message to more than one user (for instance, so all users in your group can review a Visio drawing). To add a routing slip to an e-mail message, follow these steps:

1. **Open Visio and the drawing that you want to send.**

2. **Choose File⇨Send To⇨Routing Recipient to display the Routing Slip dialog box shown in Figure 14-5.**

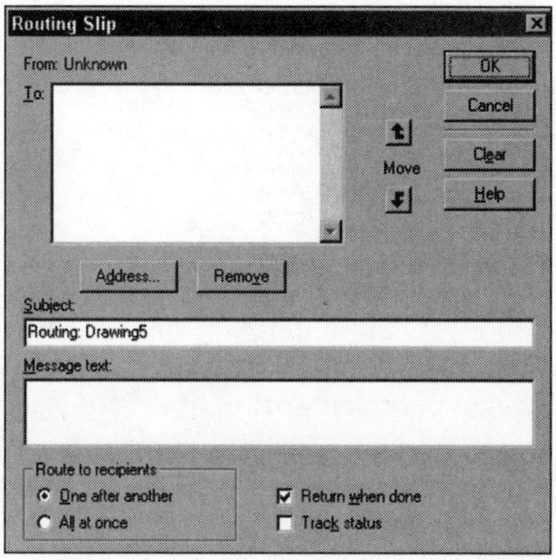

Figure 14-5:
Use the
Routing Slip
dialog box
to send a
Visio
drawing to
several
people.

3. **Click the Address button to display the Address Book dialog box and choose the recipients that you want to send the Visio drawing to and then click the OK button.**

4. **To route the drawing in a specific order, click a name in the list and then click the Move arrow (either up or down) to reorder the names.**

   Do this for all names until they are in the order that you want.

5. **In the Route to Recipients box, click the One After Another option if you're ordering the routing. If not, click the All at Once option.**

6. **Choose Return When Done to have the drawing sent back to you after everyone views it, or choose Track Status to receive an update after each person on the list views the drawing.**

7. **To add a message to the drawing, type the text in the Message Text box.**

8. **Click the OK button to close this dialog box.**

9. **Choose File⇨Send To⇨Next Routing Recipient to send the message.**

To store a drawing in a Microsoft Exchange folder, open the Visio drawing and choose File⇨Send To⇨Exchange Folder. Choose the folder that you want and click the OK button.

Using Visio Drawings on the Internet

Okay, admit it. You're so proud of your Visio drawings that you want to publish them on your Web site so that all the people who picked on you in high school can gawk in disbelief, right? You can save your drawings in HTML (Hypertext Markup Language) format when you create them, or you can convert existing files to HTML format. Either way, your drawings look as cool on your Web page as they do in Visio.

Adding hyperlinks to a drawing

A *hyperlink* is nothing more than a techie-sounding word for a leap. With just a click of the mouse, you can jump from the current page in your Visio drawing to another location. Using a hyperlink is sort of like setting a shape's double-click behavior, which lets you jump to another *page* in a drawing. (I show you all about this in Chapter 13.) But if you want to jump to another Visio drawing, to a file in another program, or to a Web site on the World Wide Web, follow these steps:

1. **Open the saved Visio drawing in which you want to create a hyperlink.**

   Your Visio drawing must be a saved file because the link is created by referencing your drawing's filename.

2. **To create a hyperlink from a page in the drawing, make sure that no shapes in the drawing are selected. To create a hyperlink from a specific shape, select the shape.**

3. **Choose Insert⇨Hyperlinks.**

   Visio displays the Hyperlinks dialog box shown in Figure 14-6.

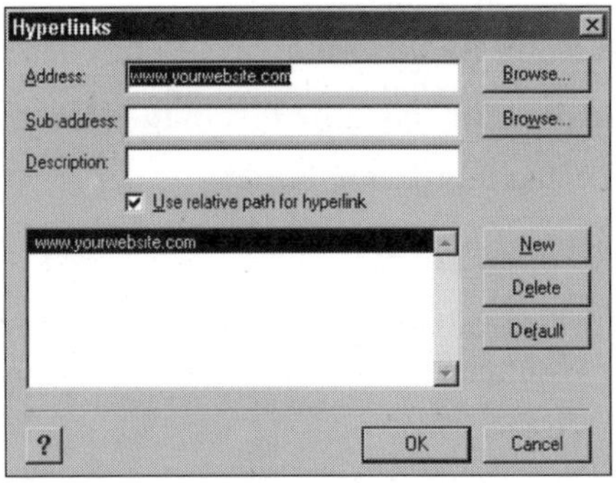

Figure 14-6:
In the Hyperlinks dialog box, tell Visio where you want to jump.

4. **In the Address box, either type the full path name to the file that you want to open or type the URL (Uniform Resource Locator).**

The location you name is called the *linked file.*

- **To enter a file path name:** Type the full directory name for a file on your own computer's hard disk or one that you have access to on a local network.

- **To enter a URL:** Type a Web site address on the World Wide Web, such as `http://www.visio.com` or `http://www.microsoft.com`. It's important that you include the `http://` in the URL; it indicates the protocol used to access the site. (Some sites use `ftp://` or other protocols.) If you don't know the path or URL, click the top Browse button. After you type your entry, the full path name appears in the Path box.

5. **(Optional) In the Sub-Address box you can enter an exact location in a file or Web site that you want to link to. If you are linking to a Visio drawing, you can click Browse to open the Hyperlinks dialog box and select a drawing page from a list.**

6. **(Optional) In the Description box, you can type a name that describes the location that you're linking to.**

7. **Click the OK button.**

To use your hyperlink, right-click the shape or drawing page, choose Hyperlink, and then choose Open or Open in New Window. Open in New Window lets you see the hyperlink as well as your Visio drawing.

Saving a drawing as an HTML page

If you want Visio to create a Web page for you and to include your drawing, saving the drawing as an HTML page is the way to go. If you save a multi-page drawing as an HTML page, Visio creates a separate HTML page for each page in the drawing. If your drawing includes hyperlinks — pointers in your drawing to other locations in the drawing, to other files, or to other locations on the World Wide Web — saving it in HTML format preserves the links, making it an *image map,* another name for a graphic file that has hyperlinks.

Use these steps to save a drawing as an HTML page:

1. **Start Visio and create or open the file that you want to save.**

2. **Choose File⇨Save As to display the Save As dialog box shown in Figure 14-7.**

3. **In the Save In box, choose the folder in which you want to save the file.**

4. **In the File Name box, type a name for the file, including the *.htm* file extension.**

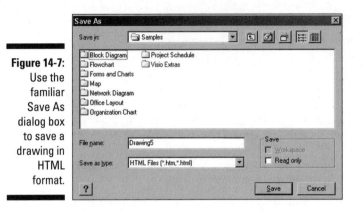

Figure 14-7:
Use the familiar Save As dialog box to save a drawing in HTML format.

5. **In the Save As Type box, choose HTML files (*.htm, *.html).**

6. **Click the Save button.**

   The Save As HTML dialog box appears, as shown in Figure 14-8, appears.

7. **Click the Filter Settings button.**

   The Filter Settings dialog box comes up. Now you can specify zoom percentage, dots per inch (dpi), or screen resolution on the Web page and then click the OK button.

Figure 14-8:
Click the Filter Settings button in the Save As HTML dialog box.

8. **If your drawing includes hyperlinks that you don't want to appear in the Web page, click the Options button.**

   The Export Options dialog box appears. Uncheck the Enable Image Maps check box, then click the OK button.

9. **Click the OK button to close the Save As HTML dialog box.**

   Visio displays a message asking if you want to view the HTML page. Click Yes to view the page using your Web browser.

Part V
The Part of Tens

The 5th Wave   By Rich Tennant

"Correction, Dad—Mom goes at the top of the organizational chart."

In this part . . .

The Part of Tens — a mysterious name that indicates you're going to learn at least ten things about *something*! Here, you discover answers to the ten most frequently asked questions from Visio's top trainers; survey ten of Visio's more interesting stencils and wizards; discover ten terrific tips for using Visio; and see ten sample drawings.

Chapter 15

Answers to Ten (Or So) Burning Questions about Visio

*T*he questions in this chapter come directly from Visio Corporation's top trainers. They say these are the top 10 (well, lucky 13, actually) most frequently asked questions by new users.

Can I Work with Other File Types Inside Visio?

You can open, or *import*, other file types with the Visio program, including AutoCAD drawings and Windows metafiles. To see a list of file formats that you can open, click the Open button and browse the Files of Type list in the Open dialog box.

Can I Change the Number of Recently Opened Files Listed at the Bottom of the File Menu?

The File menu typically lists the four most recently opened files, but you can change this number by choosing Tools⇨Options. On the General tab, the Recently Used Files box is under User Options. Type a new number in the Recently Used Files box.

Can I Customize My Drawing Environment?

You can customize your Visio drawing environment so that it suits your needs. For example, you can hide the grid and rulers if you don't care about precisely positioning your shapes and you want more screen space. (On the View menu, remove the check mark from the Ruler and Grid options.) You can change the Stencil view to display icons and names, icons only, or names only. (Right-click anywhere on the stencil's green background and then choose a view style.) You can also view page breaks while creating your drawing so that you can take care not to position shapes too close to the page's edge of the page. (See Chapter 3 for more information on printing.)

How Many Times Can I Undo?

By default, Visio can undo the last ten actions you have performed. To specify fewer or more actions, choose Tools⇨Options. On the General tab, type a new number in the Undo Levels box (under User Options).

How Do I Search for a Shape?

What? You don't want to open every stencil searching for a shape? Use Shape Explorer to find the shape. Choose Tools⇨Macros⇨Shape Explorer. In the Search For box, type what you are looking for and then click the Find Now button. For more information, see Chapter 11. (By the way, Shape Explorer isn't installed with a typical installation. You may have to reinstall Visio and choose the Custom/Complete option to get Shape Explorer.)

How Do I Unlock a Shape?

If you select a shape and it has gray padlock selection handles, the shape is locked to prevent changes. To unlock a shape, select the shape and then choose Format⇨Protection. For more information, see Chapter 13.

How Do I Copy Formatting from One Shape to Another?

Use the Format Painter to quickly copy formatting from one shape to another. Select a shape that's already formatted, click the Format Painter tool (it looks like a paintbrush) on the Standard toolbar and then click the shape that you want to format. For more information, see Chapter 8.

How Do I View Multiple Pages at the Same Time?

You can view multiple pages at the same time by opening pages in separate windows and then tiling the windows. Choosing Edit⇨Go To⇨Page displays the Page dialog box. At the bottom of the dialog box, choose Open Page in New Window. To tile the windows, choose Window⇨Tile.

How Do I Check a Drawing for Page Breaks?

You can quickly check to see whether your drawing fits within the printable area by choosing View⇨Page Breaks. For more information about printing and page breaks, refer to Chapter 3.

How Can I Let Visio Know that I Always Save My Files in the Same Folder?

Choose Tools⇨Options, click the File Paths tab, and then type the path in the Drawings box. You can also set default file paths for other files, such as templates and stencils.

Okay, just a few more favorite questions!

How Can I Draw Shapes Precisely?

When you're drawing irregular shapes using the Pencil or Freeform tools, the snap feature can make you crazy, snapping shapes and lines everywhere! To turn off the snap feature, choose Tools➪Snap & Glue and then uncheck the Snap check box (under Currently Active). For more information about using snap and glue, see Chapter 8.

Can I Count Shapes on a Layer?

To see how many shapes are assigned to a layer, choose View➪Layer Properties and then click the # column (which is in the Layer Properties dialog box). The numbers tell only how many shapes are on each layer; they don't provide an accurate count of how many shapes are in your drawing. This is because a single shape may be assigned to two or more layers. For more information about working with layers, see Chapter 10.

How Do I Rotate Shapes to a Specific Angle?

You can use the Size & Position window to specify the angle of rotation to a precision of 0.01 degree. To specify a precise angle, select a shape and then choose View➪Windows➪Size & Position to display the Size & Position window. Alternatively, simply select a shape and then click the status bar. The Size & Position window appears. For more information on working with shapes, see Chapter 8.

Chapter 16

Ten of Visio's Coolest Stencils and Wizards

*B*y now you're probably getting the idea that all of Visio's shapes are organized by category and stored on stencils. This arrangement makes shapes easy to find and keeps stencils to a manageable size. Wizards make the job of creating drawings as easy as possible by providing step-by-step instructions for completing a specific task (such as creating a project time-line or an organization chart from existing data). But when you have a spe-cific task to do, you probably don't want to spend a whole lot of time snooping around in Visio just to see what's there — save your snooping for your big sister's diary! This chapter is designed to show you some examples of stencils and wizards that you might otherwise overlook.

Check Out These Stencils

Regardless of the type of drawing you create, you can open any stencil any time and use its shapes in the current drawing. Don't ever let the name of a stencil pigeonhole you. You can find all sorts of shapes to use on seemingly unrelated stencils. For a quick view of the myriad of shapes included in many of the Visio stencils, see Appendix A.

Many of the shapes that you see in the stencils in this chapter have more than one control point. To find out what a control point is for, float the mouse pointer over the control point — do not click the mouse. A tip pops up and tells you what the control point is for. See Chapter 4 for more detailed infor-mation on control points.

Remember that you can get pop-up tips on any shape just by floating the mouse over the shape in the stencil. If you need more help, drag the shape onto the drawing and right-click it. Choose Help from the shortcut menu. You can always delete the shape later.

Organization Chart stencil

The Organization Chart stencil is by far one of the slickest new features in Visio 2000. Reading your mind would be the only quicker way to create an organization chart! This stencil works by having you drop subordinate shapes (that would be the worker bees) on top of their superior shapes (that would be the suits). When you do this, Visio automatically connects the boxes and spaces and aligns them perfectly. This stencil also includes a few new shapes that let you drop multiple shapes at once. For example, assume a customer service manager has six worker bees reporting to him or her — you can drag and drop one shape for all six employees. Visio just asks you how many shapes you want and automatically adds and aligns them all at once.

When you choose the organization charts type for your drawing, Visio automatically adds an Organization Chart menu to the menu bar and displays the Organization Chart toolbar. On the toolbar you find buttons that let you change a chart's horizontal, vertical, or side-by-side layout. You can also quickly move a misplaced shape up or down in the organization chart. Be sure to check out the Organization Chart menu, which offers the following options and more:

- **Compare Organization Data** lets you compare one version of an organization chart with an updated version.

- **Convert Shape** lets you change a shape from one type to another (such as a Consultant shape to a Staff shape) without having to drag out a new shape.

- **Export Organization Data** lets you send all the data stored in an organization chart to an Excel file, a .TXT file, or a .CSV (comma-delimited) file. The data uniquely identifies each person and who they report to. If you enter custom properties data for each person, this information automatically exports as well.

- **Find Person** lets you find *any* text, not just a name. This is a great way to find someone in a large organization.

- **Hide Subordinates** lets you display only the levels you want in the organizational structure.

Visio offers the Organization Chart Wizard as well. Typically, you use the wizard if you have data already stored in another file, but you can use the wizard to create an organization chart using new data, too. Refer to Chapter 14 for examples.

Geographical Maps stencil

Visio has a bunch of stencils for drawing geographical maps. Just pick the part of the world that you want to draw:

- ✔ Africa
- ✔ Asia
- ✔ Europe
- ✔ North and South America
- ✔ Middle East
- ✔ United States and Canada

In addition to the first six stencils listed here, which contain shapes for the countries, states, or provinces that make up a region, the Maps of the World stencil contains world and continental maps. (See Figure 16-1.) These stencils are great for creating drawings that show sales or branch offices, service centers, carrier routes (for airlines or transport companies), wide area network locations, video conferencing facilities, weather patterns, temperature zones — the possibilities are endless. The "Build Region Wizard" section later in this chapter shows you how to use this wizard to create regions automatically from a selection of state, province, or country shapes.

Figure 16-1:
It takes only one shape from the Maps of the World stencil to create this map.

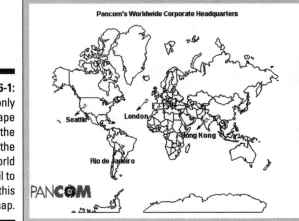

Directional Maps stencil

The Directional Maps stencil contains every shape you can imagine for creating roads, bridges, three-way and four-way intersections, cloverleafs, railroad tracks, metro lines, traffic signs, emergency services (such as hospitals and fire departments), landmarks, and bodies of water. This stencil is the one that you want for creating various maps: sightseeing, directional, area, tour, public transit, and so on. (Figure 16-2 shows a directional map.) If you're creating a city map in which streets run at odd angles, be sure to refer to Chapter 9 to see how you can rotate the page to make these streets easier to draw.

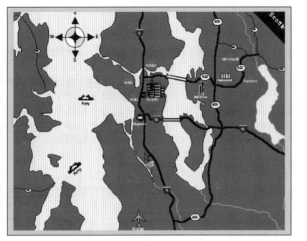

Figure 16-2:
All shapes used in this map are created using the Directional Maps stencil.

Marketing Diagrams stencil

Ever notice how marketeers (that's marketeers, not Mouskateers) are experts at illustrating data? They come up with some pretty snazzy looking charts, graphs, and diagrams. If you're not a marketing-type person, you may never think to look at the Marketing Diagrams stencil, but you should — this stencil has shapes you might find useful even outside of marketing; they have a generic structure. Take, for example, a matrix, which is a classic marketer's tool. This stencil has several matrices, which are shown in Figure 16-3, but you don't have to use them to present marketing information only. You can use any of these matrices to present growth/development data, diet/nutrition data, sales training data, academic requirements, or a hundred other types of information.

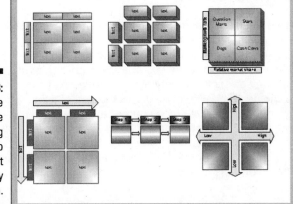

Figure 16-3:
Use one of these marketing matrices to present almost any type of data.

Figure 16-4 has examples of other shapes from the Marketing Diagrams stencil. Although these stencils were designed for marketing purposes, they can be used for any type of data. Think about the relationships they represent: The circle/spoke diagram can represent parts that contribute to a whole; the pyramid can represent building blocks or a hierarchical relationship; the arrows represent a continuous cycle. Use your imagination with these shapes. Each one is customizable; when you drag them into the drawing, Visio prompts you for the number of circles, pyramid levels, or arrows you want.

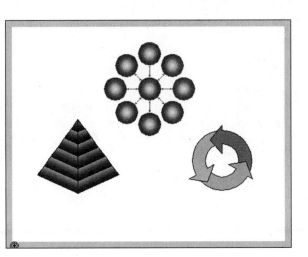

Figure 16-4:
Use these marketing shapes to present other types of information.

Form Design stencil

Have you ever tried to create a form using a word processor? You know, the kind with boxes of all different shapes and sizes, borders, grids, horizontal and vertical lines, and check boxes. If you have, then you know — it's a *nightmare*. Word processors are decidedly *text oriented* rather than *object oriented*, which means that they understand only how to move text from left to right and wrap text to the next line when you get to the end of a line. They don't understand anything else, and they beg you not to make them try! (If you do, you're only asking for major frustration.)

When you need to create a form, the Visio Form Design stencil is just what you're looking for. It contains all sorts of useful shapes, such as:

- Arrows
- Borders
- Data boxes (you know, those silly little boxes that are usually too small to write just one character in — not so in Visio)
- Date/time/page number box
- Grids
- Logo placeholder
- Text boxes (plain, shaded, or with a black background and white characters)
- Title box
- Vertical lines
- Work order forms (see Figure 16-5)

Because Visio is object-oriented, moving all those little shapes into place wherever you want them is easy. Use the Form Design stencil to create purchase orders, invoices, fax cover sheets, packing slips, application forms, warranty cards, customer surveys — basically any kind of a form that is difficult to create with a word processor.

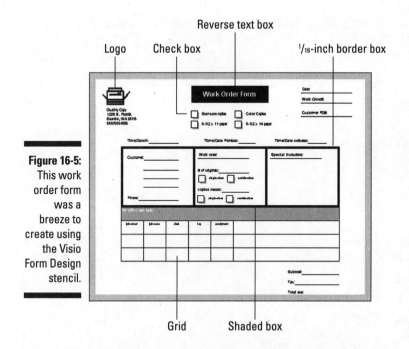

Figure 16-5:
This work order form was a breeze to create using the Visio Form Design stencil.

Charting Shapes stencil

The Charting Shapes stencil is designed to help you create just about any type of business chart — pie chart, bar graph, line graph, row/column matrix — and do it quickly. Granted, these types of shapes aren't all that exciting, but I show them here because Visio makes them so easy to create and modify.

Figure 16-6 shows an ordinary bar graph, but you don't have to create the pieces of this graph yourself. Just drag the bar graph shape from the Charting Shapes stencil onto your drawing. A dialog box lets you specify the number of bars you want. Use the control points on the graph to change the height and width of bars. To change bar percentages and bar height, width, color, and text, click an individual bar (don't worry about the padlocks it displays), right-click, and select the command you want from the shortcut menu.

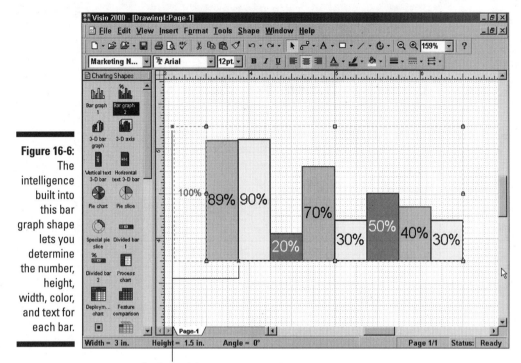

Figure 16-6:
The intelligence built into this bar graph shape lets you determine the number, height, width, color, and text for each bar.

Control points

You can create an impressive 3-D bar chart like the one shown in Figure 16-7 using the 3-D axis shape and the 3-D bar shape. Drag the axis onto your drawing page and use control points on the 3-D axis to vary the box depth and the number/frequency of gridlines. Now drag as many 3-D bars as you want on top of the axis. Use the control point on each bar to change the bar depth. To change bar color, click the bar and then choose a fill color from the Fill tool, which is on the Standard toolbar.

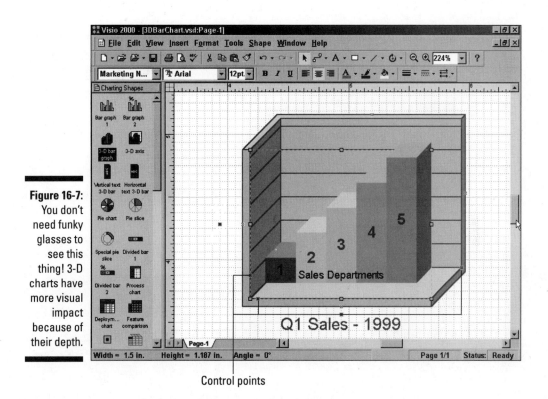

Figure 16-7:
You don't
need funky
glasses to
see this
thing! 3-D
charts have
more visual
impact
because of
their depth.

Control points

Blocks with Perspective stencil

Like 3-D shapes, block diagrams have a lot of visual impact. They're even
more interesting when you use shapes from the Blocks with Perspective
stencil. Each shape in this stencil is 3-D with an adjustable *vanishing point*
(the imaginary point where the lines of a three-dimensional shape converge).
You can adjust the vanishing point of any shape to any direction or depth
just by moving the control point. (See Figure 16-8.)

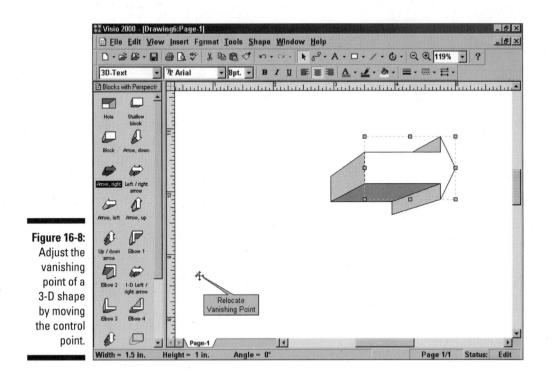

Figure 16-8:
Adjust the
vanishing
point of a
3-D shape
by moving
the control
point.

If you start a new drawing by choosing the Blocks Diagram with Perspective drawing type, Visio automatically opens the Blocks with Perspective stencil and puts a vanishing point shape in your drawing, as shown in Figure 16-9. This shape represents a vanishing point for the entire page, displaying two perpendicular lines that cross each other. The vanishing point is marked at the point where the lines cross. Move the vanishing point shape anywhere on the drawing page. When you drag other shapes into the drawing, Visio automatically glues their vanishing points to the page vanishing point. This makes each shape appear to be pointing to the page vanishing point. (See Figure 16-9.) You can change an individual shape's vanishing point by dragging its control handle away from the page vanishing point. (By the way, the page vanishing point crosshair doesn't print with the drawing.)

The vanishing point in Figure 16-10 has been moved. Can you tell where it is now?

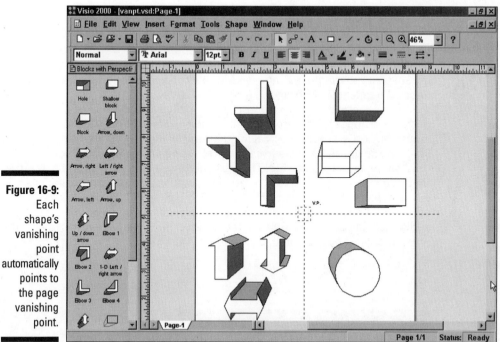

Figure 16-9:
Each shape's vanishing point automatically points to the page vanishing point.

Figure 16-10:
The vanishing point for each shape now points to the new location of the page vanishing point.

Flowchart stencil

When you use the Flowchart stencil, Visio automatically turns on one of its new features: dynamic grid. Dynamic grid aids you in aligning and distributing shapes. For example, drag one flowchart shape onto the drawing. Nothing unusual happens. Now drag the next flowchart shape into the drawing. When the two shapes get close to becoming vertically aligned, you see a faint dotted line appear that helps you align the shapes vertically. Release the mouse button when the vertical line passes through the center of the shape. Place the shape as far away from the first shape as you want it. Now drag the third shape onto the drawing. The vertical dotted line appears again, but this time you also see a horizontal dotted line appear when the third shape is equally spaced from the second shape. (See Figure 16-11.) Visio keeps track of how far apart you space the first and second shapes so you can distribute additional shapes evenly. Release the mouse button when both vertical and horizontal lines pass through the center of the shape.

Dynamic grid lines

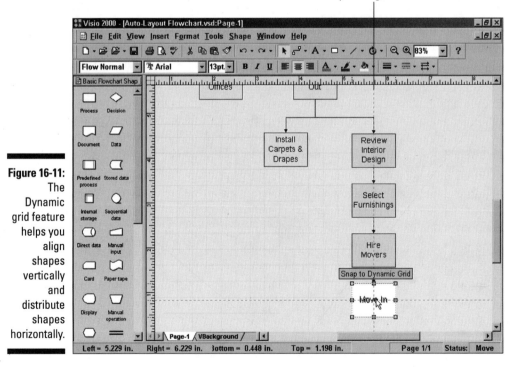

Figure 16-11: The Dynamic grid feature helps you align shapes vertically and distribute shapes horizontally.

Of course, if you don't want your shapes aligned or distributed evenly, that's your choice. Just release the mouse button when the shape is where you want it. If you want to turn off the dynamic grid feature altogether for this drawing, do so by choosing Tools⇨Snap & Glue. In the Snap & Glue dialog box, remove the check mark from the Dynamic Grid box and then click the OK button.

Try Some Great Wizards

Visio has lots of great wizards that are designed to help you accomplish tasks easily and quickly. Some great Visio wizards are the Organization Charts Wizard and the project schedule wizards Gantt Chart and Import Project Data. You won't see these wizards listed in this chapter; see Chapter 14 where you find out how to use data stored in other programs to create organizational charts and timelines. You see some other interesting — and very different — wizards in this chapter.

To use any of the Visio wizards, choose Tools⇨Macros. Pick a wizard from one of the categories on the submenu or click Macros to choose from an alphabetized list of wizards and macros.

Organization Chart Converter Wizard

The Organization Chart Shapes stencil in Visio 2000 has new built-in behavior (like automatically connecting and positioning shapes) and new features (like exporting and comparing data in two files). Because of this, Visio includes the Organization Chart Converter Wizard to help you convert older organization charts that you created using previous versions of Visio. The converter brings your old organization charts up to date so you can take advantage of all the automated behavior and new features of organization charts with Visio 2000. Just supply the old organization chart's filename, and Visio takes care of the rest. To use this wizard, choose Tools⇨Macros⇨Organization Chart⇨ Organization Chart Converter.

Chart Shape Wizard

Ever get tired of typical business bar charts that represent quantity with — what else — bars? You can jazz up your bar charts by creating *extendable* or *stackable* shapes via the Chart Shape Wizard. Visually, your charts are more interesting because the boring bars are replaced with other shapes — whatever shape you choose or create.

✔ An *extendable* shape is one that stretches, without distortion, when you resize it. The shape usually consists of two or three sections with only one of the sections that stretch. The other sections don't stretch, and that keeps the shape from being distorted. (See Figure 16-12.) Visio contains some shapes that are already extendable, such as the pencil, flower, extend-o-hand, people, person, and umbrella shapes on the Marketing Clip Art stencil. You can use these, or you can create your own extendable shapes by using the Chart Shape Wizard. Shapes that make good extendable shapes are those that have straight-line elements without a lot of complexity or detail. Extendable shapes that you create can run horizontally or vertically.

✔ A *stackable* shape is one that duplicates itself when you stretch it. For example, if your chart depicts numbers of people who own a cow, you can make the cow shape from the Marketing Clip Art stencil a stackable shape (like that shown in Figure 16-13). The larger the quantity shown in your chart, the more cow shapes are stacked on top of one another. Like extendable shapes, stackable shapes of your creation can run horizontally or vertically.

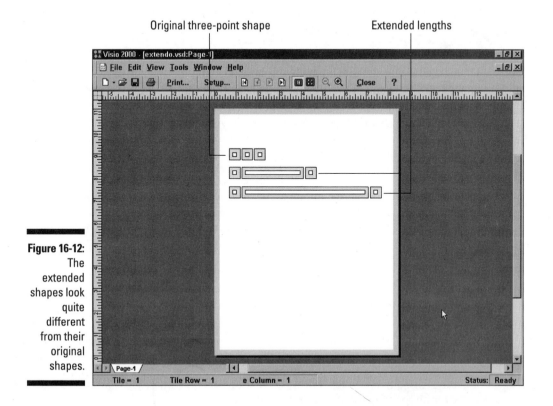

Original three-point shape   Extended lengths

Figure 16-12:
The extended shapes look quite different from their original shapes.

Figure 16-13:
How about a
stackable
cash cow?

To create an extendable or stackable shape, use the Chart Shape Wizard:

1. **Open a new Visio file and drag into the drawing area the shape that you want to use.**

   You can use just about any shape to create a stackable shape. If you're creating an extendable shape, drag onto the drawing page the two or three shapes that will make up the extendable shape.

2. **Choose Tools➪Macros➪Forms and Charts➪Chart Shape Wizard to start the wizard.**

3. **Click Next to move to the second screen.**

4. **Choose Extendable or Stackable and then click Next.**

5. **Follow the remaining wizard screens to finish your shape.**

After you create an extendable or stackable shape, you extend or stack it by dragging a selection handle. If the shape runs horizontally, drag any of the right resize handles to the right or left. For shapes that run vertically, drag any top handle up or down.

Build Region Wizard

The Build Region Wizard is a nifty little tool that helps you create a geographic map. If you're creating a map of adjoining states or countries, it can save you from having to align each piece of the jigsaw puzzle. If you're creating a map of non-adjoining states or countries, it can make what could have been a nearly impossible task a breeze.

The Build Region Wizard works with any of the following stencils. (For more information on these stencils, take a look at the earlier section "Geographical maps.")

- ✔ Maps of Africa
- ✔ Maps of Asia
- ✔ Maps of Europe
- ✔ Maps of the Middle East
- ✔ Maps of North America and South America
- ✔ Maps of the United States and Canada

To create a map, use any of the stencils and drag into the drawing area the shapes that you want. (See Figure 16-14.) You don't need to waste any time arranging the shapes; the wizard automatically does it for you.

To use the Build Region Wizard, follow these steps:

1. **Open one or more of the geographic maps stencils or use the geographic maps template to create a new drawing.**
2. **Drag all the shapes that you want into the drawing.**
3. **Select all the shapes that are part of the region you're building.**
4. **Choose Tools➪Macros➪Maps➪Build Region.**

   The wizard creates the map for you from the shapes you selected.

If you want to add more states, countries, or provinces to the drawing, just drag them in and place them anywhere in the drawing area. Select all the new shapes, along with the old, and run the wizard again. The wizard arranges the new shapes into the existing drawing. Figure 16-15 shows the result of running the Build Region Wizard on the drawing shown in Figure 16-14.

Adding more flair to Visio

Want to add even more flair to your Visio documents than a stencil or wizard can provide? Check out the following pages in the Visio Corporation Web site to find out more about other products you can use with Visio.

- ✔ For information about add-on products: Select Help➪Visio on the Web➪Visio Solutions Library or go directly to www.visio.com/solutions. Click the Product Directory for a list of add-on products that you can purchase on the spot.

- ✔ For free add-on products: Go directly to www.visio.com/support/downloads/visio.html for free add-on products, wizards, and other utilities from the Visio Development Team.

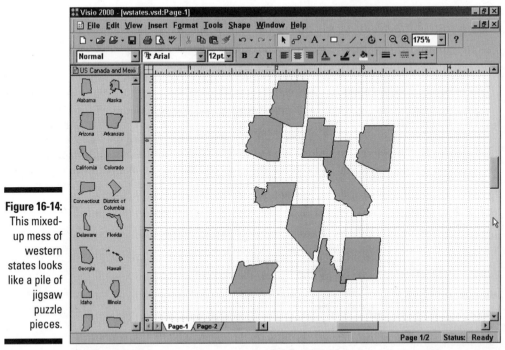

Figure 16-14:
This mixed-up mess of western states looks like a pile of jigsaw puzzle pieces.

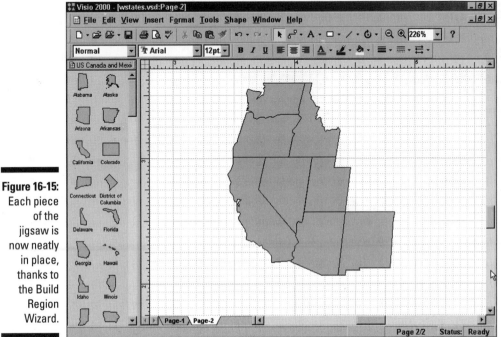

Figure 16-15:
Each piece of the jigsaw is now neatly in place, thanks to the Build Region Wizard.

Stencil Report Wizard

Think of the Stencil Report Wizard as a tool for creating a stencil reference sheet. Suppose that you manage a group of network engineers who are just learning to use Visio to create drawings and network diagrams. You could have your engineers study each stencil on the screen, but it would make much more sense to create a reference sheet that includes descriptions of all the shapes included in the network equipment stencils. (See Figure 16-16.) When you choose the stencil, the Stencil Report Wizard creates a drawing that shows an example of each shape, its name, and a description of the prompt shown on the status bar when you select the shape in the stencil.

To use the Stencil Report Wizard, choose Tools➪Macros➪Visio Extras➪ Stencil Report Wizard and then follow the prompts on the screen.

Figure 16-16:
The Stencil Report Wizard creates a nice, printable drawing showing all shapes on the selected stencil.

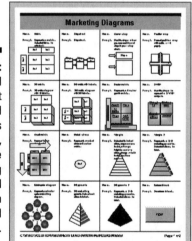

Chapter 17

Ten of the Best Visio Tips

In This Chapter

▶ Handy tips from the makers of Visio

▶ Features that you should play around with

*T*ips can be some of your greatest assets when you figure out how to use a new application. Here are ten valuable tips from the pros at Visio.

Use Your Pasteboard

"Pasteboard? What's that?" you ask. You may not have noticed the blue area surrounding a newly created drawing page. (In fact, you don't see the pasteboard if you zoom in on the drawing page.) When it's visible, you can drag shapes onto the pasteboard and use it as a type of holding area for shapes that you're not ready for yet — sort of like waiting room at your doctor's office. This is a great way to store shapes when you're opening a lot of stencils. You can drag the shapes onto the pasteboard and then close the stencils that you're not using anymore. The shapes are stored with the drawing, but they don't print. When you're ready to use the shapes, just drag them into the drawing area.

Preview Your Drawings in Windows Explorer

A fast way to view a drawing before opening it in Visio is to use the Quick View feature in Windows. It is available in Windows Explorer. (Before you get frustrated, understand that you may not have Quick View installed on your computer. If not, dig out and dust off your Windows disk and install it!)

Go to the directory where your Visio file is located, right-click the file, and choose Quick View from the drop-down menu that appears. Windows displays the file in a Quick View window so that you can identify the file quickly. To open the file in Visio, click the Visio tool (it looks like the Visio company logo: dark blue with bright green shapes) on the Quick View toolbar. To close the Quick View window, click the window's close button (the button with the X in the upper-right corner of the window).

Group Shapes

The more adept that you become at creating shapes, the more you realize that a good shape is often a combination of many shapes. When you spend a lot of time creating the various components, you don't want to lose any of the pieces when you start dragging and copying them. The best way to avoid losing anything is to group the pieces. (Sort of like when your first grade teacher made you hold hands and walk two by two on your way to the museum field trip.) Refer to Chapter 8 for details on grouping shapes.

Use Guides to Position and Move Shapes

A guide is sort of like a Visio clothesline — or maybe *shapeline* is more appropriate! Use a guide when you want to "hang" shapes from the same line — horizontal, vertical, or diagonal. It's a great way to position and align shapes, but you can also move them easily using a guide. Just drag the guide, and all the attached shapes move along with it. To review guide use, see Chapter 7.

Work with Drawing Layers

Drawing layers are one of the most useful Visio features. Think of them as transparent pages on which to place your drawing shapes. Layers help you organize your work, particularly with complex, detailed drawings. Group similar or related shapes onto the same layer; duplicate shapes that you want to appear on multiple layers. Stack the layers together to see your complete drawing. You can print or view layers selectively, and you can lock layers to protect them from change. See Chapter 10 for details on creating and using layers.

Fool Around with Snap and Glue

Snap and glue are two of the of most powerful Visio features; they make creating drawings a whole lot easier. But they can be confusing when you're first checking them out because there are so many choices. Dynamic or static? Snap and glue to what? Connection points? Handles? Grid? Guides? All or none? Set snap and glue strength? Yikes!

Don't worry. The best way to figure out snap and glue is to *play with them*. Create a drawing that you don't care anything about and go wild! Try every combination of snap and glue options that you can think of. Drag some shapes in. Move them around. Reset the snap and glue strength. Turn off some of the snap and glue options. Move shapes around. Turn *all* the options off. Now move shapes around again. You get the idea. Just play around with snap and glue to see what happens. The more you experiment, the more comfortable you'll feel.

Set Undo Levels

Many computer programs have only one level of the Undo command. That means if you want to take back a mistake, you better do it right away, before you do anything else — otherwise you lose your chance! Other programs have *levels* of the Undo command, which means that you can choose Edit⇨ Undo repeatedly and the command can undo the last few actions that you took. Visio defaults to ten levels of undo, but you can set the level if you want. If you think you'll never want to undo more than the last five actions, set the level to 5. If you want to be able to undo the last 50 commands, Visio lets you set the level to 50. To set this option, choose Tools⇨Options and click the Advanced tab. Type a number — up to 99 — in the Undo Levels box. (Be aware that the higher the number you enter, the more memory resources you use on your computer.)

Quickly Edit the Text in Your Document

You can either press F7 to quickly run the spell checker or choose Tools⇨ Spelling. Choose Edit⇨Find to find text in a drawing; choose Edit⇨Replace to search for and replace text in a drawing.

Use Keyboard Shortcuts

You can significantly speed up your work if you take the time to memorize some of the Visio keyboard shortcuts for menu commands. They are listed on every menu, just to the right of the command name. (Some commands have none.) You also find other keyboard shortcuts that aren't listed in any one place where you can easily find them. You just sort of pick them up as you go. See the Cheat Sheet for a list of helpful shortcuts.

Gluing Shapes to Shapes

In previous versions of Visio, you could glue connectors only to shapes. With Visio 2000, some shapes can be glued to other shapes. The capability of a shape to glue to another shape is preprogrammed into the shape. Look for this capability where it seems logical. For example, in an office layout drawing, you can glue adjacent pieces of furniture together so that when they're moved, they move together.

Chapter 18

Ten Really Slick Drawings from the Makers of Visio

In This Chapter

▶ See great examples of office, building, and landscape layouts

▶ Check out the cool city map of Seattle

▶ Look at the detail in the network diagrams

▶ View a Web diagram that looks like an organization chart

*T*he drawings in this chapter are samples intended to inspire, inform, motivate, and impress you! All of them were created by experts at Visio Corporation — who better to show off the capabilities of Visio than the makers of Visio themselves? Each drawing has a brief description of the product and stencils used to create the drawing. Sample drawings were done in Visio Standard, Visio Professional, and Visio Technical.

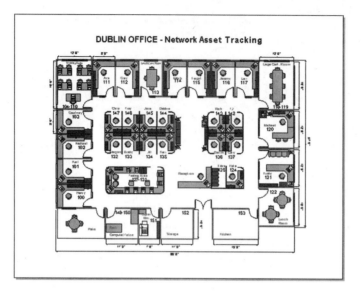

Visio Product: Visio Standard

Stencils Used: Office Layout/Office Layout Shapes; Network Diagram/Basic Network Shapes; Visio Extras/Callouts

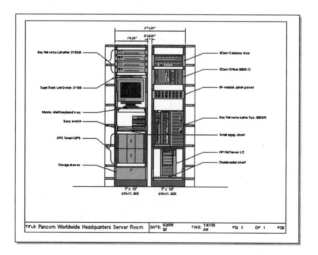

Visio Product: Visio Professional

Stencils Used: Network Diagram/Basic Network Shapes; 3Com Equipment; Bay Networks Equipment; Cabletron Equipment; Cisco Equipment; HP Equipment

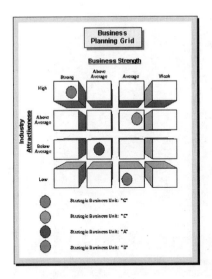

Visio Product: Visio Standard

Stencils Used: Block Diagram/Blocks with Perspective; Forms and Charts/Marketing Diagrams

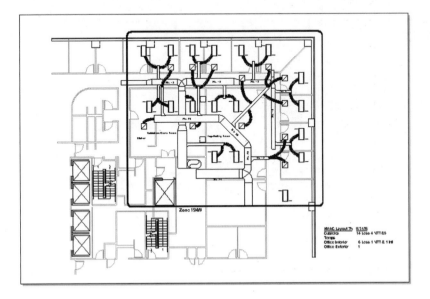

Visio Product: Visio Technical

Stencils Used: AEC/HVAC Controls; AEC/HVAC Equipment; AEC/HVAC Single Line; AEC/HVAC Double Line; AEC/Building Core; AEC/Walls; Shell and Structure

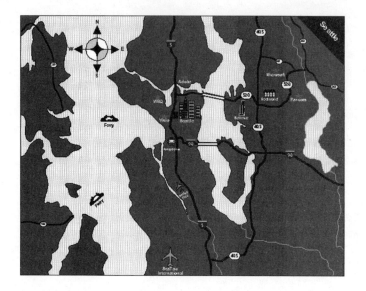

Visio Product: Visio Standard

Stencils Used: Map/Landmark Shapes; Map/Road Shapes

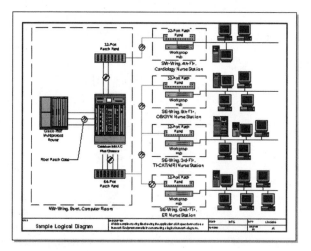

Visio Product: Visio Professional

Stencils Used: Network Diagram/General Equipment; Network Diagram/General Manufacturer Equipment; Network Diagram/Logical Symbols 1; Network Diagram/Logical Symbols 2

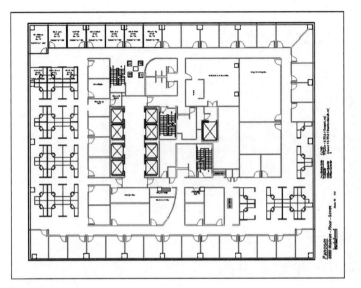

Visio Product: Visio Technical

Stencils Used: Facilities Management/Building Core; AEC/Electrical and Telecom; Annotations/General – Annotations; Annotations/General – Dimensioning; Architectural Facilities Management/Office Equipment – Electronic; Facilities Management/Office Equipment – Accessories; Facilities Management/Office Equipment – Services; Facilities Management/Office Furniture; Facilities Management/Resources; Equipment/Office Furniture/Steelcase; AEC/Walls; Shell and Structure; Facilities Management/Modular Office Furniture

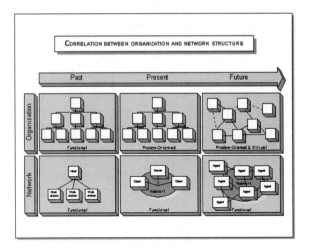

Visio Product: Visio Standard

Stencils Used: Block Diagram/Blocks; Block Diagram/Block with Perspective; Block Diagram/Blocks

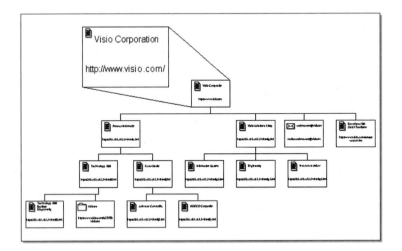

Visio Product: Visio Professional

Stencils Used: Internet Diagram/Web Diagram Shapes; Flowchart/Basic Flowchart Shapes 1; Flowchart/Basic Flowchart Shapes 2

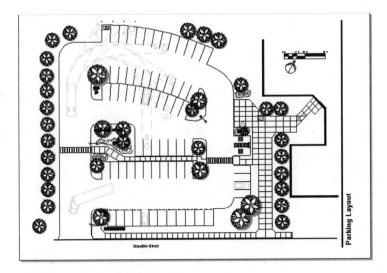

Visio Product: Visio Technical

Stencils Used: Facilities Management/Site – Parking and Roads; Facilities Management/Site Accessories; Facilities Management/Landscape Watering; Facilities Management/Landscape Plants; Annotation/Dimensioning – Engineering; Annotation/General – Annotations; Facilities Management/Vehicles

Appendix

Stencil Gallery

• •

*V*isio organizes stencils into categories to make them easier to find. In this gallery, stencils are arranged by Visio product and then by category. First you see stencils that are available in Visio 2000 Standard. At the time of printing, Visio 2000 Professional and Visio 2000 Technical weren't released yet, so the stencils shown are for Visio 5.0 Professional and Visio 5.0 Technical.

Visio contains literally thousands of shapes on hundreds of stencils. It isn't possible to show every stencil in this gallery. The stencils I include are the most unique and most interesting in each category. The names of stencils that aren't shown are listed under each category.

Stencils in Visio 2000 Standard

Category: Block Diagram

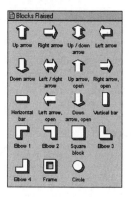

Category: Forms and Charts

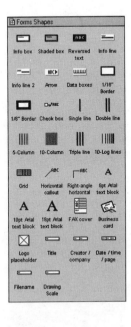

Forms Shapes

Info box	Shaded box	Reversed text	Info line
Info line 2	Arrow	Data boxes	1/16" Border
1/8" Border	Check box	Single line	Double line
5-Column	10-Column	Triple line	10-Log lines
Grid	Horizontal callout	Right-angle horizontal	8pt Arial text block
10pt Arial text block	18pt Arial text block	FAX cover	Business card
Logo placeholder	Title	Creator / company	Date / time / page
Filename	Drawing Scale		

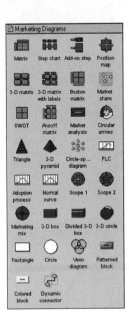

Marketing Diagrams

Matrix	Step chart	Add-on step	Position map
3-D matrix	3-D matrix with labels	Boston matrix	Market share
SWOT	Ansoff matrix	Market analysis	Circular arrows
Triangle	3-D pyramid	Circle-sp... diagram	PLC
Adoption process	Normal curve	Scope 1	Scope 2
Marketing mix	3-D box	Divided 3-D box	3-D circle
Rectangle	Circle	Venn diagram	Patterned block
Colored block	Dynamic connector		

Marketing Clip Art

Target	Dart/ Pushpin	Thermom...	Globe
Check box	Check/ Cross	Stretchable dollars	Stretchable pounds
Sign post	Extend-o hand	People	Scales
Pencil	Growing flower	Oil well	Variable stack
Variable smoke	Variable building	Umbrella	Stack of papers
Cylinder	Cash cow	Dog	Money bag
Star	Question mark	Financial institution	Factory
Wholesaler	Person	Retailer	Consumer
Building block	Rocket	Crystal ball	Sunglasses
Empty box	Full box	Tombstone	Airplane
Train	Train car	Truck	Truck 2
Ship	House	House 2	Wooden barrel
Shopping cart	Shopping cart 2	Oil barrel	Coin
VISA	American Express	MasterCard	Access
Diners Club	Delta	Switch	Eurocard
U.S. dollar	Yen	Pound	Euro
Barbells	Television set	Yin Yang	Puzzle corner
Puzzle side	Puzzle middle 1	Puzzle middle 2	Puzzle middle 3

(Stencil continued)

"NO" sign	Warning sign	Stop sign	Diamond label
Award circle	Aztec label	1st place	Clipboard
Tree	Copyright		

Charting Shapes

Bar graph 1	Bar graph 2	3-D bar graph	3-D axis
Vertical text 3-D bar	Horizontal text 3-D bar	Pie chart	Pie slice
Special pie slice	Divided bar 1	Divided bar 2	Process chart
Deploym... chart	Feature comparison	Feature on/off	Row header
Column header	Grid	Yes/No box	Normal curve
Exponential curve	Line graph	Graph line	Data point
X-Y axis	X-Y-Z axis	Graph scale	X-axis label
Y-axis label	Z-axis label	X axis	Y axis
Z axis	Text block 8pt	Text block 10pt	Text block 12pt
2-D word balloon	1-D word balloon	Horizontal callout	Annotation

Category: Flowchart

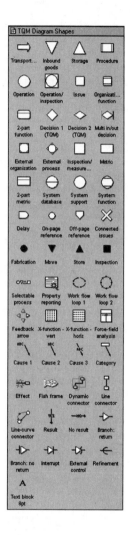

Basic Flowchart Shapes

Process, Decision, Document, Data, Predefined process, Stored data, Internal storage, Sequential data, Direct data, Manual input, Card, Paper tape, Display, Manual operation, Preparation, Parallel mode, Loop limit, Terminator, On-page reference, Off-page reference, Flowchart shapes, Auto-height box, Property reporting, Dynamic connector, Line-curve connector, Control transfer, Annotation

SDL Diagram Shapes

Start	Variable start	Procedure	Variable procedure
Create request	Alternative	Return	Decision 1
Message from user	Primitive from call	Decision 2	Message to user
Primitive to call control	Save	Off-page reference	On-page reference
Multi document	Document	Disk storage	Divided process
Divided event	Terminator	Dynamic connector	Line-curve connector

Data Flow Diagram Shapes

Data process	Center to center 1	Center to center 2	Multiple process
Loop on center	Loop on center 2	State	Start state
Stop state	Multi state	External interactor	Stop state 2
Data store	Entity relationship	Object callout	Entity 1
Entity 2	Object	Oval process	Oval process

Stencils in the Flowchart category not shown: Cause and Effect Diagram Shapes, Cross-Functional Flowchart Shapes Vertical, Cross-Functional Flowchart Shapes Horizontal, Miscellaneous Flowchart Shapes, Work Flow Diagram Shapes

Category: Map

Landmark Shapes

Town house	Suburban home	City	Building 1
Building 2	Condos	Outdoor mall	Gas station
Airport	Train station	Ferry	River
Lake	Ocean	Scale	Direction
North	Text block 8pt	Text block 10pt	Text block 18pt
Callout	Tree	Cathedral	Skyscraper
Church	Factory	Warehouse	Hospital
Barn	Park	Fire department	School
Motel	Stadium	Convenie... store	

Recreation Shapes

Restroom	Potable water	Campgro...	SCUBA diving
Skating	RV	Marina	Snowmobile
Parking	Swimming	Supplies/...	Campfire
Shower	Canoe access	Golf	Fishing
Downhill skiing	Horseback riding	Amphithe...	Boat launch
Cross-co... skiing	Hiking	Climbing	Kayaking
Snowboar...	Tennis	Volleyball	Racquetb...

Transportation Shapes

Stop light	Stop	Yield	No entry
No parking	One way	Street	Speed limit
HOV	Airport	Bus stop	Freeway exit
Train station	Information	Construct...	Pedestrian crossing
School zone	Railroad crossing	Truck	Car
Rest area	Sanitation dump	Parking	

(continued)

(Map continued)

Flags

Albania · Andorra · Argentina · Australia
Austria · Belgium · Bosnia-Herzegov... · Brazil
Bulgaria · Canada · Chile · China
Croatia · Czech Republic · Denmark · Estonia
European Council · Finland · France · Germany
Greece · Greenland · Hong Kong · Hungary
Iceland · India · Indonesia · Ireland
Israel · Italy · Japan · Latvia
Luxembo... · Macedonia · Malaysia · Mexico
Monaco · Netherlands · New Zealand · Norway
Pakistan · Poland · Portugal · Puerto Rico
Qatar · Romania · Russia · Singapore
Slovakia · South Africa · South Korea · Spain
Sweden · Switzerland · Taiwan · Thailand
Turkey · Ukraine · United Arab Emirates · United Kingdom
United States · Vietnam · Yemen · Yugoslavia (Serbia-

US Canada and Mexico

Alabama · Alaska · Arizona · Arkansas
California · Colorado · Connecticut · District of Columbia
Delaware · Florida · Georgia · Hawaii
Idaho · Illinois · Indiana · Iowa
Kansas · Kentucky · Louisiana · Montana
Maine · Massach... · Maryland · Michigan
Minnesota · Missouri · Mississippi · Nebraska
Nevada · New Hampshire · New Jersey · New Mexico
New York · North Carolina · North Dakota · Ohio
Oklahoma · Oregon · Pennsylv... · Rhode Island
South Carolina · South Dakota · Tennessee · Texas
Utah · Vermont · Virginia · Wisconsin
Wyoming · Washington · West Virginia · Alberta
British Columbia · Manitoba · New Brunswick · Newfoun... and
Northwest Territories · Nova Scotia · Ontario · Prince Edward
Quebec · Saskatch... · Yukon Territory · Aguascali...
Baja California · Baja California · Campeche · Chiapas
Chihuahua · Coahuila De · Colima · Distrito Federal
Durango · Guanajuato · Guerrero · Hidalgo

(Stencil continued)

Jalisco · Mexico · Michoacan de Ocampo · Morelos
Nayarit · Nuevo Leon · Oaxaca · Puebla
Queretaro de Arteaga · Quintana Roo · San Luis Potosi · Sinaloa
Sonora · Tabasco · Tamaulipas · Tlaxcala
Veracruz-... · Yucatan · Zacatecas

Europe

Albania · Austria · Belgium · Bosnia and Herzegov...
Bulgaria · Belarus · Croatia · Cyprus
Czech Republic · Denmark · Estonia · Finland
France · Germany · Greece · Iceland
Ireland · Italy · Hungary · Latvia
Lithuania · Luxembo... · Macedonia · Moldova
Montenegro · Netherlands · Norway · Poland
Portugal · Romania · Russia · Serbia
Slovakia · Slovenia · Spain · Sweden
Switzerland · Turkey · Ukraine · United Kingdom
Lake Ladoga · Lake Onega · Lake Vanem · Danube
Dnieper · Don · Gota Alv · Neva
Rhine · Suir

Stencils in the Map category not shown: Metro Shapes, Middle East, Asia, Africa, North and South America, World

Category: Network Diagram

Category: Visio Extras

Embellishments

Wave section	Wave corner	Braid section	Braid corner
Braid end-cap	Egyptian section	Egyptian corner	Egyptian end-cap
Greek section	Greek corner	Greek border	Cross section
Cross corner	Cross end-cap	Wave section 2	Wave corner 2
Wave corner 3	Roman section	Star section	Triangle section
Chiseled frame	Square frame	Photo frame	Art deco frame
Jewel frame	Classic frame	Fun frame	Art deco circle
Art deco tile	Wave tile	Weave tile	Zigzag tile
Op-art tile	Diamond tile	Graphic tile	Celtic ornament
Button ornament	Arc ornament	Checker section	Single line frame
Multi line frame			

Clip Art

Business woman	Man walking	Meeting	Woman with
Presentat...	Handshake	Man running	Man with chart
Man with folder	Audience	Politician	Large Macintosh
Small Macintosh	IBM PS/2	Dumb terminal	Workstation
IBM PC AT	Tower	Detailed IBM PS/2	Laptop computer
LaserJet printer	LaserWriter	Dot matrix printer	Facsimile machine
Flatbed scanner	Button	CD	Disk
Video cassette	Business telephone	Telephone	3.5" disk
5.25" disk	Compact car	City bus	Car pool
Jet	Cruise ship	Luggage	Train symbol
Taxi symbol	Globe 1	Governm...	Open briefcase
Diamond label	Award circle	Aztec label	Blue ribbon
1st place	Gold star	Recycle symbol	Coffee cup
Magnifying glass	Target	Clipboard	Notes
Scroll	Date book	Copyright	File cabinet
Alarm clock	Cheers	Globe 2	The big day

(Stencil continued)

Charts and Graphs	Page layout	Chess pieces	Newspaper
Time flies	Paper airplane	Vacationer	Cutting costs
Royal Chair	Tornado	Cards	Brainstorm
Money tree	Celebrate	Surprise	Dance 1
Dance 2	Dynamic globe	Man in the moon	Trophy

Borders and Titles

Border Graduated	Border classic	Border contemp.	Border binder
Border elegant	Border retro	Border neon	Border triangles
Border graphic 1	Border graphic 2	Border modern 1	Border modern 2
Border technical 1	Border technical 2	Border small	Title block deco
Title block compass	Title block bold	Title block jagged	Title block contemp.
Title block retro	Title block elegant	Title block notepad	Title block classic
Title block corporate 1	Title block corporate 2	Title block horizon	Title block sphere
Title block geometric	Note box classic	Note box contemp.	Note box triangles
Note box deco	Note box neon	Note box file	Hyperlink button
Hyperlink circle 1	Hyperlink circle 2		

Stencils in the Visio Extras category not shown: Connectors, Callouts

Stencils in Visio 5.0 Professional

Category: Database

Category: Internet Diagram

Category: Network Diagram

Cabletron MMAC

MMAC 3-slot	MMAC 5-slot	MMAC 8-slot	MMAC M3FNB
MMAC 7C03	MMAC 7E03-24	MMAC 7F06-02	MMAC 7X00
MMAC M30SM	AP2000	CRM2-R/E-C	CRM2-R/E-ENT
CRM2-R/1	CRM2-R/T-E	CRM2-R/T-E	CRM2-R/T-IP
CRM3-E	CRM3-T	CSMIM	CSMIM
CXRMIM	EMME	EMM-E6	MMAC ESX
ESXMIM-F2	ETWMIM	FDCMIM-24	FDCMIM-28
FDCMIM-34	FDCMIM-44	FDCMIM-48	FDC-08
FDM-30	FDMMIM	FDMMIM-04	FDMMIM-24
FDM-04	FO-28	FOMIM-12	FOMIM-16
FOMIM-18	FOMIM-22	FOMIM-26	FOMIM-32
FOMIM-36	FOMIM-38	FORMIM-22	IRM-3
M5PSM	PCMIM	TDR-42A	TDRMIM-22A
THN-MIM	TP-24	TP-34	TPMIM-22
TPMIM-32	TPMIM-T1	TPR-22	TPR-36
TPRMIM-20	TPRMIM-33	TPX-22	TPX-24
TR-34A	TRBMIM-T	TRF-26	TRFMIM-22
TRFMIM-26	TRFMIM-32	TRFMIM-36	TRFMIM-38
TRMIM-10R	TRMIM-20R	TRMIM-12	TRMIM-22
TRMIM-22A	TRMIM-24	TRMIM-32A	TRMIM-34A
TRMIM-42	TRMIM-42A	TRMIM-44	TRMM

(Stencil continued)

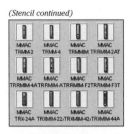

MMAC TRMM-2	MMAC TRMM-4	MMAC TRRMIM	MMAC TRRMIM-2AT
TRRMIM-4A	TRRMIM-A	TRRMIM-F2	TRRMIM-F3T
MMAC TRX-24A	MMAC TRXMIM-22	MMAC TRXMIM-42	MMAC TRXMIM-44A

3Com SuperStack

SS II Hub TR 12	SS II Hub TR 24	SS II Hub TR (Back	SS II Hub TR RMON
SS II Hub TR Adv	SS II Hub TR Cop.	SS II Hub TR Copper	SS II Hub TR Fiber
SS II Hub100	SS II Hub 100 (Back	SS II Hub100	SS II Management
SS II Switch 2000	SS II Switch 2200	SS II Switch 2700	SS II Switch 3000
SS II Switch	SS Redundant	SS UPS (US)	SS UPS (Int)
SS UPS (Japan)	1000Base-F Trans	1000Base-TX Trans	Link Switch 2000 TR
Link Switch 2200	Link Switch 2700	Link Switch 3000	Link Switch 3000TX

Telecom Symbols

Modem	Fax	Telephone	Comm. hub
PBX / PABX	Public switch	Generic rack	DSU / CSU
MUX / DEMUX	Database	Cloud	City
Satellite	Satellite dish	Radio tower	Microwave tower
Wireless net. node	C.T.S.	Room	Amplifier
ATM	Video	Service switching pt.	Signal transfer pt.
Service control pt.			

Hewlett Packard

Adv. Stack 200/400 fr.	Adv. Stack 230	Adv. Stack 240	Adv. Stack 430
Adv. Stack 440/445	Adv. Stack 470	Adv. Stack 470/480 fr.	Adv. Stack 480
Adv. Stack 650	Adv. Stack J2410A	Adv. Stack J2434A	Adv. Stack J2435A
Adv. Stack J2436A	Adv. Stack J2437A	Adv. Stack J2600A	Adv. Stack J2601A
Adv. Stack J2602A	Adv. Stack J2606A	Adv. Stack J2607A	Adv. Stack J2608A
Adv. Stack J2609A	Adv. Stack rt. eng.	Advance Sta 228669A	Advance Stack 228682A
Advance Sta 228688B	J2413A	J2414B	J2601B
Advance Sta J2602B	J2610B	J2611B	J2962A
Advance Sta J3027A	J3028A	J3030A	J3100A
Advance Sta J3102A	J3103A	J3108A	J3128A
Advance Sta J3133A	J3136A	J3137A	DesignJet 650c
DeskJet 540	DeskJet 550/560c	EtherTwist 28641B	EtherTwist 28683A
EtherTwist 28685B	HP 14" monitor	HP 15" monitor	HP 3000 9X7 fr.
HP 3000 9X8 fr.	HP 9000 17" monitor	HP 9000 20" monitor	HP 9000 712 fr.
HP 9000 715 fr.	HP 9000 725 fr.	HP 9000 735 fr.	HP 9000 755 fr.
HP 9000 827+ fr.	HP 9000 8X7 fr.	Keyboard	LaserJet 4+/4M+
LaserJet 4L	LaserJet 4P/4MP	LaserJet 5P	Net Server LC fr.
NetServer LF / LM fr.	NetServer LH fr.	Vectra M2 fr.	Vectra N2 fr.
Vectra VE fr.	Vectra VL2 fr.	Vectra VL3 fr.	Vectra XM2 fr.
Vectra XU fr.			

(continued)

(Network Diagram continued)

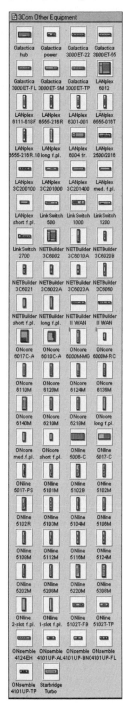

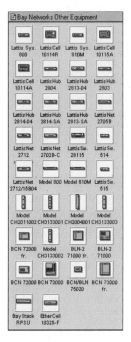

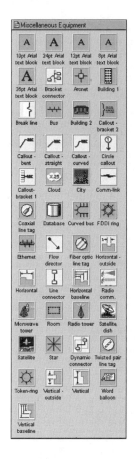

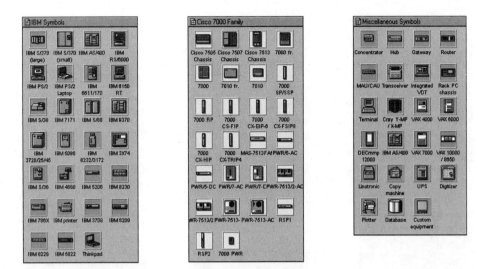

Stencils in the Network Diagram category not shown: 3Com Linkbuilder, Bay Networks Centillion, Bay Networks BayStack, Bay Networks Accessories, Cabletron Micro MMAC, Cabletron MMAC Plus, Cisco Catalyst Switches, Structured Racks

Category: Software Diagram

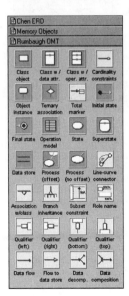

(continued)

(Software Diagram continued)

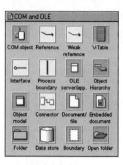

Stencils in the Software Diagram category not shown: Express-G, Gane-Sarson DFD, Jacobson Use Cases, Language Level Shapes, Martin ERD, Nassi-Schneiderman, Shlaer-Mellor OOA, UML- Static Structure Shapes

Category: Visio Extras

Stencils in Visio 5.0 Technical

Category: AEC

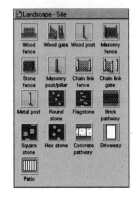

(continued)

(AEC Diagram continued)

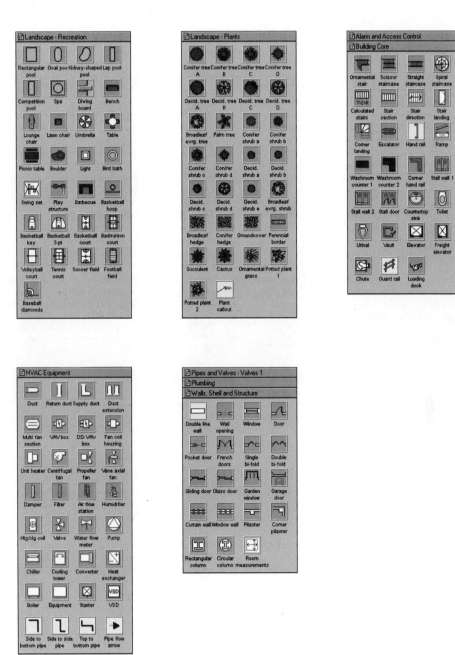

Stencils in AEC category not shown: Home - Appliance, Home - Cabinets, Home - Furniture, HVAC - Single Line and HVAC - Double Line, Initiation and Annunciation, Landscape - Watering, Pipes and Valves - Pipes 2, Pipes and Valves - Valves 2, Video Surveillance.

Category: Annotation

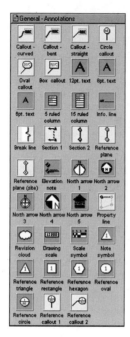

Stencils in the Annotation category not shown: General - Title Blocks, General - Drawing Tool Shapes

Category: Electrical & Electronic

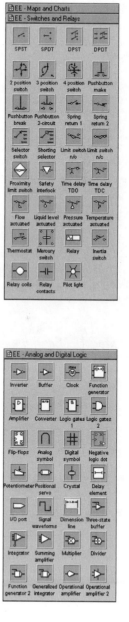

(continued)

(Electrical & Electronic continued)

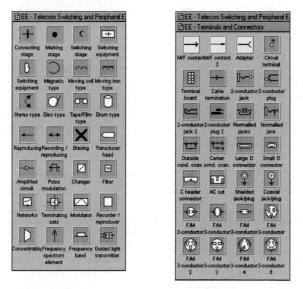

Stencils in the Electrical & Electronic category not shown: Composite Assemblies, Fundamental Items, Maintenance Symbols, Qualifying Symbols, Rotating Equipment and Mechanical Functions, Transformers and Wingdings, Transmission Paths

Category: Equipment

Category: Facilities Management

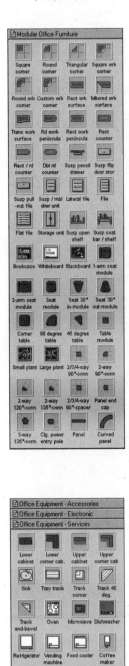

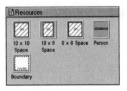

(continued)

(Facilities Management continued)

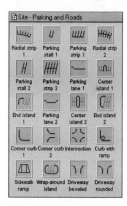

Category: Industrial Process

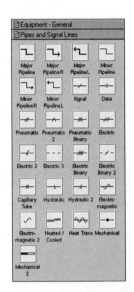

Shop Floor - Machines and Equipment
Shop Floor - Storage and Distribution

Diesel forklift	Electric forklift	Rising cab forklift	Stacking forklift
Order picker	Manual pallet jack	Powered pallet jack	Standard pallet
Conveyor belt	Roller conveyor	Angled roller	Bridge crane
Overbrace jib crane	Underbrace jib crane	Wall jib crane	Floor crane
Gantry crane	Mobile shelf	Freestanding shelf	Standard shelf
Standard rack	Rack section	Push back rack	Sloped rack
Drive-in rack	Mezzanine floor	Storage drum	

Equipment - General

Breaker	Roll crusher	Hammer crusher	Crushers
Ball mill	Various mills	Mixer	Blender
Kneader	Double blender	Filter	Rotary filter
Screen	Electromagnet	Cyclone	Centrifuge
Briquetting machine	Prill tower	Dryer	Conveyor wheel
Scraper conveyor	Screw conveyor	Overhead conveyor	Hoists
Electric motor	Boom loader		

Valves and Fittings

Gate valve	Globe valve	Screw-down valve	Check valve
Stop check valve	Diaphragm valve	Powered valve	Needle valve
Relief valves	Angle valve	Float operated	Flanged valve
Butterfly valve	Wedge / Parallel	Ball valve	Relief (angle)
Reducing valve	Plug valve	3-way Plug Valve	Mixing valve
Character. port	Reducer	General joint	Butt weld
Flanged/ bolted	Soldered/ Solvent	Screwed joints	Socket w/ spigot
Sleeve joint	Socket weld	Swivel joint	End caps 1
End caps 2	Electrically bonded	Electrically insulated	Bursting disc
Flame arrester	Strainer	Separator	Exhaust silencer
Tundish	Bell mouth	Exhaust head	Open vent
Siphon drain	Hydrant	Drain silencer	Y strainer
Liquid seal open/closed			

Equipment - General
Pipes and Signal Lines

Major Pipeline	Major Pipeline R	Major Pipeline L	Minor Pipeline
Minor Pipeline R	Minor Pipeline L	Signal	Data
Pneumatic	Pneumatic 2	Pneumatic Binary	Electric
Electric 2	Electric 3	Electric Binary	Electric Binary 2
Capillary Tube	Hydraulic	Hydraulic 2	Electro-magnetic
Electro-magnetic 2	Heated / Cooled	Heat Trace	Mechanical
Mechanical 2			

Stencils in the Industrial Process category not shown: Annotations, Vessels, Warehouse - Shipping and Receiving

Category: Mechanical Engineering

Stencils in the Mechanical Engineering Category not shown: Fasteners 2, General, Welding, Seals

Index

• U •

Underline tool, 99
Undo
  levels of, 274, 297
  to restore deleted shape, 232
  to restore text, 84
ungrouping, 181
Union tool, 151
units of measurement, 91–92, 141
unlocking shapes, 70–71, 275
updating linked file, 262
URL, 269

• V •

vanishing point of three-dimensional
    shape, 54, 285, 286, 287
variable grid, 134
vertical alignment
  of shapes, 147
  of text, 89–91
vertices
  adding, 166–168
  basics, 65–67, 159, 160, 167
  changing, 165–168
  gluing connectors to, 113
  snapping shape to, 139
View menu
  Connection Points, 70, 107
  Full Screen, 193
  Header and Footer, 49
  Layer Properties, 204, 205, 207, 210, 214
  Page Breaks, 46, 275
  Toolbars, Customize, 17, 18
  Windows, Drawing Explorer, 36, 251
  Windows, Pan & Zoom, 34
  Windows, Size & Position, 170, 172, 276
  Zoom, 33
View toolbar, 132, 204

Visio
  closing, 18
  features, 11
  product variations, 10
  starting, 13–14, 22
  terminology, 12
  uses of, 9–10
Visio Corporation Web site, 222, 292
Visio on the Web command in Help, 19
Visio screen, 15–16
.VSD file extension, 28
.VSS file extension, 228
.VSW file extension, 29

• W •

Web page, saving drawing as, 269
Web site address, for hyperlink, 269
weight of line, 175
Welcome to Visio dialog box, 13, 22,
    30–31
white fill, versus transparent, 161
Whole Page button (Preview toolbar), 43
Window menu
  Cascade, 192
  Show Document Stencil, 226
  Tile, 192, 275
Windows Clipboard, 85
Windows Explorer, to preview drawings,
    295–296
Windows menu
  Cascade, 31
  Tile, 31
wizards
  basics, 217–218
  Build Region, 218, 291–293
  Chart Shape, 289–291
  Custom Properties Editor, 240–241
  finding, 220–221
  Organization Chart Converter, 289

Notes

Notes

Notes

Notes

Notes

Notes

Notes

Notes

Notes

Notes

Notes

Dummies Books™
Bestsellers on Every Topic!

GENERAL INTEREST TITLES

BUSINESS & PERSONAL FINANCE

...counting For Dummies®	John A. Tracy, CPA	0-7645-5014-4	$19.99 US/$27.99 CAN
...siness Plans For Dummies®	Paul Tiffany, Ph.D. & Steven D. Peterson, Ph.D.	1-56884-868-4	$21.99 US/$29.99 CAN
...siness Writing For Dummies®	Sheryl Lindsell-Roberts	0-7645-5134-5	$16.99 US/$27.99 CAN
...nsulting For Dummies®	Bob Nelson & Peter Economy	0-7645-5034-9	$21.99 US/$29.99 CAN
...stomer Service For Dummies®, 2nd Edition	Karen Leland & Keith Bailey	0-7645-5209-0	$21.99 US/$29.99 CAN
...anchising For Dummies®	Dave Thomas & Michael Seid	0-7645-5160-4	$19.99 US/$27.99 CAN
...tting Results For Dummies®	Mark H. McCormack	0-7645-5205-8	$19.99 US/$27.99 CAN
...me Buying For Dummies®	Eric Tyson, MBA & Ray Brown	1-56884-385-2	$16.99 US/$24.99 CAN
...use Selling For Dummies®	Eric Tyson, MBA & Ray Brown	0-7645-5038-1	$19.99 US/$29.99 CAN
...man Resources Kit For Dummies®	Max Messmer	0-7645-5131-0	$29.99 US/$44.99 CAN
...vesting For Dummies®, 2nd Edition	Eric Tyson, MBA	0-7645-5162-0	$21.99 US/$29.99 CAN
...w For Dummies®	John Ventura	1-56884-860-9	$21.99 US/$29.99 CAN
...adership For Dummies®	Marshall Loeb & Steven Kindel	0-7645-5176-0	$19.99 US/$27.99 CAN
...anaging For Dummies®	Bob Nelson & Peter Economy	1-56884-858-7	$21.99 US/$29.99 CAN
...arketing For Dummies®	Alexander Hiam	1-56884-699-1	$21.99 US/$29.99 CAN
...utual Funds For Dummies®, 2nd Edition	Eric Tyson, MBA	0-7645-5112-4	$19.99 US/$27.99 CAN
...gotiating For Dummies®	Michael C. Donaldson & Mimi Donaldson	1-56884-867-6	$19.99 US/$27.99 CAN
...rsonal Finance For Dummies®, 3rd Edition	Eric Tyson, MBA	0-7645-5231-7	$21.99 US/$28.99 CAN
...rsonal Finance For Dummies® For Canadians, 2nd Edition	Eric Tyson, MBA & Tony Martin	0-7645-5123-X	$19.99 US/$27.99 CAN
...blic Speaking For Dummies®	Malcolm Kushner	0-7645-5159-0	$21.99 US/$29.99 CAN
...les Closing For Dummies®	Tom Hopkins	0-7645-5063-2	$16.99 US/$25.99 CAN
...les Prospecting For Dummies®	Tom Hopkins	0-7645-5066-7	$16.99 US/$25.99 CAN
...lling For Dummies®	Tom Hopkins	1-56884-389-5	$16.99 US/$24.99 CAN
...all Business For Dummies®	Eric Tyson, MBA & Jim Schell	0-7645-5094-2	$21.99 US/$29.99 CAN
...all Business Kit For Dummies®	Richard D. Harroch	0-7645-5093-4	$29.99 US/$44.99 CAN
...xes 2001 For Dummies®	Eric Tyson & David J. Silverman	0-7645-5306-2	$15.99 US/$23.99 CAN
...me Management For Dummies®, 2nd Edition	Jeffrey J. Mayer	0-7645-5145-0	$21.99 US/$29.99 CAN
...riting Business Letters For Dummies®	Sheryl Lindsell-Roberts	0-7645-5207-4	$21.99 US/$29.99 CAN

TECHNOLOGY TITLES

INTERNET/ONLINE

...merica Online® For Dummies®, 6th Edition	John Kaufeld	0-7645-0670-6	$19.99 US/$27.99 CAN
...anking Online Dummies®	Paul Murphy	0-7645-0458-4	$24.99 US/$34.99 CAN
...Bay™ For Dummies®, 2nd Edition	Marcia Collier, Roland Woerner, & Stephanie Becker	0-7645-0761-3	$21.99 US/$32.99 CAN
...Mail For Dummies®, 2nd Edition	John R. Levine, Carol Baroudi, & Arnold Reinhold	0-7645-0131-3	$24.99 US/$34.99 CAN
...enealogy Online For Dummies®, 2nd Edition	Matthew L. Helm & April Leah Helm	0-7645-0543-2	$24.99 US/$34.99 CAN
...ternet Directory For Dummies®, 3rd Edition	Brad Hill	0-7645-0558-2	$24.99 US/$34.99 CAN
...ternet Auctions For Dummies®	Greg Holden	0-7645-0578-9	$24.99 US/$34.99 CAN
...ternet Explorer 5.5 For Windows® For Dummies®	Doug Lowe	0-7645-0738-9	$19.99 US/$29.99 CAN
...esearching Online For Dummies®, 2nd Edition	Mary Ellen Bates & Reva Basch	0-7645-0546-7	$24.99 US/$37.99 CAN
...b Searching Online For Dummies®	Pam Dixon	0-7645-0673-0	$24.99 US/$34.99 CAN
...vesting Online For Dummies®, 3rd Edition	Kathleen Sindell, Ph.D.	0-7645-0725-7	$24.99 US/$37.99 CAN
...ravel Planning Online For Dummies®, 2nd Edition	Noah Vadnai	0-7645-0438-X	$24.99 US/$34.99 CAN
...ternet Searching For Dummies®	Brad Hill	0-7645-0478-9	$24.99 US/$34.99 CAN
...ahoo!® For Dummies®, 2nd Edition	Brad Hill	0-7645-0762-1	$19.99 US/$29.99 CAN
...he Internet For Dummies®, 7th Edition	John R. Levine, Carol Baroudi, & Arnold Reinhold	0-7645-0674-9	$21.99 US/$32.99 CAN

OPERATING SYSTEMS

...OS For Dummies®, 3rd Edition	Dan Gookin	0-7645-0361-8	$21.99 US/$32.99 CAN
...NOME For Linux® For Dummies®	David B. Busch	0-7645-0650-1	$24.99 US/$37.99 CAN
...INUX® For Dummies®, 2nd Edition	John Hall, Craig Witherspoon, & Coletta Witherspoon	0-7645-0421-5	$24.99 US/$34.99 CAN
...lac® OS 9 For Dummies®	Bob LeVitus	0-7645-0652-8	$21.99 US/$32.99 CAN
...ed Hat® Linux® For Dummies®	Jon "maddog" Hall, Paul Sery	0-7645-0663-3	$24.99 US/$37.99 CAN
...mall Business Windows® 98 For Dummies®	Stephen Nelson	0-7645-0425-8	$24.99 US/$34.99 CAN
...NIX® For Dummies®, 4th Edition	John R. Levine & Margaret Levine Young	0-7645-0419-3	$21.99 US/$32.99 CAN
...Windows® 95 For Dummies®, 2nd Edition	Andy Rathbone	0-7645-0180-1	$19.99 US/$27.99 CAN
...Windows® 98 For Dummies®	Andy Rathbone	0-7645-0261-1	$21.99 US/$32.99 CAN
...Windows® 2000 For Dummies®	Andy Rathbone	0-7645-0641-2	$21.99 US/$32.99 CAN
...Windows® 2000 Server For Dummies®	Ed Tittel	0-7645-0341-3	$24.99 US/$37.99 CAN
...Windows® ME Millennium Edition For Dummies®	Andy Rathbone	0-7645-0735-4	$21.99 US/$32.99 CAN

Dummies Books™
Bestsellers on Every Topic!

GENERAL INTEREST TITLES

FOOD & BEVERAGE/ENTERTAINING

Bartending For Dummies®	Ray Foley	0-7645-5051-9	$15.99 US/$23.99 CAN
Cooking For Dummies®, 2nd Edition	Bryan Miller & Marie Rama	0-7645-5250-3	$21.99 US/$32.99 CAN
Entertaining For Dummies®	Suzanne Williamson with Linda Smith	0-7645-5027-6	$19.99 US/$27.99 CAN
Gourmet Cooking For Dummies®	Charlie Trotter	0-7645-5029-2	$19.99 US/$27.99 CAN
Grilling For Dummies®	Marie Rama & John Mariani	0-7645-5076-4	$19.99 US/$27.99 CAN
Italian Cooking For Dummies®	Cesare Casella & Jack Bishop	0-7645-5098-5	$19.99 US/$27.99 CAN
Mexican Cooking For Dummies®	Mary Sue Miliken & Susan Feniger	0-7645-5169-8	$21.99 US/$29.99 CAN
Quick & Healthy Cooking For Dummies®	Lynn Fischer	0-7645-5214-7	$19.99 US/$27.99 CAN
Wine For Dummies®, 2nd Edition	Ed McCarthy & Mary Ewing-Mulligan	0-7645-5114-0	$21.99 US/$29.99 CAN
Chinese Cooking For Dummies®	Martin Yan	0-7645-5247-3	$21.99 US/$29.99 CAN
Etiquette For Dummies®	Sue Fox	0-7645-5170-1	$21.99 US/$29.99 CAN

SPORTS

Baseball For Dummies®, 2nd Edition	Joe Morgan with Richard Lally	0-7645-5234-1	$19.99 US/$27.99 CAN
Golf For Dummies®, 2nd Edition	Gary McCord	0-7645-5146-9	$21.99 US/$29.99 CAN
Fly Fishing For Dummies®	Peter Kaminsky	0-7645-5073-X	$21.99 US/$29.99 CAN
Football For Dummies®	Howie Long with John Czarnecki	0-7645-5054-3	$19.99 US/$27.99 CAN
Hockey For Dummies®	John Davidson with John Steinbreder	0-7645-5045-4	$19.99 US/$27.99 CAN
NASCAR For Dummies®	Mark Martin	0-7645-5219-8	$21.99 US/$29.99 CAN
Tennis For Dummies®	Patrick McEnroe with Peter Bodo	0-7645-5087-X	$21.99 US/$29.99 CAN
Soccer For Dummies®	U.S. Soccer Federation & Michael Lewiss	0-7645-5229-5	$21.99 US/$29.99 CAN

HOME & GARDEN

Annuals For Dummies®	Bill Marken & NGA	0-7645-5056-X	$16.99 US/$24.99 CAN
Container Gardening For Dummies®	Bill Marken & NGA	0-7645-5057-8	$16.99 US/$24.99 CAN
Decks & Patios For Dummies®	Robert J. Beckstrom & NGA	0-7645-5075-6	$16.99 US/$24.99 CAN
Flowering Bulbs For Dummies®	Judy Glattstein & NGA	0-7645-5103-5	$16.99 US/$24.99 CAN
Gardening For Dummies®, 2nd Edition	Michael MacCaskey & NGA	0-7645-5130-2	$19.99 US/$29.99 CAN
Herb Gardening For Dummies®	NGA	0-7645-5200-7	$16.99 US/$24.99 CAN
Home Improvement For Dummies®	Gene & Katie Hamilton & the Editors of HouseNet, Inc.	0-7645-5005-5	$19.99 US/$26.99 CAN
Houseplants For Dummies®	Larry Hodgson & NGA	0-7645-5102-7	$16.99 US/$24.99 CAN
Painting and Wallpapering For Dummies®	Gene Hamilton	0-7645-5150-7	$16.99 US/$24.99 CAN
Perennials For Dummies®	Marcia Tatroe & NGA	0-7645-5030-6	$16.99 US/$24.99 CAN
Roses For Dummies®, 2nd Edition	Lance Walheim	0-7645-5202-3	$21.99 US/$32.99 CAN
Trees and Shrubs For Dummies®	Ann Whitman & NGA	0-7645-5203-1	$16.99 US/$24.99 CAN
Vegetable Gardening For Dummies®	Charlie Nardozzi & NGA	0-7645-5129-9	$16.99 US/$24.99 CAN
Home Cooking For Dummies®	Patricia Hart McMillan & Katharine Kaye McMillan	0-7645-5107-8	$21.99 US/$27.99 CAN

TECHNOLOGY TITLES

WEB DESIGN & PUBLISHING

Active Server Pages For Dummies®, 2nd Edition	Bill Hatfield	0-7645-0603-X	$24.99 US/$37.99 CAN
Cold Fusion 4 For Dummies®	Alexis Gutzman	0-7645-0604-8	$24.99 US/$37.99 CAN
Creating Web Pages For Dummies®, 5th Edition	Bud Smith & Arthur Bebak	0-7645-0733-8	$24.99 US/$37.99 CAN
Dreamweaver™ 3 For Dummies®	Janine Warner & Paul Vachier	0-7645-0669-2	$24.99 US/$37.99 CAN
FrontPage® 2000 For Dummies®	Asha Dornfest	0-7645-0423-1	$24.99 US/$34.99 CAN
HTML 4 For Dummies®, 3rd Edition	Ed Tittel & Natanya Dits	0-7645-0572-6	$24.99 US/$34.99 CAN
Java™ For Dummies®, 3rd Edition	Aaron E. Walsh	0-7645-0417-7	$24.99 US/$34.99 CAN
PageMill™ 2 For Dummies®	Deke McClelland & John San Filippo	0-7645-0028-7	$24.99 US/$34.99 CAN
XML™ For Dummies®	Ed Tittel	0-7645-0692-7	$24.99 US/$37.99 CAN
Javascript For Dummies®, 3rd Edition	Emily Vander Veer	0-7645-0633-1	$24.99 US/$37.99 CAN

DESKTOP PUBLISHING GRAPHICS/MULTIMEDIA

Adobe® In Design™ For Dummies®	Deke McClelland	0-7645-0599-8	$19.99 US/$27.99 CAN
CorelDRAW™ 9 For Dummies®	Deke McClelland	0-7645-0523-8	$19.99 US/$27.99 CAN
Desktop Publishing and Design For Dummies®	Roger C. Parker	1-56884-234-1	$19.99 US/$27.99 CAN
Digital Photography For Dummies®, 3rd Edition	Julie Adair King	0-7645-0646-3	$24.99 US/$32.99 CAN
Microsoft® Publisher 98 For Dummies®	Jim McCarter	0-7645-0395-2	$19.99 US/$27.99 CAN
Visio 2000 For Dummies®	Debbie Walkowski	0-7645-0635-8	$21.99 US/$32.99 CAN
Microsoft® Publisher 2000 For Dummies®	Jim McCarter	0-7645-0525-4	$19.99 US/$27.99 CAN
Windows® Movie Maker For Dummies®	Keith Underdahl	0-7645-0749-1	$19.99 US/$27.99 CAN

Notes

Notes